Tools & Trades

The 25th Anniversary Collection

1983 – 2008

The Tools & Trades History Society
Reg. Charity No. 290474

was founded in 1983 to further the knowledge and understanding of hand tools and the people and trades who used them.

The Society publishes a quarterly Newsletter and an occasional Journal which the members receive as part of their membership benefits.

The Tools & Trades History Society web site: www.taths.org.uk

ISBN 978 0 947673 19 2

Edited by Jane Rees
Printed by The Charlesworth Group, Wakefield.

From the Editor

This special publication of the Tools and Trades History Society is a reprint of selected articles from the Society's Journals and Newsletters. It is being published in celebration of the Society's twenty-fifth anniversary in 2008.

On 16th April 1983, Philip Walker invited a group of tool enthusiasts, academics, historians and others he thought might be interested to attend a meeting at the Science Museum in London where he introduced his idea for the Tool and Trades History Society (TATHS). The idea was enthusiastically received. W. L. Goodman, the author of *British Planemakers from 1700, The History of Woodworking Tools* and many other works, was elected President; R. A. Salaman, author of *The Dictionary of Woodworking Tools*, and Kenneth Kilby, author of *The Cooper and his Trade,* were elected Vice-Presidents. Philip Walker became the first Chairman, W. R. Fowle, the Treasurer, and P. R. West, the Secretary. A management committee of nine members was also chosen. After the meeting and over the next few months, 216 members signed up for the new Society. Of these, 32 were from the U.S.A; 8 from Canada; two each from Australia, South Africa and Germany; and one each from France, Belgium and Norway.

The first Newsletter was published in May 1983, shortly followed by the first volume of *Tools & Trades,* the Journal of the Society. To date a total of 105 Newsletters and 15 Journals have been published. The Society has also produced a number of special publications: *The Tool Chest of Benjamin Seaton* in 1994; a reprint of the *James, Isaac and John Fussell Catalogue* in 2001; and a reprint of the 1787 *Directory of Sheffield* in 2004. In addition there have been two CDs of collections of tool catalogues and a technical leaflet on handsaws. The Society also assisted the Hawley Collection in Sheffield with the publication of a booklet about spokeshaves.

The cover illustration of the first Journal was the picture of the wheelwright from the *Book of Trades* published in London by Tabart & Company in 1804, which continued to be used for many years. Drawing inspiration from this, Matthew Carter, a founder member of TATHS and a leading typeface designer, produced a logo and a typeface designed specially for the Society.

From the wealth of information contained in Newsletter and Journal articles, choosing what to include in this volume was a difficult task. Many of the later Journals and Newsletters are still in print, so only material from publications produced during the first eighteen years was considered. It was decided to have as many authors as possible represented, so there is only one contribution per author. The intention was to cover a wide range of subjects of interest to the Society, so the volume includes firm's histories, studies into specific tool types, tool usage, historic inventories and countryside matters. Virtually none of the original illustrations are available, so the quality of reproduction that could be achieved was also a factor in the choice of articles to be included.

In 1997 the format of the Journal was

Philip Walker, the founder of the Tools and Trades History Society.

The three-legged chair – thoughts on construction, function and purpose by the Society's first Chairman.

Philip Walker

Newsletter No. 8: Winter 1985

Being about to vacate this curious piece of furniture, the Chairman's seat, I think I should come clean. Not that I have ever concealed my motives for founding TATHS, indeed I have trumpeted them on many occasions. Nevertheless, some members have been conned, there is no doubt about that. I took a deliberate gamble that they would come to love their Society – well, perhaps to feel that it was worth their annual ten quid – before they realised exactly what it was!

When I invited you all to come to the Science Museum in London, in April 1983 (Yes, it really was less than two years ago, but certainly to me it seems much longer) in order to form a society for the history of tools and the trades, it was because I had become increasingly aware of a great need and because I saw a great opportunity.

The need was to get recognition for a huge, and highly important, subject – a subject which had never been approached in an organised and comprehensive way before. The opportunity was the existence of many thousands of people – including you, dear reader – who were already involved with the subject in some way or another.

Let me start with the subject. I usually think of it as: "How Things Were Made in the Past" – before the arrival of fossil fuels, of machines and electricity. Tools are the starting point, but the subject includes the methods and skills of using them, and how people got themselves, their trades and their workshops organized. Why include these other bits? Tools by themselves have a wide enough appeal. They look nice; if you are looking for something to collect there are still

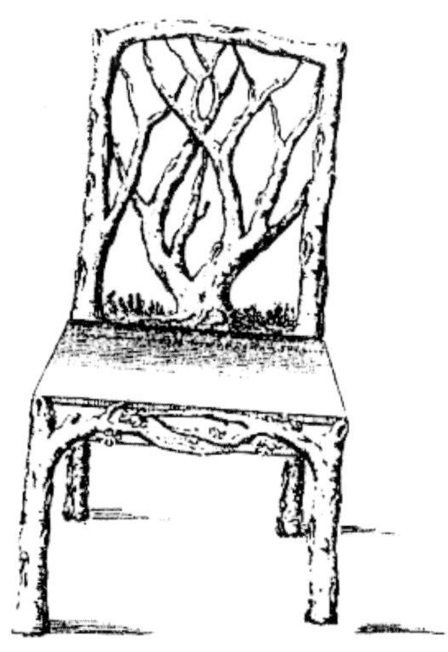

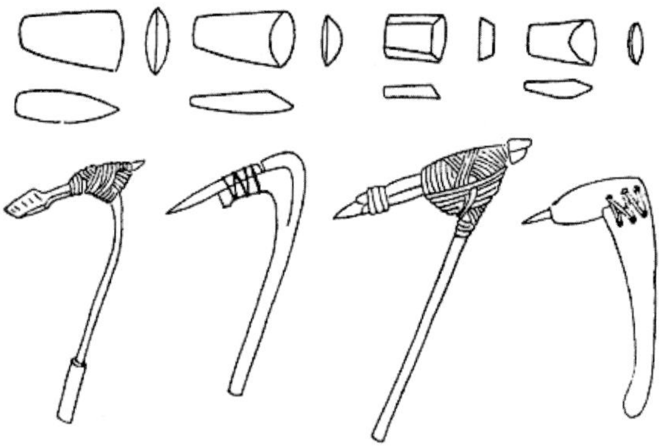

plenty of them about; they are a good investment; they recall the old times; their forms are very characteristic of particular cultures or periods – almost as much so as costume; often they can actually be used, at no detriment to themselves and giving great satisfaction to the user.

Certainly tools have many attractions. But essentially they are for making things. They are technical, to do with techniques, a part of technology. Unless we recognise their technical nature tools are mere baubles. If we do recognise it, we find that they have enlightening connections with almost all of human activity.

There are other ways of arriving at this subject. For example: just under 30 years ago another subject was recognised (I nearly said "was invented" – but that would have been disparaging, and quite wrong. Subjects exist, they just have to wait until somebody recognises them). This other subject, an important one and kindred to ours, is Industrial Archaeology. Industrial archaeology has arrived – in a big way. Scores of books are published every year; you can take an M. A. degree in it; one industrial archaeology centre alone employs twenty inspectors.

Industrial archaeologists study how industry developed; they record and preserve its relics; they seek to understand its processes. In short, their subject is "How Things Were Made" – but only during the last 250 years!

We might, therefore, call our subject Pre-industrial Industrial Archaeology. If the name sounds a bit daft, it is surely no more daft than devoting so much attention to the technology of the last couple of hundred years whilst virtually ignoring the technology of all previous human history!

Of course modern technology is vastly

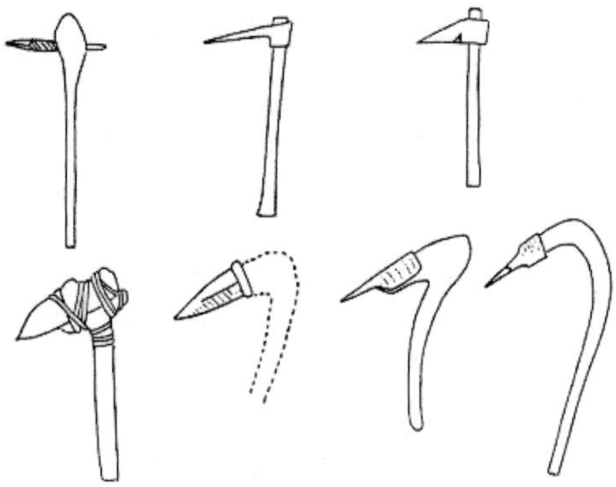

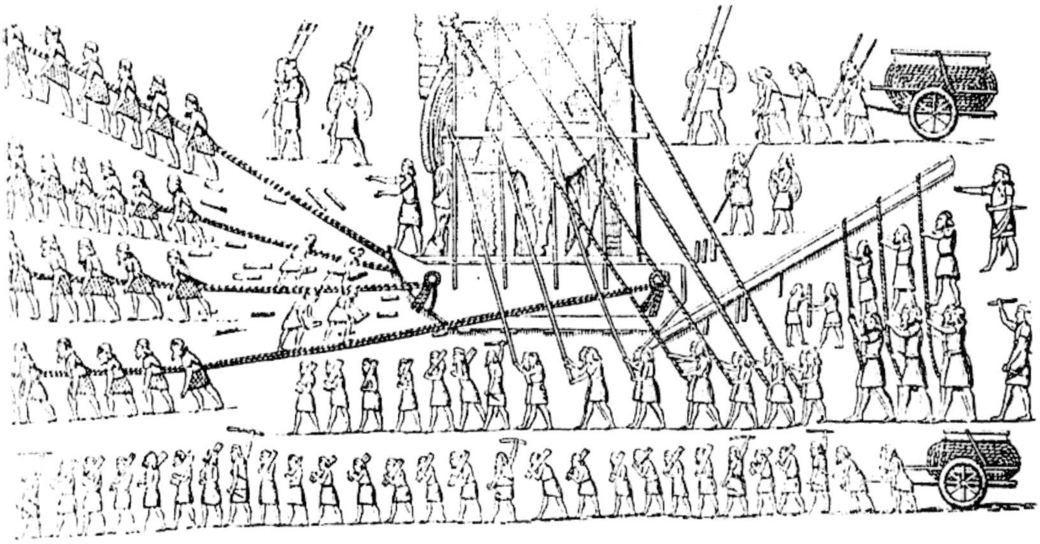

more complex, in its engineering and in its organisation. But it all started from the basic pre-industrial trades which worked stone, iron, wood, leather and textiles – with hand tools alone. The industry of the Industrial Revolution depended on the ancient trades to get its plant built, as it continues to depend on them for its development and its maintenance. Moreover, those trades, which had evolved over many thousands of years, had learned things by practice which are still now only partly explained by theory.

Throughout the stumbling progress of the science of metallurgy, blacksmith toolmakers had successfully produced fine steel cutting edges. The double-bearing crank, on which much machinery still depends, was not invented by a mechanical engineer but by a humble carpenter seeking to convert the reciprocal motion of his hand into rotary motion for a boring bit. I have no wish to belittle the scientists and engineers who have made our "advanced society" possible. The history of their achievements is fascinating and important. I am all in favour of industrial archaeology. An eminent industrial archaeologist, Kenneth Hudson, hits the nail on the head by quoting the remark that the basis of culture is technology. I just feel that we should look seriously at the whole of the basis, not only at its recent super-structure.

Since I accept that the subject matter I am promoting is relatively simple, why do I feel that it needs an organised and systematic approach? There are several answers to this. Much of hand technology is not as simple as it looks. The traditional tools and techniques have evolved very slowly, over the whole of human history. Consequently, each generation is apt to take for granted the technology which it inherits. Certainly, the proverbial castaway on the desert island would soon discover how helpless he is without a spade, without a knife or an axe. But even he has an idea of what these tools are and, if appropriate materials were miraculously washed ashore, he can try to reproduce them. So it takes a considerable act of imagination to appreciate the huge technological advance which even

the most basic manufactured tools represent over the unshaped, unhafted sticks and stones which alone were available to man, the first tool-user – as contrasted with man the tool-maker. But the fact is that the simple-looking tools which have been handed down to us are often quite complex in their construction, subtle in their function, and sometimes obscure in their purpose. Our task, in understanding them now, is made the more challenging by the fact that the people who made them, and the people who used them, rarely wrote down what they were doing. The evidence, therefore, is largely indirect, and it is the practical, technical approach that is favoured in the quest. If answers have to be found in the tools themselves, and in the surviving artefacts made with those tools, it is the enquirer with practical experience of using tools who can best pose the three essential questions: How was it made? How did it work? What was it for? – Construction, Function & Purpose.

However, although I believe that it is the practical men who are most likely to ask the right questions, they are unlikely, unaided, to find the information and the connections which will take us beyond

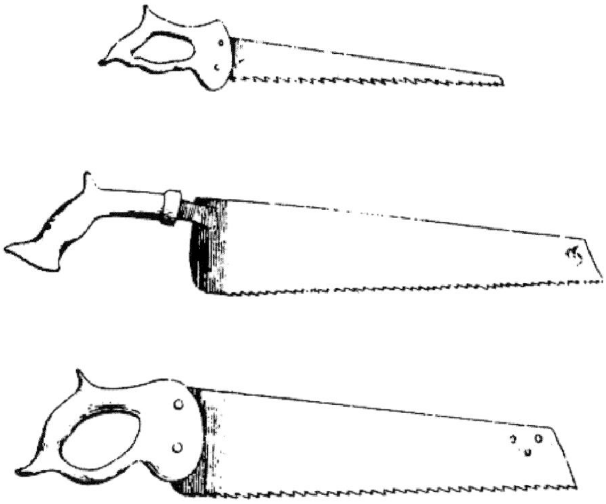

the solution of a few intriguing but isolated conundrums into a coherent and enlightening field of study. It is not that working craftsmen lack the opportunity or inclination to read widely. Many such practical men (in every instance of the word "men" it must be understood that I include women. The word is generic, and it would an abuse of the reader to pepper my message with conjunctions and alternatives. A glance at our first Journal will show how important women are to us.) are very well read indeed. Nor is it even because information has to be gathered

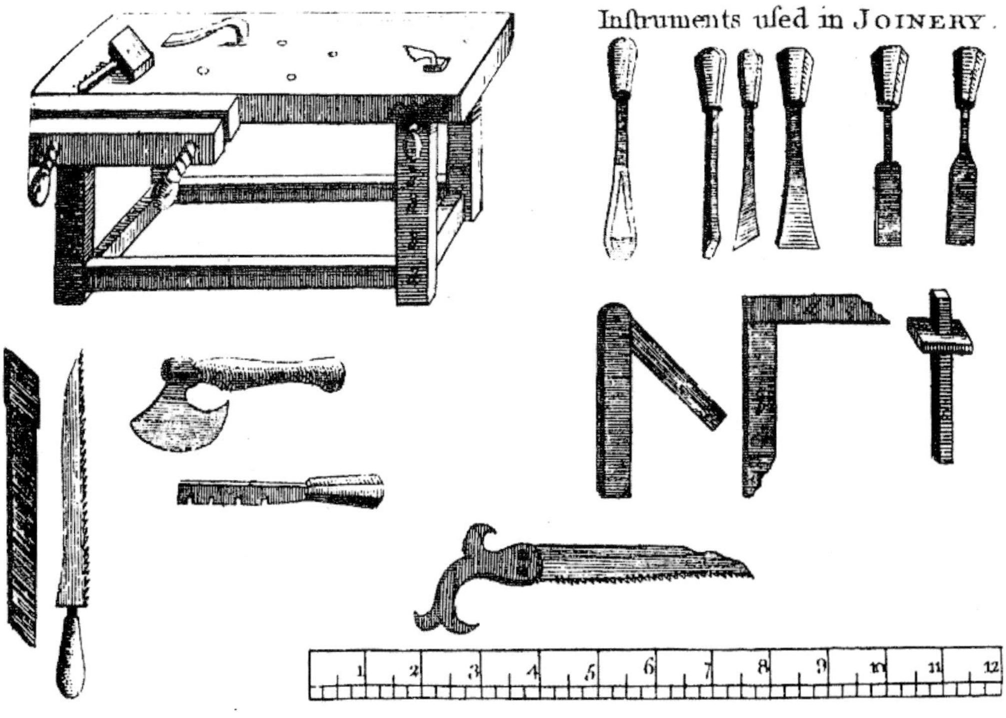

from remote periods and distant places – through the barriers of unfamiliar language and difficult accessibility. No, it is because the most promising sources have still to be mined: on archaeological sites, in ancient documents, in the formation of language itself, in metallurgy and other physical sciences – and this mining has to be done with a sense of direction, with an awareness of what is being sought. So, are we caught in a circle? In a "Catch 22" situation? Am I saying that we need information from sources which are closed to us, and that those who do have the keys are unable to extract it because they do not already share our interests?

It isn't really such a paradox. I am simply highlighting the distinction between an enquiry – the search for the answer to a specific question – and a field of study, where each new discovery often does no more than point to further areas requiring

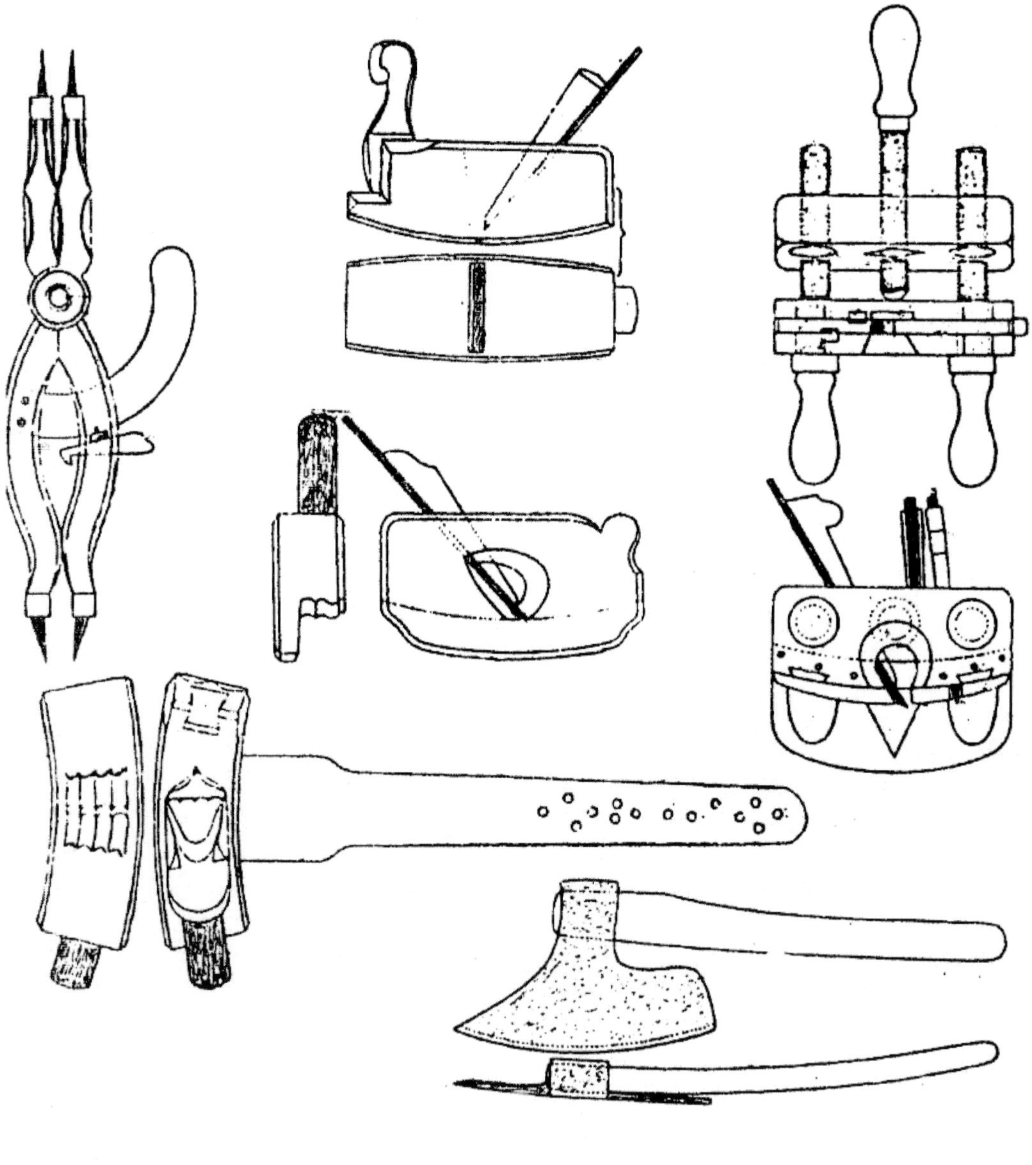

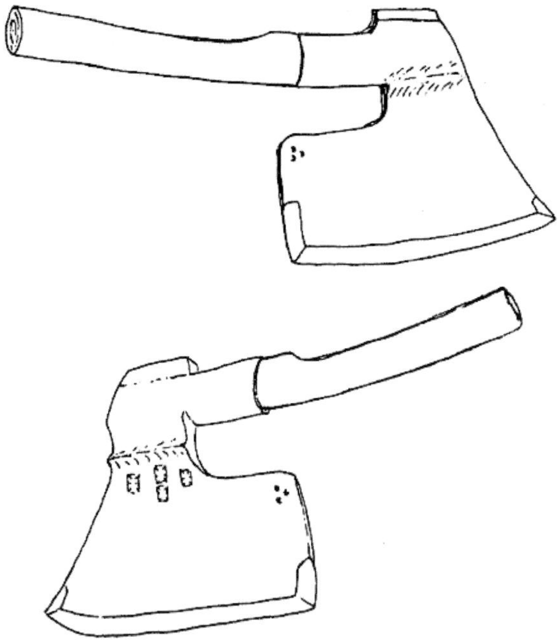

investigation. In other words, and I suppose it is a truism, a "subject" is open-ended. It is not a jig-saw puzzle, where all the parts exist and will eventually be assembled into a complete picture. Our picture's frame will constantly expand and alter shape. It needs not so much some super information-retrieval system as a climate of interest and awareness, to pick up the light reflected from many other disciplines. In its turn it will reflect light back.

So much for the need: At the beginning I described my vision as having another facet – the opportunity presented by the existence now of thousands of people already involved with tool and trades history, although most of them don't yet see it as a distinct subject. Let me say at the outset that I am aware of the danger that I am being arrogant in taking it upon myself to classify the interests and motivations of others. However, the needs of the subject and the possible benefits to its adherents make the risk worth running. After all, nobody is forced to join our Society – and some of those who won't be doing so have already made their views crystal clear!

So, I will be presumptuous, to the extent of looking at some of the main groups which I see as forming the Society's constituency.

There is the ever-growing army of tool collectors. Their reasons for choosing this field of collecting are as various as are the collectors themselves. I have already pointed to some of the possibilities in mentioning the attraction which tools undoubtedly possess for a considerable section of the population. But, as I see them, the collectors are the preservers of the vital material relics of the subject. One has only to imagine the number of man-hours that collectors put in to seeking-out and rescuing, examining and preserving, to realise that few other classes of object are served by such a strong force of voluntary field-workers! In addition to the tools themselves, relevant books, catalogues and other papers – often apparent ephemera which for many decades had been the first candidates for the fire – or worse (see *The Specialist* by Lem Putt), are carefully preserved by enthusiastic collectors.

Since there are collectors there are also, of course, dealers. They too have an essential role. It has been well established, in other fields, that whole categories of familiar objects from the daily life of the past remain unseen and almost forgotten until specialist dealers get to work. As it is said in the trade "the stuff is beginning to come out of the woodwork", with the result that we now have an understanding of the frequency and importance of many types of tool which, a mere decade or so ago, would have seemed freakish survivals. Because dealers, in the course of their business, see such a quantity and variety of tools they are in a better position than most individual collectors to get a true perspective on the subject. Moreover, in the nature of things, theirs will often be the first eyes to see important relics (complete tool kits, undisturbed old workshops, and the like). In short, dealers can – many do – play a vital role in the conservation process, and some make an active contribution to research as well. Yes, we must embrace the dealers into our circle.

Then there are the skilled, time-served, tradesmen. A few have both intimate knowledge of an ancient trade and the ability to write about it. TATHS President and joiner, Bill Goodman, and TATHS Vice-President and cooper, Ken Kilby, both tradesmen first then historians and teachers, are outstanding examples. Many more, while possessing valuable knowledge and skills, grieve silently at the seemingly inevitable devaluation and disappearance of the trades to which they have devoted their lives.

Antiquarians, recorders and lovers of the country scene (TATHS Vice-President Raphael Salaman is representative of a long line: Sturt, Massingham, George

BEADING ROUTER.

FENCE ROUTER.

BOXING ROUTER.

FENCE ROUTER, LONDON PATTERN

JIGGER ROUTER

PISTOL ROUTER.

LONDON PATTERN JIGGER ROUTER

WHEELER'S JARVIS.

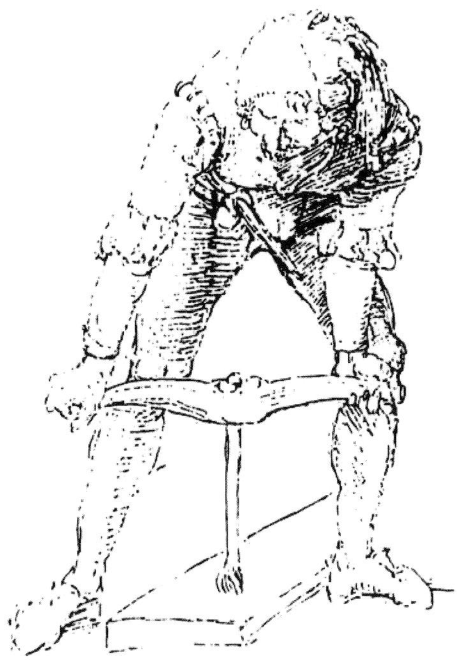

Ewart Evans ...) preserve not only the material details of a vanished world but, even more importantly, they evoke for us an atmosphere, a distinctive way of life. Some people would dismiss these intangible aspects as having no part in modern, scientific, statistical, history making. But those of us who have been lucky enough to experience the scene of ancient trades and their workshops, without the noise of machinery, free of neon strips and plastic bags, with the dust caught in cobwebs rather than extracted by whirring fans, know that work then had its special flavour – it also, of course, particularly in trades organised on a larger scale, had its special horrors. This flavour is a valid part of the history. It should be remembered, and it is not easy to associate it with the tools alone once they have been sanitised, polished up, and neatly displayed.

When I come to look at the people more specifically regarded as scholars and academics I see specialists in many different fields whose work has some connection with the history of tools and trades. Some social and economic historians; archaeologists of many different specialisations; museum curators: they labour at their chosen speciality, usually without being aware that their subjects do have this common theme. The sad part is not only that opportunities for constructive collaboration have been lost through this isolation of the "academic" world from the practical, technical world, but also that the more intellectual disciplines have often exposed themselves to ridicule by those who could have helped them, and have thereby further widened the gap. Our subject has to win recognition and support from these people: the museum curators who have quantities of tools and equipment deposited in their storerooms; the archivists whose ancient documents contain precious clues for dating and understanding tools and processes; the archaeologists who control the sites of human life and work. The benefit will be mutual.

The old-established museums are, these days, showing much more concern for the practical, everyday evidence of life in the past, and they are beginning to welcome help with questions of identification and interpretation. But they have not yet fully appreciated the relevance of these things to the treasures which have traditionally constituted their exhibits. Almost every hand-made artefact, whether it is a piece of furniture, a weapon, ceramic or an historic building, contains evidence of the way it was made. Understanding this evidence can throw light on the tools and techniques of the period: it can also illuminate the history of the object itself. This is something which the specialist historians of the various classes of antiques have scarcely begun to appreciate. Equally, in the field of archaeology, it is almost axiomatic that every human community, whether it was a town, village, or the company of a sea-going ship, included tradesmen, their tools and their workshops. Indeed one might regard these as the defining centre of the community. The palaces and the churches and the gun-deck may have survived more prominently, but every community since the wandering tribes has existed by the things that were made and exchanged, even if only on a level of local barter. In this sense the workshop is always the most significant site – and it was the workmen who built those palaces and churches and cannon! Agriculture may have a more direct importance for the consumer, and we do not regard

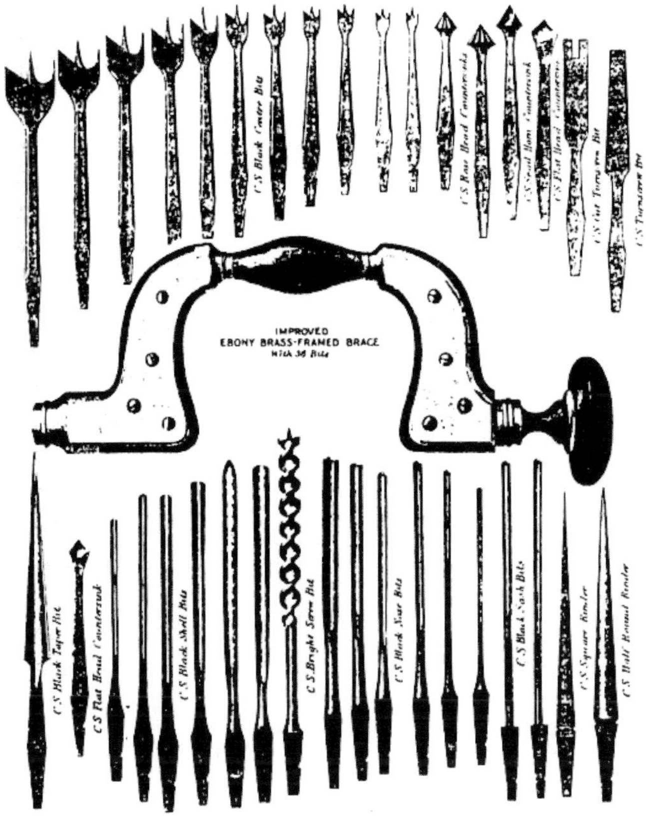

agriculture as a trade (it is, in any case, well looked after by its own historians), but agriculture itself depends absolutely upon the smiths and the carpenters, the leather-workers and the basket-makers, to make and maintain its implements, containers and vehicles.

We can help all these historians of man and his prestigious artefacts. And we need their help in giving us access to the relevant objects and sites in their care, and also to the expert resources of metallurgy, chemistry, dendrology and the like.

I could go on. There are other groups: the manufacturers of new tools; the organisers of the new generation of open-air or village museums; those concerned with the training of future tradesmen, who rightly see trades history as an encouragement to the establishment of high standards now. But I think I have said enough, both of my hopes for the subject, and of the human constituencies which, I believe, will support our Society. So, back to this three-legged chair, which calls for a sitter with a fine sense of balance – a finer one than I think I possess.

To get recognition for the subject we need the Society, and the Society is people. I have disclosed my ulterior motive in launching TATHS. I have said it was a bit of a con. It was also a gamble. The human constituencies I have listed are very diverse. Even those people who will forgive me for my deception and my presumption will not always see eye to eye with each other. The centrifugal tendencies are there, and they have already made themselves felt, as some of you will have seen in one instance or another. I therefore want to take this last opportunity as Chairman to look at some of the critical comments that have been made in these two years. I hope that my explanations may reduce the chances of anyone being deterred by them from supporting the Society.

1. Do we really need a large society?
I hope I have said enough to show that the "subject" is vast, and open-ended. A widespread awareness is therefore needed so that ideas and scraps of information, often from apparently irrelevant quarters, can be caught up and woven into the big picture.

2. Shouldn't we get away from London, or the South-East of England?
We will go wherever our members take us. London is a centre (we already have members in 17 different countries) and a powerful magnet. So it is up to members to devise counter-attractions. I suggest a start by arranging local meetings. Tell us about them, so that we can publicize them in advance and report them afterwards.

3. Do we really need a Journal? – even if it is unreadable (almost)?
The Journal is not intended to be a "good read". It is a record of original work, observations, ideas. It will be a tool for people working on the subject in the future. It is already taken by many libraries, so it is as permanent as anything in this world can be.

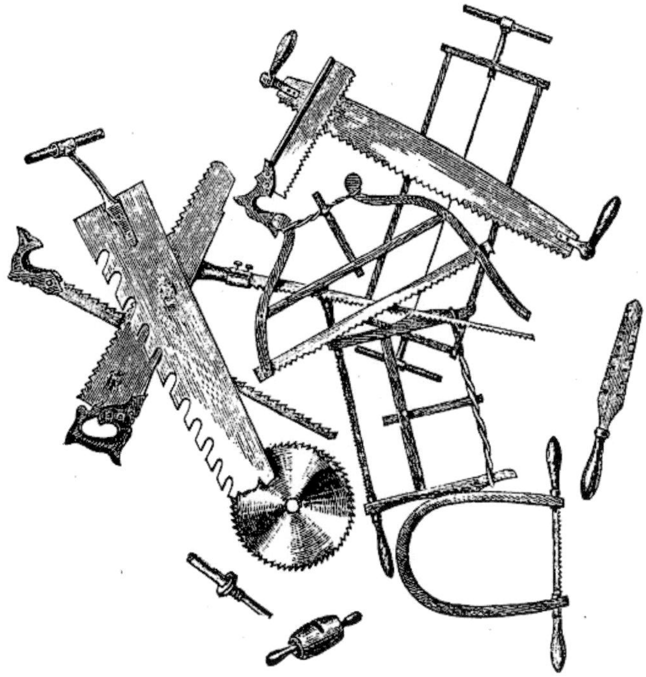

4. Isn't our main need a computer to store all the information centrally?

Some aspects of the subject can be reduced to lists of facts. Richard Harris is already using a computer to store our information about books (The Bibliography). But a "subject" lives on angles and connections, not only on facts. For example, a computer would have been a useful tool for Bill Goodman when pursuing his pioneering work on tool-makers, but it would not have grasped the significance of all those names on tools in the first place, nor figured out how to distinguish the names of makers from those of owners.

5. Shouldn't we steer clear of controversial matters?

I think there are three distinct areas.

i) Controversy unfortunately seems inevitable when establishing a new subject. In pointing to the absurd consequences of not giving this subject attention in the past, I have refrained from quoting actual examples because I would much rather win people over than alienate them.

ii) Controversy between conflicting ideas within a subject can be very fruitful.

iii) Controversy will certainly arise if we accept that we have a role in conservation.

Personally I think we should. When the world's oldest known, complete, workshop environment, with full tool kits and equipment of several trades, is handled in an uninformed and secretive way I think we should protest. Other societies, very properly, fought to save Euston Arch and the Coal Exchange. When they were demolished, two particular monuments were lost. Until it becomes as unthinkable to dismantle an ancient workshop without special knowledge of period tools and techniques as it would

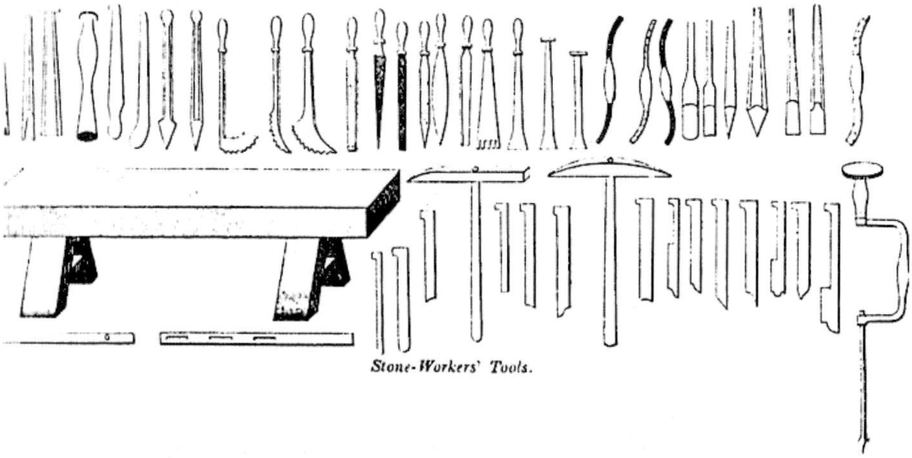

Stone-Workers' Tools.

be to unwrap a mummy without knowledge of anatomy, or to excavate Roman inscriptions without reading Latin, it is knowledge itself that is lost.

6. Shouldn't we pay more attention to trades other than the woodworking trades?

Certainly we should. The Editor, and the organisers of Society meetings, will welcome contributions bearing on the trades which worked stone, iron, leather, etc. It just happens that woodworking is very popular amongst amateurs, its tools are numerous – and it is probably the oldest trade of all!

Even with woodworking tools can't we get away from the concentration on planes?

The amount of material on planes which appears in the Newsletter and Journal does, of course, reflect the interest in them. Perhaps this interest is not surprising. After all, the plane was the earliest form of automation. The

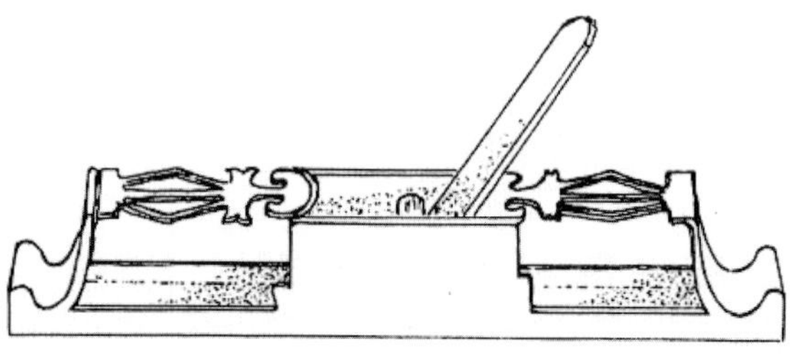

ROMAN c.350 A.D.

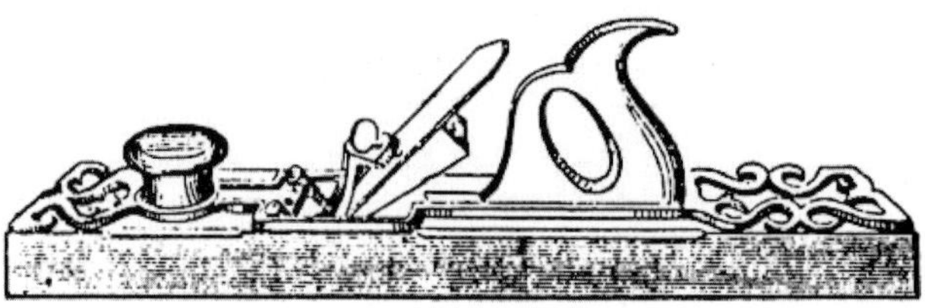

AMERICAN 1868 A.D.

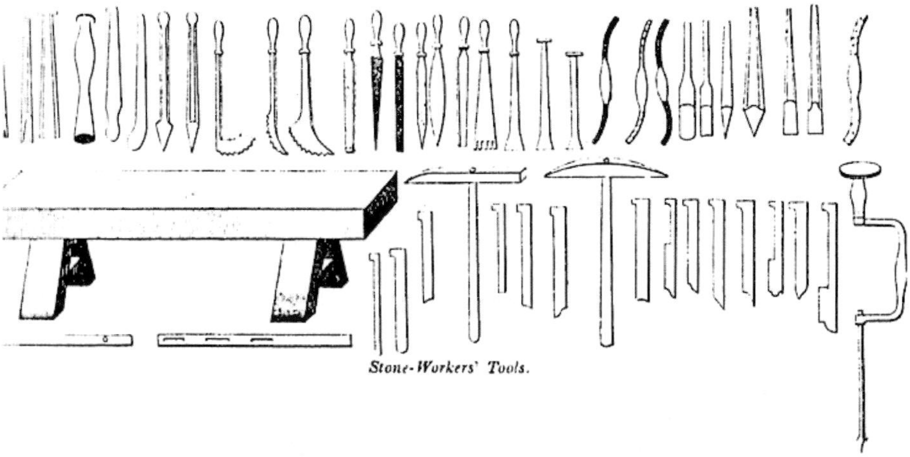

Stone-Workers' Tools.

user simply keeps pushing and the tool produces a flat or profiled surface just as it has been programmed to do. But, here again, tell us about your own interests.

As most members join in order to enjoy themselves, couldn't we arrange meetings etc. more with the aim of having fun? In particular couldn't we have swapping and marketing sessions?

We are a history society and we are a recognised charity with an educational purpose. I think we must get these essential aspects of our nature firmly established before we can turn our attention to the side-shows, perfectly harmless though they might be. In any case, it has been my impression that members have had a good deal of fun, at meetings and in the Newsletters, in spite of having the spectre of a "serious purpose" hanging over their heads!

Richard Crips the wheeler – a Medieval craftsman and his tools

John Clark

Tools and Trades Volume 2: 1984

Documentary sources

Anyone interested in the early history of tools and the ways in which they were used must be prepared to look at a great variety of types of evidence.[1] Some of the tools themselves exist, as odd survivals, stray finds or discoveries from archaeological excavations. Usually incomplete or in poor condition, they are rarely found in a context that tells much about their use. Finds not of single tools but of tool-kits are extremely rare – the Viking Age tool-chest of an itinerant metal- and wood-worker from Mastermyr, Sweden; the finds from the *Mary Rose*; the abandoned equipment of the 1596 Novaya Zemlya expedition – these are very much the exception. Archaeological finds of workshop scrap and of part-finished products can reveal on close study many details of technology and technique, which also leave their traces even on the finished object. Contemporary pictorial evidence also survives, in forms such as the lively scenes in the margins of medieval manuscripts, which include craftsmen at work among other characters from daily life. In interpreting such scenes both the style of drawing and the probable lack of specialised knowledge (and interest) on the part of the artist have to be borne in mind. In turning to documentary sources one finds a few "technical treatises", though most technical knowledge was obviously passed on by word of mouth from master to apprentice. Other documents include a great variety of "lists" made for specific purposes, one of which is the particular subject of this article.

It is apparent, even from the first volume of this Journal, that such early inventories or lists of tools and equipment are a major source of information – indeed it seems a source of delight – to those interested in the history of particular trades and crafts: "Any woodworker's inventories are food and drink to me".[2] Naturally, the further back into the past one pursues such history the scarcer these lists become and the more often their interpretation and the identification of the tools listed become matters of dispute. Yet as early as the 11th century an Anglo-Saxon writer provided, in a treatise on the duties of the steward of a large rural estate, a list of the equipment, from ploughs, saws and axes to winnowing fans and cheese-vats, required for the maintenance of a large farm.[3]

Latin-English dictionaries or vocabularies of the same date and later, devised for the use of those learning the language which was to remain for so many years the language of both Church and Law, are also useful, since they are often arranged by subject headings such as *de instrumentis agricolarum* (concerning farmers' tools) or *nomina artaficium cum suis instrumentis* (the names of craftsmen with their tools) and provide the medieval Latin words for many common tools with their translations into Old or Middle English.[4] Yet they must be used with care, for the men who compiled them, usually churchmen, would hardly have been experts on tools and their uses, and their equation of obscure Latin words with obscure English words should not be relied on too closely.

Notional lists such as these are clearly of interest, but they cannot compare with lists of equipment actually purchased or valued for some specific purpose, which survive among documents of the later medieval period. Royal and other building accounts, for example, list not only materials but equipment for use on particular building projects, and L. F. Salzman made excellent use of such accounts for the invaluable chapter on "Tools" in his book *Building in England Down to 1540*.[5] Yet among the wealth of archives carefully preserved in record offices throughout this country anything that can be regarded as an inventory of the equipment of an individual and identifiable craftsman is extremely rare before the probate inventories of the 16th century and later, and even these often contain a mere entry such as "his workinge tooles" without further details.[6] The purpose of this article is to consider one rare survival and its circumstances.

Fortunately for those of us who lack the skill to tackle the complexities of medieval documents in their original script and language, many have been published in modern versions, either in full or as "calendars", detailed summaries in English of the (usually Latin) originals. Among the records for which there are published calendars of this type are the *Plea and Memoranda Rolls of the City of London*.[7] These Rolls, 102 in number and beginning in 1323, each consist of a series of parchment membranes, sewn together at the top and rolled up for storage, and they contain the records of a variety of legal cases decided by the Mayor and Aldermen of London, together with copies of correspondence and notes of various decisions and ordinances.

Among the cases recorded in some detail are many in which a debtor's goods, held in "foreign attachment", were valued and handed over to his creditor in payment of a debt on which he had defaulted. Foreign attachment, or in the delightful medieval Latin phrase *attachiamentum forinsecum*, is not a term likely to be met with outside such by-ways of medieval jurisprudence. It was, in origin, the procedure by which a creditor could lay legal claim to goods belonging to a debtor in settlement of the debt even when those goods were in the hands of a third party. In practice, in many cases the goods are described as already being in the possession of the plaintiff; the creditor is in effect himself the third party and wishes to acquire legal ownership of goods which, in some cases at least, had been pledged to him as security for a loan – a somewhat cumbersome procedure necessitated by the absence of a system like modern pawnbroking.[8] Should the debt not be paid, and the lender be able to prove his case before the Mayor and Aldermen, he could claim ownership of the "attached" goods – subject only to the condition that if the defendant could prove within a year and a day that he owed no debt he could reclaim his goods. To avoid any possibility of a later dispute, a full list of the goods involved, with valuations made by independent assessors, would be attached to the record of the court's decision.

In some cases, where foreign attachment is used in its original sense, it might involve property, rents or cash, but in some 85 instances calendared between 1365 and 1482 it is movable goods that are listed and valued. In about 30 cases the debtor is either explicitly identified as a merchant or is clearly engaged in trade. In most of these the sums involved are large, presumably representing business loans and reflecting the large scale of medieval trade. Sums of £200, £400 and £700, at a time when a day's wages for a skilled craftsman might be at best six old pence, need to be multiplied by a factor of up to 1000 before they can be compared with modern values. The goods attached are merchandise, in most cases bales of cloth, England's staple export. The other cases, however, involve more personal possessions: items of intrinsic value, of course, such as plate and jewellery, but also household goods, furniture and clothing. Among these cases are a few where the debtor is a craftsman, and his tools and equipment are among the items appropriated – a baker in 1384, a spurrier (maker of spurs) in 1412, and, in 1454, the "wheeler" or wheelwright, Richard Crips.

Richard Crips the wheeler

One cannot be positive of the identity of men who make brief appearances in medieval legal records, but Richard is almost certainly the same man as appears as a plaintiff in a lawsuit in the City ward of Farringdon Without in 1445 – perhaps the beginning of his financial troubles – and, as Richard Crispe, is found making a "gift" of his goods and chattels to one Robert Fissher in 1452.[9] By one of those tortuous legal manoeuvres common in the medieval period, Richard, in making that "gift", was pledging his goods as security for a loan, while retaining the use of them.[10] When the loan was repaid the deed of gift would be cancelled. Unfortunately, though such "gifts" may be registered in the City's Rolls, their cancellation is not usually recorded. Presumably it was regarded as sufficient if the original deed was returned to the borrower or destroyed. Thus we have no record of the final outcome of this financial dealing on the part of Richard Crips, nor how he came to be in debt two years later, for the very large sum of £40, to the Priory of St. Bartholomew, Smithfield.[11] Since he had been involved in a law-case in Farringdon Ward Without, the ward in which Smithfield lies, outside the City walls on the north-west, it seems likely that he lived in this area, and the Priory, owning much landed property, like all monastic houses, may have been his landlord. £40 could represent several years' rent. Smithfield, site of London's great cattle and horse market, would be a suitable place for a wheelwright to set up his business: as early as the 1170s a writer describing the market mentions the sale of farm-tools as well as live-stock.[12] There are other references to wheelwrights in this area: Robert the Wheeler, living in Smithfield, in the 1330s, and even earlier, Richard the Wheeler, who had property in the parish of St. Sepulchre between 1240 and 1260.[13] But we cannot locate the workshop of Richard Crips; certainly not on the basis of the events of 24 February 1454 when Reginald Colyer, the Prior of St. Bartholomew's, affirmed the bill of debt before the Mayor and Aldermen, and Richard's goods, already in the possession of the Priory, were valued, and their ownership, subject to the usual conditions, handed over in payment of the debt. What follows seems to be a fairly complete and very detailed inventory of the contents – materials, stock, tools and equipment – of a large and busy workshop, making and repairing not just wheels – the term "wheeler" is misleading – but, like the famous wheelwright's shop described nearly 500 years later by George Sturt,[14] complete vehicles.

The inventory

As in all such cases, specialists were called in to value the goods, and it is an indication of the range of materials and products that Richard dealt with that the valuers included not just another wheeler, Thomas Swerdebreke, but an iron-monger, a carpenter, and a smith. With such specialist advice we may expect not only that the valuations reflect contemporary market values but also that the terms used to describe tools and parts of carts are accurate. The list, like all legal documents of the period, is framed in Latin, but in most cases, rather than try to find a Latin equivalent, the clerk drawing it up has put the names of individual objects in English – though in a spelling unfamiliar to us – presumably adopting the terms used by the craftsmen valuing them.

The inventory (see Appendix below) follows a fairly logical sequence. It begins by listing ironwork, both completed cart fittings and over a hundredweight of scrap iron, moves on to tools and equipment, then to stocks of timber, to finished wheels and carts and their constituent parts, and finishes with miscellaneous pieces of furniture and other odds and ends. The arithmetic is a little suspect in places, but the total valuation, at £20 13*s* 5*d*, falls far short of the £40 Richard owed.

The list of tools and equipment is obviously of great interest; the obscure terminology used for parts of carts and carriages deserves study in its own right; and the inventory contains some clues to workshop practice and technique in the wheeler's craft that are not immediately obvious. For example, the medieval cart contained little ironwork – like the 19th century farm-cart as described by George Sturt.[15] What ironwork there was could be made in the wheelwright's workshop, and Richard Crips was suitably equipped. He owned no stock of new iron; the raw material of the everyday smith making such rough utilitarian objects as cart fittings was presumably scrap-iron, like the 1 cwt. 1 qr. 8 lbs. owned by Richard and valued at 9*s* 2*d*. Much of the timber he had in stock is unspecified, but the "10 elm trunks" (2*s* 6*d*) were almost certainly destined to be made into wheel naves, being the favourite wood of later times for this purpose. As well as "2 new worked *navys*" (naves) there are "12 rough *navys*". Presumably, as in Sturt's time, naves were cut roughly to size before being left to season until considered ready for final shaping.[16] Wheels were clearly produced to standard sizes and patterns; the inventory includes 1000 spokes (together with a considerable number of "refuse" spokes, discussed below) and 680 *fyles* (felloes), enough to make over 80 wheels.

Richard's tools fall clearly into two groups: those for ironworking and those for woodworking. The blacksmith's tools are listed first. No forge is mentioned; this would obviously be a fixture, not part of Richard's goods and chattels, but its presence is indicated by a pair of smith's bellows, valued at 6*s* 8*d*, as well as a *shovyll* for the *herthe*. A trough that is listed later might also be part of the smith's equipment, standing by the hearth with water for quenching the hot iron.

Three anvils are listed; the largest, weighing 402 lbs., being heavy even by modern standards. Listed and valued together with one of the anvils is a *bykeron*. In more recent practice the term "bickern"

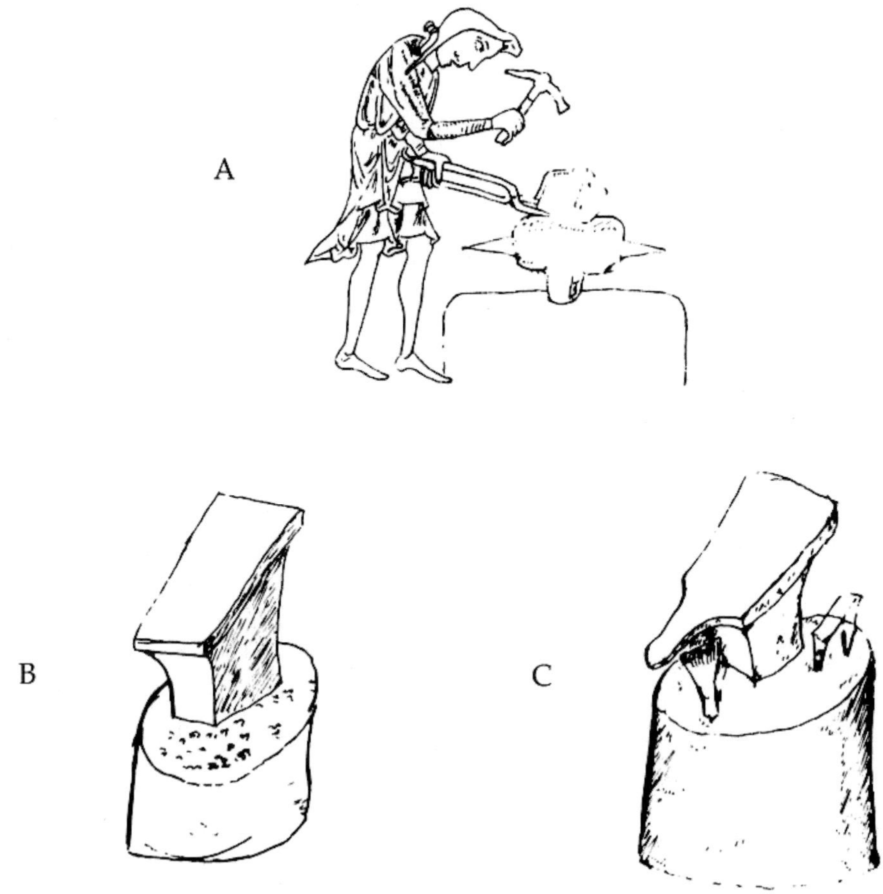

Fig. 1. Medieval blacksmiths' anvils.

A. 13th-century armourer using anvil with two horns (Trinity Coll. Cambridge Ms. 0.9.34, f.24; cf. Harvey 1975, pl.121).

B & C. German anvils of about 1425, of plain rectangular and horned form, used respectively by a smith and a farrier; Housebook of the Mendel Fraternity *(Stadtbibliothek, Nuremberg, "Mendel I", 1.47 and 46; cf. Treue 1965, pls.81 and 79).*

or "beak iron" has been applied to the projecting horn on a large anvil of the modern "London Pattern" or of similar shape.[17] Here it is a separate piece of equipment. Similarly a list of smiths' tools in use at Rochester Castle in 1363 includes both an *anuell* and a *bicorne*.[18] In discussing the Rochester list, Salzman concurred with the *Oxford English Dictionary's* definition of the latter: "properly an anvil with two horns, or cones, at its ends, for shaping iron to a curve", (from *bi-corne*, "two-horn"), presumably to be distinguished from an anvil of simple rectangular form. Certainly, in medieval illustrations, examples can be found of rectangular anvils and of anvils with one or two horns (Fig. 1). However, there is other evidence that the Rochester smith's *bicorne* and Richard Crips' *bykeron* may have been quite distinct from their anvils. In his *Dictionary of Tools Used in the Woodworking and Allied Trades*, R. A. Salaman illustrates a cooper's anvil or "bick iron", a T-shaped anvil or "stake" with a long stem set in a block of wood, used in particular when riveting cask hoops.[19] The term "bickiron" is also applied to a particular type of T-shaped stake, held in a wooden block or in a vice, used when shaping a bowl or hollow vessel by "raising" it from a sheet of metal.[20] It is therefore not surprising to find it occurring elsewhere, among an armourer's equipment. A list of equipment in the Tower of London Armouries in 1660 includes "small bick-ernes" as well as a variety of stakes ("tramping", "round" and "welting") and "a great square anvill", while a 15th century treatise, "How a man shall be armed at his ease when he shall fight on foot," includes among items that need to be available at a joust "an hamer and pynsons and a bicorne"– presumably for running repairs between the events.[21] To be available in the field at a joust, a *bicorne* must have been fairly light and portable: it is unfortunate that no separate weight is given for Richard Crips' *bykeron* that would allow us to estimate its size. T-shaped stakes of various types, either made to fit into a square hole in the top of the main anvil or set into a block of wood and floor-standing, are common enough in more recent smith's workshops; although, as far as I am aware, there is no archaeological or pictorial evidence to confirm the existence of such a tool in the 15th century, it seems highly likely that Richard's *bykeron* was of this type, and was used for the shaping of curved ironwork.

The hand tools for ironworking consisted of nine pairs of tongs, a pair of *pynsons* (pincers) and seven hammers, large and small. Seven *vyles* (files) are listed later separately.

The woodworking tools were more varied. The tool of most general usefulness was the *paryn* (paring) axe, a short-handled broad-axe or side-axe used like a modern wheelwright's axe for much of the shaping of parts of wheels and cart timbers (Fig. 2). An *addes* (adze) would be used in particular for shaping the inside curve of wheel felloes. Richard also owned a *hak hamer* – a problematic tool. The Oxford English Dictionary defines a hack-hammer as an adze-like tool used for dressing stone, quoting a 19th century reference to the dressing of mill-stones. What the term means when applied to an item in a woodworker's tool-kit is far from clear. "Hack" certainly implies a cutting or chopping tool, being a dialect term for various types of pick or mattock, and, as Salaman indicates, a Scots word for a small adze.[22] Perhaps we should picture a tool combining hammer-head and adze-blade – an adze-hammer, common enough as a carpenter's tool in the Roman period, there is also evidence for such an implement in medieval times.[23] Four *chesels* and two *percers* (presumably some form of awl) require little comment. A spoke shave and a two hand shave, however, listed together, require discussion. The latter is presumably a simple draw knife or drawing knife, a straight blade with a handle set at right angles at each end. A tool of this type appears in the foreground of the 15th century illustration of a German wheelwright in Figure 2; it is an essential tool of the more

Fig 2. 15th century German wheelwright at work. Ulrich von der Hul, waggon-maker, pictured in 1451 in the Housebook of the Mendel Fraternity of Nuremberg *(Stadtbibliothek, Nuremberg, "Mendel I", f.73; cf. Trent.1965, pl. 111).*

recent wheelwright, and is used in a number of other crafts.[24] Here it is clearly distinguished from the spoke shave. The appearance of the latter term in our inventory predates by over 50 years the earliest reference recorded in the Oxford English Dictionary. Its function is presumably implied by its name – a specialised shave for the shaping of spokes (although this has been doubted).[25] Its form is uncertain. It would be unwise to assume that it necessarily resembled the later tool of that name, which has a blade set into a wooden stock extending into a handle at each end; identity of name need never imply identity of form. Yet the possibility remains that this very early reference is to a tool like the modern one.

Richard owned four saws of different types. The first listed is a *whyppe* (whip) saw, the large two-man cross-cut saw seen in medieval illustrations (Fig. 3A) and quite expensive at 20*d*.[26] His *putte* (pit) saw, used for cutting logs into planks, would have had a long narrow blade fixed centrally into a rectangular wooden frame (Fig. 3C) like several in medieval and modern illustrations in Goodman's *History of Woodworking Tools*.[27] In two German pictures of 1425 showing sawyers at work the timber is clearly placed on low trestles over a saw-pit in which the bottom sawyer stood, [28] rather than on the high trestles of most illustrations and recent European practice – a much earlier view of a saw-pit in use than any known to Goodman. There would seem little doubt that the English pit-saw, as its name implies, was used with a saw-pit, and that one of the unmentioned features of Richard Crips' premises was such a pit. Richard's *bowe* saw would have been a simple framed saw, the blade tensioned by a twisted cord, of the type common in medieval illustrations and modern Continental practice (Fig. 3B),[29] but the form of his *tenan* saw is less certain. Its purpose, the cutting of tenons, is clear from its name, but not its shape. There is certainly no evidence for backed saws like the modern English tenon saw till several hundred years later. "Was it a frame saw like the modern French *scie a tenons* – as Goodman has suggested is implied by the confused description of a "Tennant Saw" in Joseph Moxon's *Mechanick Exercises*, [31] or a simple handsaw of the common medieval "breadknife" form (Fig. 3D)?

Apart from a wrest, whose nature is uncertain – a saw-set is one possibility – the last items in the list that can safely be identified as woodworking tools appear as a single entry: "4 *awgers* & 1 *byrse*, value 12*d*" The augers should include both the large tool used for boring the axle hole through the nave and smaller ones for starting the mortices in nave and felloes to take the spokes. In this context the *byrse* is presumably the oddly-named wheelwright's "bruzz" or "buzz", a long chisel with a V-shaped blade used in particular for chopping out the corners of the spoke mortices.[32] This tool here makes what seems to be its earliest recorded, but previously unnoticed, appearance in circumstances that allow us to be fairly sure of its identification. However, no tools of this form are known from archaeological excavations, nor are they recognisable in medieval illustrations, and it is as well to remember the warning in the case of the tenon saw, that it is unwise to assume that tools with the same name are, in different times and places, also the same in shape.

A number of other pieces of workshop equipment appear scattered through the rest of the list, including a grindstone with a trough. The three *stokkes*, the *clam stok* and the *chypping stoke* were presumably various forms of bench or cradle on which the work could be placed, like the chopping blocks, morticing cradles and wheel frames of modern wheelwrights,[33] while the two *stepyng stoles* (stepping stools) no doubt had many uses around the workshop.

A major, and essential, piece of equipment to be found in a more recent wheelwright's shop is a large lathe, used for the turning of naves. George Sturt records that the lathe in his own workshop had only been installed by his grandfather, shortly before 1810, and he had been told that before that naves made in the workshop had been merely rounded up with an axe.[34] Surviving wheels, however, archaeological finds from the Celtic, Roman and early medieval periods in northern Europe, have turned naves, while some very elegantly turned naves make their appearance in medieval illustrations of carts.[35] There is considerable evidence for the use of

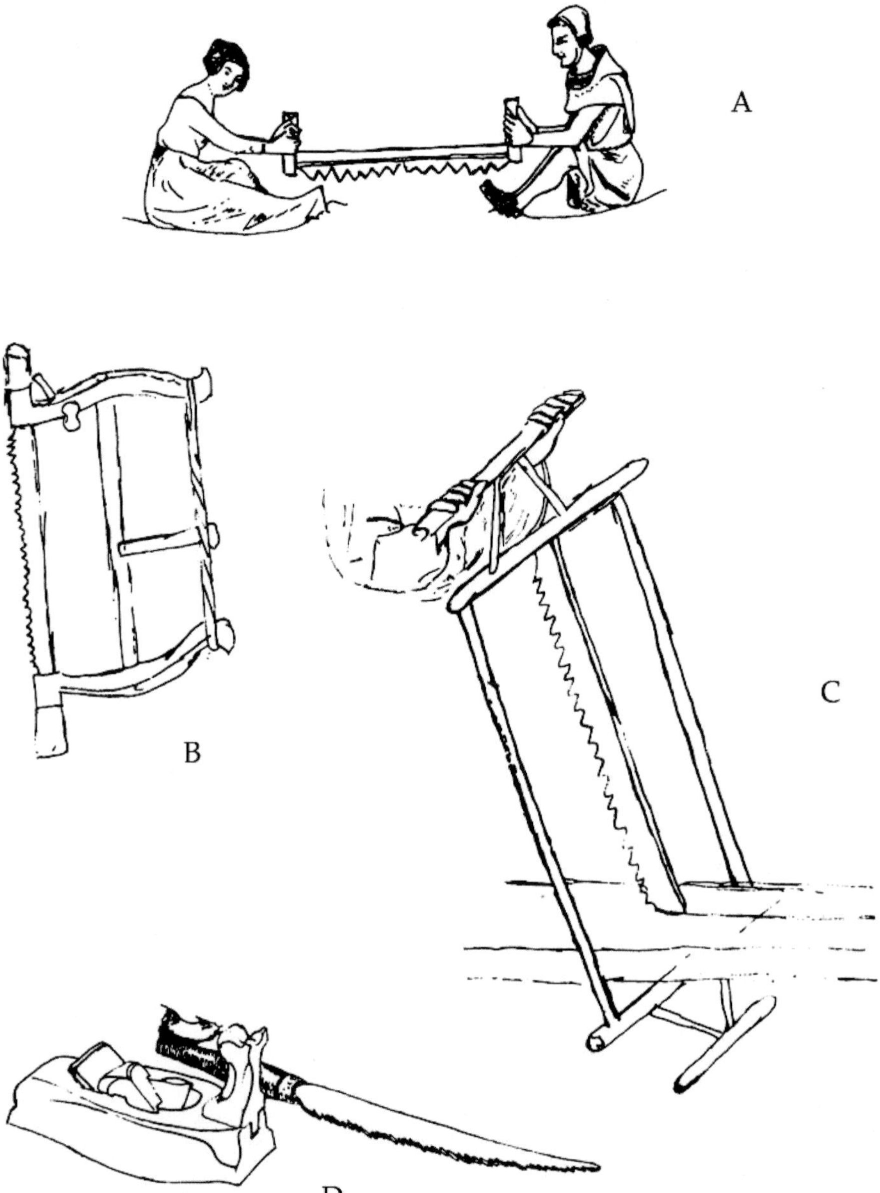

Fig. 3. Medieval saws.

A. Whip saw in humorous use in Flemish "Romance of Alexander", c. 1337 (Bodl. Lib., Ms. 264, f.63v; cf. James 1933, p.20).

B & C. Bow saw (possibly tenon saw) and pit saw as shown in the 15th-century Housebook of the Mendel Fraternity *(Stadtbibliothek, Nuremberg, "Mendel I", f.21 and 39; cf. Treue 1965, pis.40 and 70).*

D. Small hand saw shown in Albrecht Dürer's engraving "Melencolia I", dated 1514 (cf. Strauss 1972, p.167). Its size can be estimated from that of the plane lying alongside it.

the turning-lathe in medieval England;[36] whether there was one in Richard Crips' workshop seems to depend on an obscure philological crux. Flanking the stepping stools and the chipping stock in the list are a lathe valued at 2*d* and three small lathes together worth 1*d*. These are interpreted in the printed Calendar as "laths"; lathe is certainly a normal medieval spelling for "lath", a thin strip of wood. However, in the light of the low values given elsewhere in the inventory for timber and wooden objects – an elm trunk for 3*d*, for example – it seems unlikely that a strip of wood could be worth as much as 2*d*.[37] On the other hand identifying these lathes as turning-lathes presents equal difficulties. Whatever form it took one would expect a lathe to be worth rather more – the chipping stock and the stepping stools were 1*d* each, the clam stock 6*d*. But the crucial question is whether "lathe" could at this period denote a turning-lathe. The Oxford English Dictionary quotes no use of the word in this sense before the 17th century; the term in use earlier seems to have been "turn" or "turne" (Latin *tornus*). "Lathe" does seem to have an earlier meaning of some form of supporting structure or scaffolding, and it seems wisest to leave open the question of what exactly these lathes of Richard's were.

There are other anomalies. The smith's toolkit is far from complete, for example, lacking at least chisels and punches of various types. Perhaps Richard employed a journeyman smith who used and retained many of his own tools. Richard had in stock enough spokes and felloes to make over 80 wheels, yet only 14 naves ("rough" and "new") altogether. Most repair work on wheels would probably involve the replacement of spokes or felloes, and it may have been for such work that such large stocks were required.[38] In fact a large number of spokes are described as "refuse" spokes, presumably salvaged from broken or worn-out wheels. George Sturt explains how such second-hand spokes still had a use and value: "I sold thousands of them, at a penny a piece, for ladder rounds, but the better of them were set aside to be worked up again for smaller spokes or in barrow wheels".[39] Once again "modern" practice seems to throw light on the work of the medieval craftsman.

Conclusions

It is difficult from this document to assess the extent of Richard's business before his financial difficulties. His materials and stock-in-trade listed in the inventory were quite extensive, and at a valuation of some £15 compare well with the value of the property of others who found themselves in a similar situation, if we except the wealthy merchants with debts of £200 or £400. Indeed one might suggest that any craftsman who could run up a debt of £40 in 1454 must originally have had a large business! The premises on which he worked, perhaps rented from St. Bartholomew's Priory, were clearly quite spacious, incorporating a workshop, a forge, a yard with a saw-pit and room for storage, some no doubt under cover, of timber, complete and part-finished wheels, and carts and carriages in various stages of construction and repair. George Sturt employed eight craftsmen and apprentices; it is difficult to compare Richard Crips' establishment. It is noticeable that the inventory contains only one each of those essential, and personal, tools of the wheelwright, the side-axe and the adze; any journeyman employed by Richard must have had his own.

Richard may have managed with one or two journeymen, one of them a smith, and an apprentice; but without further documentation or comparative evidence that must remain speculation.

It is unwise to expect too much of any medieval document. We know too little of the way in which the wheelers of London, who had no craft guild of their own, organised their trade, too little of the circumstances that led to the making of this inventory, to be surprised that there are loose ends. We can only be grateful for the legal system of medieval London and the thoroughness with which it was applied, which created a document we are able to put to a use for which it was never intended.

Appendix: The inventory of Richard Crips

The inventory of Richard Crips' goods appears on membranes 8 and 8v of Roll A79 of the Corporation of London's Plea and Memoranda Rolls. A very full summary is printed in the *Calendar* edited by P. E. Jones (Jones 1954, pp. 139-41). The following translation, which is published by courtesy of the Corporation of London, is the result of a fresh consideration of the original document, and I am grateful to J. R. Sewell, Deputy Keeper of the Corporation of London Records Office, for permission to consult the original Roll.

The Latin of the 15th century text has been translated, standard Latin formulae being somewhat abbreviated and some punctuation being inserted. Two particularly obscure phrases have been left untranslated, and indicated by question marks. Where English words occur in the original they are transcribed here in their original spelling and are printed in italics.

The entry begins some way down membrane 8 with some 38 lines of Latin text giving the circumstances of the case; the inventory then follows:

Firstly. . . *hengys hokes chare nayles boltes for charis doweleges* 1 small iron spade *cheynes styroppys lachetes gametes lensys carte clowtes wroght ware* in all weighing 100 lbs. and a quarter value 1¼*d* per lb., total 13*s* 8*d*. Also 1 cwt. 1 qr. 8 lbs. of old iron value 3*s* per cwt., total 9*s* 2*d*. Also 9 pairs of iron *tongys* 1 pair of *pynsons* 7 *hamers* large & small 1 iron *bykeron* 1 iron *anvill* weighing 114 lbs. value 1*d* per lb., total 10*s* 6*d*. Also 1 *shovyll* for 1 *herthe* 4*d*. Also 4 *awgers* & 1 *byrse* value 12*d*. Also 1 *whyppesawe* 20*d* 1 *bowe* same 1*d*

1 *tenan sawe* & 1 *putte sawe* value 2*s*. Also 1 *paryn* axe value 8*d*. Also 1 *addes* 4 *chesels* & 1 *hak hamer* value 8*d*. Also 2 *percers* value 1*d*. Also 1 *spoke shave* & 1 *two hand shave* value 2*d*. Also 1 *wrest* value 1*d*. Also 7 *vyles* value 5*d*. Also 8 lbs. of lead value 4*d* 1 pair of *smythes bellows* value 6*s* 8*d*. Also 1 thousand new tiles & more value 6*s* 8*d*.

(membr. 8v)

Also 3 *stokkes* & 1 *trowgh* value 12*d* 1 *chest* & 1 *coffer* value 8*d* 1 folding table with 2 stools value 8*d*. Also 3 *shelfes* value 3*d* 1 *offeryng box* without a key value 12*d* 1 pair of *weyng scalis* value 6*d*. Also 2 *anvyles* 1 weighing 314 lbs. & the other weighing 402 lbs. value 6*s* per cwt., total 42*s*. Also 10 trunks of *elme* value 2*s* 6*d*. Also 1000 *spokes* 16*s*. Also 600 & 1 quarter of *refuse spokes* value 16*d* per 100, total 8*s* 4*d*. Also 680 *fyles* value 8*s* per 100, total 54*s* 4*d*. Also 2 *sydes* for 1 *water carte* 16*d*. Also 2 pairs of *lymers* value 6*d*. Also 15 *rayles* value 2*d* each, total 2*s* 6*d*. Also 1 new *corse* of 1 *chare* value 15*s*. Also 12 *rough navys* value 2*s*. Also 2 new worked *navys* value 8*d*. Also 1 *clam stok* value 6*d*. Also 1 pair of small wheels of *elme* value 2*s* 8*d*. Also 1 *corse* of 1 new *close carre* value 40*s*. Also 3 new *chariett wheles* value 9*s*. Also 4 pairs of new large *chariet wheles* value each 4*s* 6*d*, total 18*s*. Also 1 new *corse* of 1 *chariet* value 8*s*. Also 1 pair of *tonges* for 1 *chare* with a box value 12*d*. Also 1 old *trayse* for 1 *chare* value 2*s*. Also 2 *bordes* & 2 quarters of *tymber* value 6*d*. Also 1 old *perche* of 1 *chare* with 1 *extre* value 20*d*. Also 26 pieces of "corbe pro plumb"(?) value 3*d* each, total 6*s* 6*d*. Also 1 *stabler* value 4*d*. Also 1 new *lemer* value 12*d*. Also 1 old *corse* of 1 *chare* with 1 quarter value 6*d*. Also 2 *lodys* of *tymber* value 8*s*. Also 1 *gryndestone* with 1 *trowgh* value 4*s*. Also 1 *lode* of *carte laddyrs ere bredes* & *crosse bredes* value 13*s* 4*d*. Also 100 *extres* value each 3*d*, total 25*s*. Also 3 new *carte bodyes* value 12*s*. Also 1 pair of new *lugge wheles* value 2*s*. Also 4 pairs of *chariot wheles* value 3*s* 4*d* each pair, total 13*s* 4*d*. Also 4 pairs of *chariette wheles* value 3*s* 8*d* each pair, total 14*s* 8*d*. Also 2 pairs of wheels for 1 *carre* value 2*s*. Also 2 *sydes* for 1 horse *lytter* value 20*d* 1 old *borde* value 2*d*. Also 1 *evesborde* value 1*d*. Also 1 *perche* & 1 *sege* for 1 *chariett* value 6*d*. Also 1 *whele barowe* value 6*d* 1 pair of *olde shodde wheles* value 3*s* 4*d*. Also 1 old *corse* of 1 *chare* value 12*d*. Also 1 *lathe* value 2*d*. Also 2 *stepyng stoles* value 2*d*. Also 1 *chyppyng stoke* ld. Also 3 small *lathes* value 1*d*. Also 1 *wasshyng bolle* value 1*d*. Also 2 *tubbys* value 4*d*. Also 22 boxes value 22*d*. Also 2 old *bankeres* value 4*d*. Also 1 cloth painted with "pavys et al pes pict"? value 8*d*. Also 1 *cheker bord* 1 *ioyned stoole* & 1 *treye* value 8*d*. Also 1 *ryle* with *yerne* value 2*d*. Also 2 standing beds value 20*d* each, total 3*s* 4*d*. Also 1 chest barred with iron value 20*d*. Also 1 long cloth painted with 1 picture of the Blessed Mary value 12*d*. Also 1 other cloth with a Salutation value 2*d*. Also 1 *forme* with 2 *trestyles* value 2*d*. Also 1 long chest value 4*d*. Also 1 *buffet* value 1*d*. Also 1 *kylderkyn* with *alegyr* value 4*d*. Also 2 pairs of old *bedbordes* value 8*d*. Also 100 *doollpynnes* value 4*d*. Also 4 old *bordes* for 1 *weynskott* value 8*d*. Also 1 case for candles 5*d*. Also 94 spokes of refuse value 12*d*.

Notes

1. In his paper on "The tools available to the medieval woodworker" (1982) Philip Walker discussed the range of evidence that could be used. I am grateful to him also for his encouragement and his helpful comments on a number of the tools mentioned in the Richard Crips inventory.
2. W. L. Goodman quoted in Marcil 1983, p.49.
3. *Be gesceadwisan gerefan* ("On the competent reeve") in Liebermann 1903-16, vol. 1, pp.453-55.
4. A good range of vocabularies of this type, from the end of the 10th century to the 15th, is collected in Wright, 1873–82.
5. Salzman 1952, pp.330-48.
6. The usefulness of these probate inventories is discussed in Hoskins 1972, particularly pp.116-18, Steer 1950, pp.4-7 and 42-44, and Williams 1982.
7. Published as *Calendar of Plea and Memoranda Rolls of the City of London* in six volumes between 1926 and 1959, under the editorship of, at first, A. H. Thomas and later P. E. Jones.
8. Thomas 1929, p.26, n.l; Riley 1861, pp.183-85.
9. Jones 1954, pp.72 and 177.
10. Thomas 1943, pp.xix-xxiii.

11. Jones 1954, pp.139-41.
12. The description of London prefaced to his biography of Thomas Becket by William Fitz Stephen; translation in Stenton 1934, pp.26-33, the reference to Smithfield being on p.29.
13. Kerling 1973, pp.31 and 32 for Robert; *Ibid.* p.29 and Sharpe 1889-90, pp.7-8 for Richard.
14. Sturt 1923.
15. *Ibid.* pp.7-8.
16. *Ibid.* pp.47-48 and 100; Jenkins 1981, pp.61-63.
17. Hogg 1964, p.41.
18. Salzman 1952, p.347.
19. Salaman 1975, p.161, fig.237(b).
20. Maryon 1959, pp.87-88.
21. Bray 1808, pp.100-101; Dillon 1900, p.44. A range of armourers' stakes and bench anvils are visible in the foreground of the 16th century armourer's workshop illustrated in Hall 1957, p.352, fig.225.
22. Salaman 1975, p.218.
23. An elegant tool of this type has recently been acquired by the Museum of London (accession number 84.128/1) from a context of apparently late 13th century date in the City, while one of the late 12th century from Castle Acre, Norfolk, is illustrated in Goodall 1982, fig.38 no.1. The modern wheelwright's adze has a square poll for use as a hammer – see Salaman 1975, p.30, fig.27.
24. Salaman 1975, pp.175-83.
25. *Ibid.* p.460, quoting a suggestion by W. L. Goodman that the term "spokeshave" was a mistranslation of the Latin *radula* by confusion with radius (spoke); however, the presence of the tool here as early as 1454 in the context of a wheelwright's equipment strongly suggests that the connection with spokes is a real one.
26. Goodman 1964, pp.143-44, figs.68 and 146; Salzman 1952, pp.342-43.
27. Goodman 1964, pp.131-40, figs.137-41.
28. Treue 1965, pls.70 and 263.
29. Goodman 1964, pp.126-27, figs.68 and 134; Capet 1983.
30. Goodman 1964, pp.148-49.
31. Moxon 1703, pp.102-03, 116, plate (4); cf. Goodman 1964, pp.127-28.
32. Sturt 1923, p.102; Jenkins 1981, p.66, fig.17(b); Salaman 1975, pp.134-35, fig.202. Among the great variety of local forms taken by this word, whose etymology remains uncertain, the northern "byrse" mentioned by Salaman is obviously the closest to the form in our inventory. I am grateful to Carole Morris for pointing out that a byrse is listed among woodworking tools in the 11th century treatise referred to in note 2 – see Liebertmann 1903-16, vol. I, p.455. Its nature and function at this early date is uncertain; Toiler 1921 translates it "borer" or "chisel" on the basis of 10th and 11th century vocabularies that equate it both with the Latin *foratorium*, a boring or piercing tool, and with *scalprum*, a chisel or cutting tool.
33. Salaman 1975, pp.509-11. Wheelwrights are shown in the 13th century windows of Chartres cathedral working on wheels hung on vertical posts (Henderson 1968, fig.74); the 15th century illustrations from Nuremberg (Treue 1965, pls.20, 111 and 271) show the wheel upright in a form of cradle, supported by its nave, as in Fig. 1.
34. Sturt 1923, pp.56-57.
35. Piggott 1983, pp.162-63, 213-14.

Turned naves can be seen on vehicles in an early 15th century manuscript of Gaston Phoebus' "The Hunting Book" (Bibl. Nationale, Paris, Ms. francais 616) – see Bise 1978, p.96 – and in paintings by Bruegel – Kay 1969, pls.7, 22 and 33.

36. Morris 1982.
37. Laths for building purposes were purchased by the thousand; Salzman 1952, pp.240-41, quotes 15th century prices of between 20*d* and 5*s* per thousand.
38. I am grateful to Philip Walker for this suggestion.
39. Sturt 1923, pp.96-97.

Bibliography

Bise 1978: G. Bise, *Medieval Hunting Scenes* (Geneva, 1978).

Bray 1808: W. Bray, "Copy of a survey made of what remained in the Armouries of the Tower of London...", *Archaeologia* 11 (1808), pp.97-104.

Capet 1983: A. Capet, "The hand saw versus the frame saw", *Chronicle of the Early American Industries Association.* Vol. 36, No. 2 (June 1983), pp.44-44A.

Dillon 1900: H. A. (Viscount) Dillon, "On a Ms. collection of ordinances (of chivalry...", *Archaeologia.* 57 (1900), pp.29-70.

Goodall 1982: I. H. Goodall, "Iron objects" in J. G. Coad and A. D. F. Streeten, "Excavations at Castle Acre Castle, Norfolk 1972-77", *Archaeol.J.* 139 (1982), pp.138-301.

Goodman 1964: W. L. Goodman, *The History of Woodworking Tools* (London, 1964).

Hall 1957: A. R. Hall, "Military technology" in C. Singer *et al.* (eds.), *A History of Technology* vol. 3 (Oxford, 1957), pp.347-76.

Harvey 1975: J. Harvey, *Mediaeval Craftsmen* (London, 1975).

Henderson 1968: G. Henderson, *Chartres* (Harmondsworth, 1968).

Hogg 1964: G. Hogg, *Hammer & Tongs* (London, 1964).

Hoskins 1972: W. G. Hoskins, *Local History in England* (2nd. ed., London, 1972).

James 1933: M. R. James (ed.), *The Romance of Alexander* (Oxford 1933).

Jenkins 1981: J. G. Jenkins, *The English Farm Wagon, Origins and Structure* (3rd. ed., Newton Abbott, 1981).

Jones 1954: P. E. Jones (ed.), *Calendar of Plea and Memoranda Rolls... of the City of London a.d. 1437-1457* (Cambridge, 1954).

Kay 1969: M. Kay, *Bruegel* (London, 1969).

Kerling 1973: N. J. M. Kerling (ed.), *Cartulary of St. Bartholomew's Hospital* (London, 1973).

Liebermann 1903-16: F. Liebermann (ed.), *Die Geselze der Angelsachsen* (3 vols., Halle, 1903-16).

Marcil 1983: E. Marcil, "The tools of the Quebec cooper, 1684-1752", *Tools & Trades* 1 (1983), pp.49-74.

Maryon 1959: H. Maryon, *Metalwork and Enamelling* (London, 1959).

Morris 1982: C. A. Morris, "Aspects of Anglo-Saxon and Anglo-Scandinavian lathe-turning" *in* S. McGrail (ed.), *Woodworking Techniques before A.D. 1500* (Nat. Maritime Museum/B.A.R. International Series 129, 1982), pp.245-61.

Moxon 1703: J. Moxon, *Mechanick Exercises* (3rd ed., London, 1703, repr. Early American Industries Association, 1983).

Piggott 1983: S. Piggott, *The Earliest*

Wheeled Transport (London, 1983).

Riley 1861: H. T. Riley (ed.), *Liber Albus: The White Book of the City of London* (London, 1861).

Salaman 1975: R. A. Salaman, *Dictionary of Tools Used in the Woodworking and Allied Trades, c.1700-1970* (London, 1975).

Salzman 1952: L. F. Salzman, *Building in England Down to 1540* (Oxford, 1952).

Sharpe 1889-90: R. R. Sharpe (ed.), *Calendar of Wills Proved and Enrolled in the Court of Husting, London, A.D. 1258-1688* (2 vols., London, 1889-90).

Steer 1950: F. W. Steer (ed.), *Farm and Cottage Inventories of Mid-Essex 1635-1749* (Chelmsford, 1950).

Stenton 1934: F. M. Stenton, *Norman London* (Historical Assoc. leaflets nos. 93-94, 1934).

Strauss 1972: W. L. Strauss, *The Complete Engravings, Etchings and Drypoints of Albrecht Dürer* (New York, 1972).

Sturt 1923: G. Sturt, *The Wheelwright's Shop* (Cambridge, 1923).

Thomas 1929: A. H. Thomas (ed.), *Calendar of Plea and Memoranda Rolls... of the City of London A.D. 1364-1381* (Cambridge, 1929).

Thomas 1943: A. H. Thomas (ed.), *Calendar of Plea and Memoranda Rolls ... of the City of London AD. 1413-1437* (Cambridge, 1943).

Toiler 1921: T. N. Toiler, *An Anglo-Saxon Dictionary – Supplement* (Oxford, 1921).

Treue 1965: W. Treue *et al.*, *Das Hausbuch der Mendelschen Zwölfbrüderstiftung zu Nurnberg* (2 vols., Munchen, 1965).

Walker 1982: P. Walker, "The tools available to the medieval woodworker" *in* S. McGrail (ed.), *Woodworking Techniques before A.D. 1500* (Nat. Maritime Museum/ B.A.R. International Series 129, 1982), pp.349-56.

Williams 1982: G. H. Williams, "Probate records: a source for folk life studies", *Folk Life* 20 (1981-82), pp.7-15.

Wright 1873-82: T. Wright (ed.), *A Volume of Vocabularies* (Liverpool, 1873) and *A Second Volume of Vocabularies* (London. 1882).

An estate workshop and its chest of tools

B. H. Read

Newsletter No. 4: Winter 1984

Melbourne Hall, in the small Derbyshire town of Melbourne, has been in the ownership of the same family for over 200 years. The present owner, Lord Lothian (family name Kerr) has recently leased the outbuildings to various small "craft" industries – antique restorers, pottery makers, and a dealer in wood-burning stoves, brassware and logs. The latter took over the sawmill, intending to clear out all the "junk" and use it as a store.

However this building, which dates from 1901, was found to contain all the original machinery, the "moulds" or patterns used for making the wheelbarrows, carts, etc. used on the estate, and a chest of tools which included 84 wooden planes. The sawmill has now been turned into a living museum and its contents put on display – with the chestful of tools labelled "Victorian Woodworking Tools". I visited the place just after it had been opened to the public and, as a result of showing an interest in the tools, was invited to guess how old one of the planes was. To the surprise of all concerned (including my wife who still believes that I set the whole thing up and then decoyed her into the visit) I pulled my Goodman's *Planemakers* from my rucksack and was able to say that the plane in question had been made by John Green of York somewhere around 1800. As a result I was invited to go through the whole lot and catalogue them.

Table 1 lists the planes as they happened to come out of the box. As will be seen almost all are either stamped "EARL COWPER", branded "E.C.", or stamped "KERR". A check at the local studies library in Derby showed that Earl Cowper inherited the estate from his cousin, Lady Palmerston, in 1869 and died in 1906 leaving it to his son-in-law, Admiral Kerr. Table 2 shows the distribution by makers, and Table 3 the various combinations of owners' marks. Examination of the owners' marks, together with a few extra items culled from the 1841, 1851 and 1861 censuses, enabled me to build up the Flow Diagram showing the steps by which the kit appears to have been accumulated.

These tables are based on the preliminary notes of my first visit. There may be some gaps or inconsistencies which will need further checking, but I feel that it is worth putting the information on record straight away as it does suggest a number of intriguing lines of enquiry.

One point that particularly struck me was the recurrence of the name T. Child. I have no evidence myself that Child was a planemaker, except (a) that his stamp is always in the same place, (b) that it only occurs in this one place, although it is often over stamped, (c) if he was an owner then he pre-dated J. Widdowson who, according to the census, was 74 years old in 1841. Thus Child, as an owner, would probably be pre-1800 and would have acquired the planes from an unidentified source around, say, 1760.

(Editor's note: Since the publication of this article, T. Child has been confirmed as

a planemaker working in Stourbridge, West Midlands, around 1816.)

More generally, I wonder how usual it was for the workshop on a great estate to have its own kit of joiner's tools, in addition to those which any skilled workman would presumably have owned personally. When there were such kits would it be common for them to be made up with second-hand tools, from a number of different sources? – just as most surviving personal kits seem to have been.

I am assuming that this was an "estate kit", in the sense of being one owned by the landlord but kept for the regular use of the estate carpenter. There are, of course, other possibilities. It might be that the aristocratic owner was himself an amateur craftsman; but if that were the case here it would be an unusual coincidence that both the Earl and the Admiral, linked only by the chance of marriage, were sufficiently addicted to the hobby to have their own regular tradesman's name stamps.

The existence of these name stamps also seems to rule out the possibility that these tools just happened to have been left, without an individual owner to claim them, in the estate workshop.

I intend to go back in the spring – there are sash chisels and sash templets in the chest as well – and, if given permission, am hoping to be able to match these, and some of the planes, with joinery fittings inside the house itself.

Table 1: List of planes.

Plane No	Profile	Maker	Dates	Owners' marks
1	Quirk ogee	Gabriel ?	1770–1816	I. Widdowson, Earl Cowper
2	Quirk ogee & astragal	Mutter	1766–1812	B. Barlow, Earl Cowper
3	Side bead ?	?	modern?	none
4	Common ogee	B. Frogatt	1765–90	W. Mason, Earl Cowper
5	Quirk ogee	Gabriel	1770–1816	I. Widdowson, Earl Cowper
6	?	?		Earl Cowper
7	Sash ovolo	?	?	G. Gravnel, D. Bullock, Earl Cowper
8	Grecian ogee	Varvill & Son	1862–1906	Earl Cowper
9	Sash ovolo	?	?	G. Gravnel, D. Bullock, Earl Cowper
10	Dado	S. King, Hull	1776–1806	I. Widdowson, Earl Cowper
11	Cove & astragal sash	Gabriel	1770–1816	I. Widdowson, Earl Cowper
12	Quirk ogee	?	?	(only 8½ in. long)
13	Common ogee	?	?	Earl Cowper
14	Quirk ogee	?	?	I. Widdowson
15	Common ogee	Madox	1748–75	Earl Cowper

16	Quirk ogee	T. Child	*1816*	I. Widdowson, R. Wall, Earl Cowper
17	Side hollow and quirk	John Green	1774–1807	Earl Cowper
18	Common ogee	Gabriel	1770–1816	I. Widdowson, Earl Cowper
19	Cluster bead	John Green	1774–1807	I. Widdowson, Earl Cowper
20	Square ovolo	W. Squire	*1754–1774*	W. Nixon, Earl Cowper
21	Common ogee	John Green	1774–1807	Earl Cowper
22	Cove & astragal	T. Child	*1816*	I. Widdowson, R. Wall, Earl Cowper
23	Hollow	B. Frogatt	1765–90	W. Mason, Earl Cowper
24	Tongue	Fenton & Marsden	1841–5	R. Young, Earl Cowper
25	Quirk ogee & astragal	John Green	1774–1807	Earl Cowper
26	Square ovolo	Kaye, Notts.	1869–95	E.C. (branded)
27	Square ovolo	Hields, Notts.	1830–81	E.C. (branded)
28	Side bead	?	?	J. Bullock, Earl Cowper
29	Square ovolo	Kaye, Notts.	1869–95	E.C. (branded)
30	Quirk ogee	Gabriel	1770–1816	I. Widdowson, Earl Cowper
31	Astragal	B .Frogatt	1765–90	I. Widdowson, Earl Cowper
32	Cove & astragal sash	Gabriel	1770–1816	I. Widdowson, Earl Cowper
33	Square ovolo	Kaye, Notts.	1869–95	E.C. (branded)
34	Tongue	Varvill & Son	1862–1904	J. Bullock, Earl Cowper
35	Side bead	Varvill & Son	1862–1904	G. Cooper, R. Young,, Earl Cowper
36	Ovolo & scotia	?	?	J. Bullock, Earl Cowper
37	Cluster bead	John Green	1774–1807	J. Bullock, W. Mason, Earl Cowper
38	Sash ovolo	Hields, Notts.	1830–81	E.C. (branded)
39	Common ogee	B. Frogatt	1765–90	W.F., Earl Cowper
40	Round	T. Child	*1816*	R. Wall, Earl Cowper
41	Sash Ovolo	Kaye, Notts.	1869–95	Earl Cowper
42	?	?	?	I. Widdowson, Earl Cowper
43	Square ovolo	Kaye, Notts.	1869–95	Earl Cowper
44	Square ovolo	?	?	Earl Cowper
45	¼ side bead	B. Frogatt	1765–90	R. Young, Earl Cowper
46	?	?	?	I. Widdowson, R.Wall, Earl Cowper
47	No. 3 hollow	T. Child	*1816*	I. Widdowson, R. Wall, Earl Cowper
48	Side snipe	I. Sym	1753–1803	I. Widdowson, Earl Cowper

49	Square ovolo	?	?	I. Widdowson, Earl Cowper
50	Reverse ogee	B. Frogatt	1765–90	W. Mason, Earl Cowper
51	No. 8 round	T. Child	*1816*	I. Widdowson, R. Wall, Earl Cowper
52	Square ovolo	B. Frogatt	1765–90	W. Mason, W. Fryer, Earl Cowper
53	Hollow	T. Child	*1816*	I. Widdowson, R. Wall, Earl Cowper
54	2-bead cluster	John Green	1774–1807	I.Widdowson
55	Side round	T. Child	*1816*	I. Widdowson, R. Wall, Earl Cowper
56	No.1 hollow	T. Child	*1816*	I. Widdowson, R. Wall, Earl Cowper
57	Round	T.Child	*1816*	I. Widdowson, R. Wall, Earl Cowper
58	Scotia?	?	?	W.F., Earl Cowper
59	No. 6 hollow	T. Child		I. Widdowson, R. Wall, Earl Cowper
60	Reverse ogee?	T. Child	?	I. Widdowson, R. Wall, Earl Cowper
61	No.5 hollow	?	?	I. Widdowson, R. Wall, Earl Cowper
62	1/8 side bead	?	?	R.Young, Earl Cowper
63	No. 2 round	T. Child	*1816*	I. Widdowson, R. Wall, Earl Cowper
64	No. 6 round	?	?	I. Widdowson, R. Wall, Earl Cowper
65	No. 15? round	B. Frogatt	1765–90	W. Mason, W.F., Earl Cowper
66	No. 2 hollow	T. Child	*1816*	I. Widdowson, R. Wall,
67	Wide round	B. Frogatt	1765–90	W. Mason, R. Young, W.F., Earl Cowper
68	No. 7 hollow	T. Child	*1816*	Earl Cowper
69	No. 1 round ?	T. Child	*1816*	?
70	?	Gabriel	1770–1816	I. Widdowson, Earl Cowper
71	Side round	T. Child	*1816*	I. Widdowson, R. Wall, Earl Cowper
72	Side round	T. Child	*1816*	I. Widdowson, R. Wall, Earl Cowper
73	No. 12 round	T. Child	*1816*	I. Widdowson, R. Wall, Earl Cowper
74	No. 8 hollow	?	?	
75	Hollow	?	?	R.Young, Earl Cowper
76	Side bead	B. Frogatt	1765–90	A. Cooper, S.H., Earl Cowper
77	Side bead	?	?	R. Young
78	Sash ovolo	Kaye, Notts.	1865–95	E.C. (branded)
9	Toothing plane	Varvill, York	1796–1830	J. Bullock, Earl Cowper
80	Coffin smoother	?	?	Kerr
81	Spar plane	Atkin & Son	1843–54	
82	Compass plane	Summers Varvill	1840–62	J. Bullock, Earl Cowper
83	Compass smoother	J. Baldwin	?	Kerr
84	2 in. jack plane	C. F. Ordson, B'ham	?	Kerr

Table 2: Listing by maker's mark.

Maker	**Place**	**Plane number(s)**	**Total**
B. Frogatt	Birmingham	4, 23, 31, 39, 45, 50, 52, 65, 67, 76	10
Gabriel	London	1, 5, 11, 18, 30 ,32,70	7
Madox	London	15	1
Mutter	London	2	1
Varvill & Son	York	8, 34, 35, 79, 82	5
S. King	Hull	10	1
T. Child	*Stourbridge*	16, 22, 40, 47, 51, 53, 55, 56, 57, 59, 60,	18
		63, 66, 68, 69, 71, 72, 73	
John Green	York	17, 19, 21, 25, 37, 54	6
W. Squire	*London*	20	1
Kaye	Notts.	26, 29, 33, 41, 43, 78	6
Hields	Notts.	27, 38	2
I .Sym	London	48	1
Fenton & Marsden	Sheffield	24	1
Atkin & Son	Birmingham	81	1
Dealer marks only	Birmingham	83, 84	2
Unmarked		3, 6, 7, 9, 12, 13, 14, 28, 36, 42, 44,	21
		46, 49, 58, 61, 62, 64, 74, 75, 77, 80	

Editor's note: The dates and location for T. Child and W. Squire, which are now known, have been added in italics in Tables 1 and 2.

Table 3: Listing by owner.

1st Owner	2nd Owner	3rd Owner	4th Owner	Plane Numbers
I. Widdowson	Earl Cowper			1, 5, 10, 11, 15, 19, 30, 31, 32, 42, 48, 49, 70
I. Widdowson	R. Wall	Earl Cowper		16, 22, 46, 47, 51, 53, 55, 56, 57, 59, 60, 61, 63, 64, 71, 72, 73
I. Widdowson				14
Earl Cowper				6 ,8, 12, 13, 15, 17, 21, 25, 41, 43, 44, 68
E.C.				26, 27, 29, 33, 38, 78
R. Wall	Earl Cowper			40
B. Barlow	Earl Cowper			2
W. Mason	Earl Cowper			4, 23, 50
W. Mason	W. Fryer	Earl Cowper		52
W. Mason	W.F.	Earl Cowper		65
W. Mason	R. Young	W.F.	Earl Cowper	67
J. Bullock	W. Mason	Earl Cowper		37 (no over-stamping, so order in doubt)
J. Bullock	Earl Cowper			28, 34, 36
W. Nixon	Earl Cowper			20
R. Young	Earl Cowper			24, 45, 62, 75, 77
G. Gravnel	D. Bullock	Earl Cowper		7, 9
G. Cooper	R. Young	Earl Cowper		35
W.F.	Earl Cowper			39, 58
A. Cooper	S.H.	Earl Cowper		76

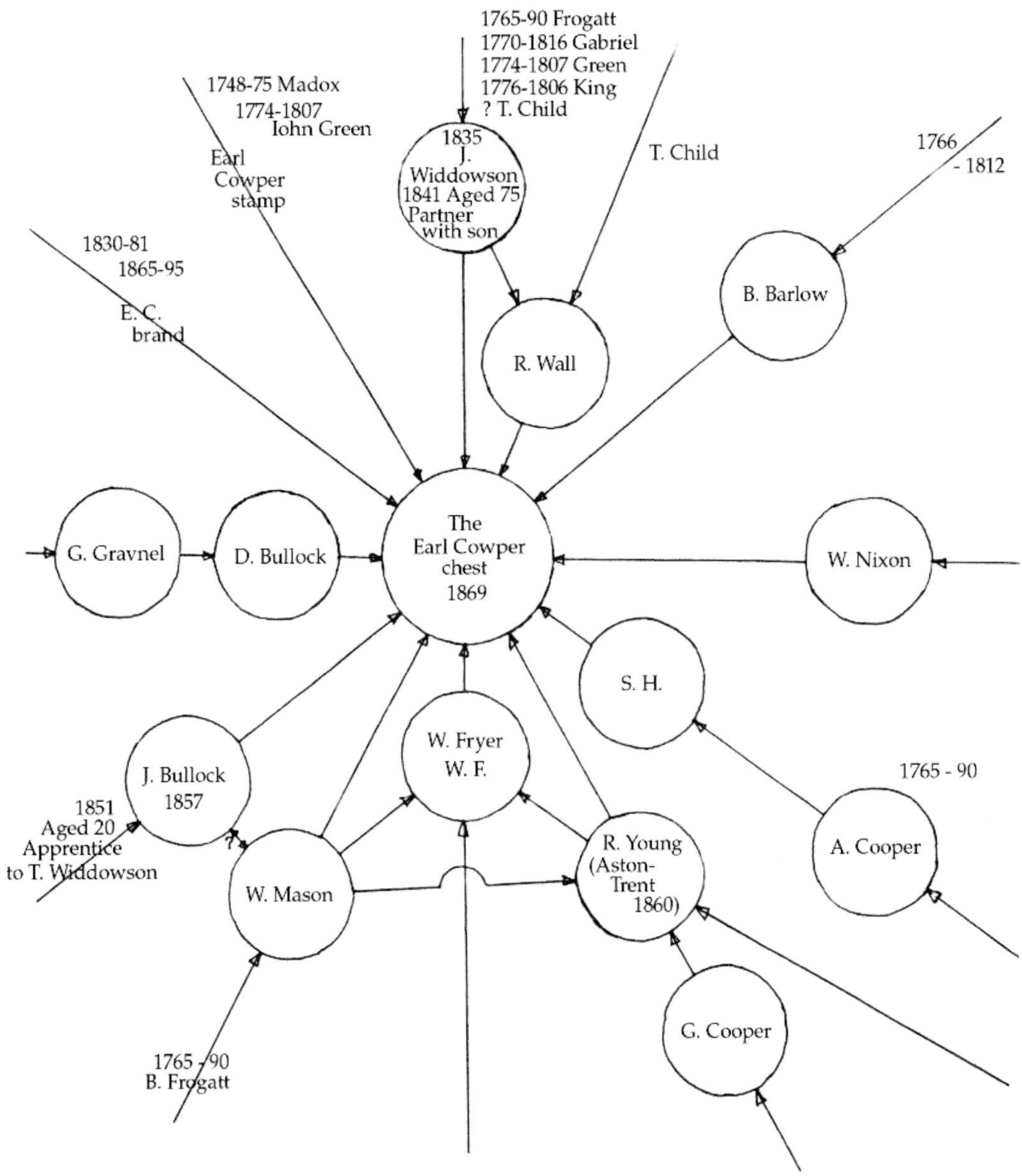

Flow diagram showing the interconnection of origins, with some postulated dates.

Compo moulds

Jane Rees

Tools and Trades Volume 3: 1985

Reverse carved moulds in boxwood or fruitwood can be seen in museums and antique shops. What they were used for and how they were used is not, however, generally known.

The majority of these moulds were used in the production of ornate gilded picture frames. They are frequently known today as "gesso" moulds. This is, however, a misnomer. Gesso is indeed used in the production of gilded picture frames, but as a base coating to take the gilding. The substance used to fill the moulds, and thus form the relief decoration for the frames, is composition, frequently abbreviated to "compo"– hence the name used in the trade: compo mould.

Before the advent of composition, picture frames were made in wood, either by carving or from profiled sections. However, during the last quarter of the eighteenth century the fashion in picture and mirror frames was much changed by the influence of the Adam brothers whose style of decoration was lighter and more repetitive. This type of decoration was difficult and expensive to produce by the traditional method of carving so the use of moulded composition in the production of the frames began. There is some evidence that during this early period, papier maché, which had been recently introduced from France, was also used. However it was lass successful than composition which, within a short time, became the accepted material for such mouldings.

A variety of recipes are used for compo but the two most common today are English compo and French compo. English compo is made by heating together rabbit or parchment glue, rosin and raw linseed oil to which is added very finely sieved whiting until the mixture acquires the consistency of soft putty. French compo is made by combining hot rabbit glue, tissue paper and, again, finely sieved whiting, and then bringing it to the same consistency. It is also possible to produce a form of compo from glue and sawdust, but this is not generally used today. Gesso is composed only of glue and whiting.

The compos used today vary very little from those of the nineteenth century, as can be seen from the recipes given in *Workshop Receipts* by Ernest Spon in 1878. Then, as now, compo had no absolutely standard formula. Spon gives no less than five recipes, although some of these are very curious and are unlikely to be successful as a base for gilding; for example, one recipe includes pitch!

However diverse the recipes are, the method of use is much the same, and has evidently remained so for a century at least; the process described in *Workshop Receipts* being exactly the same as the present day process.

Once the ingredients have been mixed, the mixture is kneaded thoroughly to ensure a totally smooth consistency and to expel air bubbles. While the compo is warm it is soft enough to be extruded. It only hardens when fully cold. During use it can be kept soft either by dipping it in, or standing it over, hot water.

Fig. 1, left. Slicing the moulding from the excess compo.

Fig. 2, right. A moulding applied flexibly over a corner.

The moulds to be used are lightly brushed with linseed oil and the compo is pressed firmly into them. It is not levelled off at this stage but left proud of the surface of the mould. After a short while, when the compo has stiffened slightly but not hardened, the filled mould is turned upside down onto a flat surface, pressed down firmly, and then lifted off leaving the compo adhering to the surface.

The actual moulding required is then delicately sliced off the excess material with a very sharp knife. Fig. 1 shows this intricate operation. The frame to which the moulding is to be applied will already have been prepared by the application of several coats of gesso painted on and sanded down to a very smooth surface.

Fig. 3, left. A mould , signed WALL, carved into a disc of boxwood.

Fig. 4, right. Reverse of the mould in Fig. 3, showing ornamental turning.

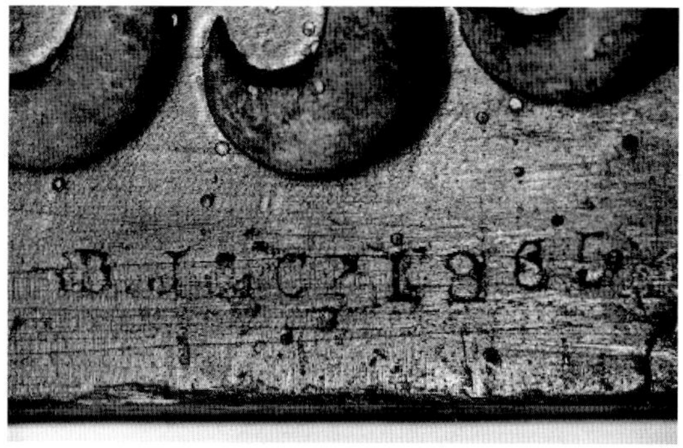

Fig. 5, left. Mould signed WALL and stamped B. J. & Co. 1865.

Fig. 6, above. Detail of mould in Fig. 5.

The moulding, which is still flexible, is then applied to the frame. It is attached to the frame simply by slightly wetting the back with water or a very weak solution of gesso, the glue in the compo providing the necessary adhesion. At this stage it is flexible enough to he placed on curved surfaces or even taken round corners if required, as shown in Fig. 2.

When all the compo ornaments have been applied they are allowed to harden. If the frame is to be water-gilded it is then lightly brushed with one or two coats of weak gesso, care being taken not to lose the definition of the moulding. This is followed by a coloured clay and size base, called bole, without which it would not be possible to burnish the gilding. If the frame is to be oil gilded, gold size may be painted directly onto the composition to receive the gold leaf.

In order to achieve the fineness of detail that was needed when carving the moulds, the intaglio carvers used boxwood or, for larger moulds, fruit-wood. The design was drawn onto the surface of the block of wood but after that the carving was done entirely freehand. The surface of the wood was lightly oiled during the carving process to help the carving tool to run smoothly, and some-times a tray of damp silver sand was kept to hand for the carver to check progress by pressing the mould onto it. It is inter-esting to note that, then as now, boxwood was an expensive commodity and not to be wasted. This is illustrated by the mould shown in Figs. 3 and 4 where the mould has been carved into the back of a piece of ornamental turning.

This mould is also unusual in that it has a name engraved on it (Wall). Only a very small proportion of the moulds I have seen bear names and of these, the name recorded above is the only one that appears to me likely to be that of a maker of moulds. The name is probably that of John Peter Wall, recorded in Kelly's *Post*

Fig. 7. Mould stamped MOUND.

Office London Directory as an "engraver on wood" working at various addresses in the Strand between 1856 and 1867. E. H. Pinto, in *Treen and Other Wooden Bygones*, (London, 1969), p. 190, names several mould makers. However, apart from the J. P. Wall mentioned above and possibly J. C. Wall, directories and other evidence suggest that they were mould users rather than mould makers. Figs. 5 and 6 also show a mould signed by Wall. Its significance is that it has also been stamped "B. J. & Co" with the date 1865. This would support the above attribution and also my belief that Wall made moulds for users other than himself.

The mould in Fig. 7 carries another name, Mound. However the way in which the name is stamped, on this and other moulds carrying the same name, using single letter punches irregularly and repeatedly struck in different positions, leads me to believe that Mound was a user and owner, rather than a manufacturer of moulds. It is, of course, possible that he produced moulds for his own use. That he was not a commercial maker of moulds is further borne out again by Kelly's *Post Office London Directories* which show no less than seven carvers and gilders named Mound (whose principal product would have been picture and mirror frames) working in London during the period from 1856 to 1940. The moulds in Figs. 3, 4 and 7 are all in the Pinto Collection of Treen and are known to have come from a firm of picture framers working in Hammersmith.

It is interesting to note that many moulds have their ends painted and marked with a workshop number and also sometimes a description of the mould.

Fig. 8 shows a selection of compo moulds for different parts of picture frames. At the right is a border mould, in the centre various medallions, swag and corner designs, and on the left a mould that would have been used to provide a patterned background on a large picture or mirror frame. This last type of mould is known in the trade as a net mould. Fig. 9 illustrates an unusual mould where brass nails have been inserted to produce a texture of small indentations. Fig. 10 shows two moulds that would have been used only for oil gilding. The carving on these is so fine and shallow that it would be lost if the moulding were painted with gesso and bole, essential in the process of water gilding but not necessary for oil gilding which can be applied direct to the compo.

Three other types of mould which

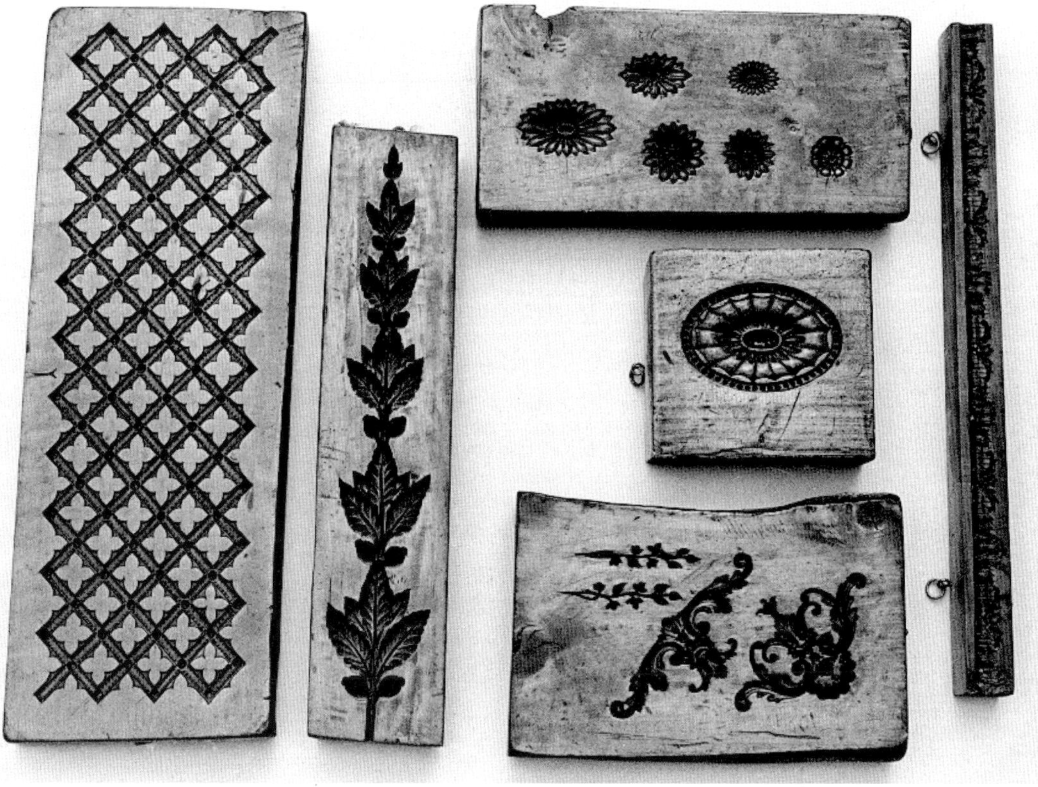

Fig. 8. Selection of moulds for various parts of frames. On the left: a "net" mould.

are similar to compo moulds are also sometimes found. These are moulds for architectural plasterwork and two types of culinary moulds. Architectural moulds are similar in style to compo moulds but always considerably larger. Culinary moulds were mostly used either for gingerbread or for fondant. The gingerbread ones are fairly easy to distinguish both by their subject matter (often people, animals or artifacts) and by their style of carving. Fondant moulds (fondant is a confection made from sugar and used in icing cakes and for sweets) more closely resemble compo moulds in subject matter but are usually very small and carved from woods other than boxwood, such as sycamore and lime which will not impart flavour to the food.

Reverse carving, as a specialised trade, is now no more. When a mould for making compo decorations is required

Fig. 9. A mould studded with brass nails, to produce indentations on the moulding.

Fig. 10. Two moulds with fine and shallow carving, suitable only for oil gilding.

these days the form is carved in positive (i.e. as it will finally appear), often simply in plaster rather than using wood at all. A reverse impression, i.e. a mould, is taken from this form. The impression is itself often made of compo or, if the form is an undercut design, stretchable latex is used.

Acknowledgements
I would like to thank Frances Binnington, gilder, for all her help and technical advice; Roy Hogben of John Cambell Picture Frames Ltd. who kindly allowed me to visit his workshops, where Figs. 1 and 2 were taken; and Richard de Peyer, curator of the Pinto Collection at Birmingham City Museum, who was extremely helpful in arranging for me to have access to the moulds and papers in the Pinto Collection of Treen and who allowed me to take Figs. 3, 4, 7 and 9 which are reproduced by permission of the Museum.

York, a centre of planemaking

J. R. Brown

Tools and Trades Volume 3: 1985

It is, perhaps, little known, other than to those with a special interest in old woodworking tools, that the City of York was amongst the most important plane manufacturing centres in the last century. Very little seems to be known about the detail of this former York industry or of the many workpeople involved. But, at one time or another from the latter half of the 18th century until the first World War, more than 60 planemakers were in business in the city and about half of these were at work at some time between the years 1820 and 1830.

Georgian, and more so Victorian, homes required miles of decorative mouldings, panelled doors and tongued and grooved boarding (there was no plywood) which at one time were all made by hand-held planes. Planemaking was very skilled work and tradesmen were required to have served a minimum of seven years apprenticeship. Their craft was slow to die, but was eventually overtaken by the introduction of machine produced mouldings and other joinery, and by the mass production of metal planes, towards the end of the Victorian era.

By 1850 York had become the centre of a railway system radiating in all directions and the city began to regain the eminence as a place of trade which it had enjoyed in the 15th century. To quote from *York and its Vicinity – A Guide* published by Thomas Brady in 1854:

"The principle manufactures carried on are glass, planes and other edge tools, soap, combs, iron-wire, confectionery and drugs and there are also some extensive iron-foundries."

Part of the demand for planes would have come from the railway carriage and wagon construction and repair workshops which were established in Queen Street in 1842. Plane bodies were later supplied to some Sheffield tool manufacturers who inserted their own plane-irons.

By 1875/76 there were only 3 planemakers left in York, but there must still have been considerable custom from the following tradesmen in the city at that time many of whom, like the planemakers, have now disappeared: boat-builders (2), cabinet makers (19), carriage builders, (13), clog makers (4), coopers (7), gun makers (5), joiners and builders (34), millwrights (8), wheelwrights (7), wood carvers and turners (17).

Most of the leading York planemakers were family concerns some spanning more than one generation. Unfortunately, in many cases the precise dates when individual planemakers were in business are not known, but the names of most with some idea of the years when they were at work are given in the list shown in Figure 1, overleaf.

The names and addresses of most of the planemakers appear in trade directories but it is difficult to be certain – unless examples of the maker's product have been traced – which of the many York planemakers were actually in business for themselves. *The Apprenticeship Register for the City of York* lists over 1211 men who were indentured as planemakers and

Fig. 1. York Planemakers

1761	**Richard Wood**
1768-99	**John Green**
	Coney Street
1771	**Green & Turner**
1771	**Phineas Turner**
	Spurriergate
1772-73	Coppergate
1772-1802	**Benjamin Dyson**
	Micklegate
1773	**Thos. & Wm. Nelson**
	Coppergate
1779	**John Spence**
	Gillygate
1784-1802	**Thomas Marsh**
1785-98	**Lancelot Tasker**
	High Ousegate
1787	**Winn & Co.**
	Bootham Bar
1787-1808	**John Green Jnr.**
	Micklegate
1791	**Middleton & Dyson**
1793-1803	**Michael Varvill**
	High Ousegate
1805-18	Feasegate
1818-29	8 New Bridge St.
1795	**John Snell**
1795-1806	**John Dyson**
	Fetter Lane
1797-1808	**George Hoyes**
1798-1812	**John Middleton**
	Peter Lane
1818-30	Nessgate
1799-1801	**Dyson & Son**
1800-20	**William Dibb**
	Peter Lane
1820-43	12 North Street
1800-07	**Thomas March**
	Davygate
1801-04	**James Hamer**
	Bishophill
1802-11	**William Ferrand**
	Bishophill
1821-30	17 Micklegate
1807	**Henry Kipling**
	Swinegate
1807	**David Brown**
	Bishophill
1807	**Richard Evers**
	Micklegate
1818-20	Peter Lane
1830	St. Martin's Lane
1807	**John Rusby**
	Micklegate
1807	**Robert Wilkinson**
	Bridge Street
1818-22	Micklegate
1807-20	**James Banks**
	Micklegate
1830	Wesley Place
1807-20	**John Burton**
	Bishophill
1807-30	**George Glaisby**
	Davygate
1808-20	**Ferrand & Wilkinson**
	17 Micklegate
1818	**Thomas Birks**
	Colliergate
1818-22	**Thomas Bean**
	Spurriergate
1846	26 Waterloo Place
1818-20	**William Buck**
	Shambles
1818-20	**Robert Darling**
	Trinity Lane
1830	Layerthorpe
1818-20	**William Simpson**
	Bishophill
1818-20	**Joseph Byram Snow**
	Skeldergate
1818-22	**John Bottomley**
	Tanner Row
1818-30	**William Kendall**
	Little Shambles
1820	**Thomas Bennett**
	Tanner Row

1820	**Glaisby & Dibb**
1820	**Robert Hardy**
	Tanner Row
1820	**William Penneyston**
	Goodramgate
1820	**Richard Flawith**
	Petergate
1820	**Robert Dalby**
	Shambles
1830	Wesley Place
1820-22	**George Robinson**
	Bishophill
1830	St. Martin's Lane
1820-30	**John Bean**
	Feasegate
1820-38	**Richard Kendall**
	2 Ogleforth
1846	7 Peter Lane
1822	**Elizabeth Hardy**
	Tanner Row
1822	**Ralph Barker**
	Fetter Lane
1829-40	**Varvill and Son**
	17 Micklegate
1830	**Richard Armitage**
	North Street
1830	**Joseph Bollands**
	North Street
1830	**Thomas Burnett**
	Bishophill
1830	**John Wales**
	North Street
1840-51	16 Goodramgate
1861-73	Scarborough Parade
1830	**James Gibson**
	Skeldergate
1830-62	**William Hustwick**
	Stonegate
1830-67	**William J. Walker**
	38-40 Micklegate
1840-62	**Summers Varvill**
	Ebor Works
1843-45	**Wm. Dibb & Son**
	12 North Street
1845-60	**Fred. Wm. Dibb**
	12 North Street
1851-76	**Charles Holmes**
	Scrivener's Court
1851-67	**George Eastwood**
	31 Walmgate
1868-89	52 Walmgate
1889-99	11 Railway Street
1855-71	**Robert Varvill**
	30 High Ousegate
1863-67	**Mary Varvill**
	34 Tanner Row
1872-98	**Varvill and Sons**
	North Street
1879-82	**Robert Ingleby**
	23 Lord Mayor's Walk
1881-83	**Thomas Banks**
	Fulford Road
1889	Hull Road
1890	**Wm. Dove & Sons**
	Lady Peckett's Yard
1899-04	**Varvill and Sons Ltd.**
	North Street
1880-10	**Holmes & Hunter**
	9 St. Saviourgate
1906-16	**Mennell Bros.**
	North Street

about half of these subsequently became Freemen. This does not mean that the remainder failed to complete their apprenticeship or remain in the City. Some would have become itinerant tradesmen and some found their way to London, where so many planemakers were established, and other important centres of the trade. Generally, York planemakers would have employed only one or two apprentices although Varvill employed large numbers of men including travellers and office staff as well as craftsmen planemakers. One such planemaker, George Underwood of Bishophill, who became a Freeman in 1825, worked for the

Fig. 2. Street locations of York planemakers 1774–1904 (the street numbers are known for only a few makers).

Varvill firm for more than 60 years. What does emerge so interestingly is that in the middle of the last century there was sufficient demand to keep so many people in the trade of planemaking and over such a long period even after the introduction of factory-made furniture, window frames, etc.

The size of this erstwhile industry of York may be judged to some extent from the number of premises in the City centre occupied by planemakers at some time over the years bearing in mind a number of premises were occupied by succeeding firms of planemakers. Again, in most cases the exact addresses are not known but the overall location of the trade may be seen from the sketch map shown.

The Varvills

Mention has already been made of the Varvills who were the largest manufacturers of planes in York. Michael Varvill who was born in 1771, the second son of Matthew Varvill, a farmer of Seaton Russ, was apprenticed to Lancelot Tasker, a planemaker in High Ousegate, York. Michael Varvill established his own business in 1793, also in High Ousegate but later moved to Feasegate. In 1829 he bought premises in Micklegate from another planemaking firm, William Ferrand, and changed his firm's name to Varvill and Son. At that time he inserted the following announcement in the *Yorkshire Gazette* of 1st August, 1829, shown in Quote 1.

Michael Varvill
Plane Manufacturer, York

> RETURNS Thanks to his Friends for the liberal Patronage experienced for 37 years, and most respectfully informs them, that he has purchased and entered upon the extensive Premises, formerly the property of the Late Mr. John Green, and recently of Mr. William Ferrand where the Business will, in future, be carried on, under the firm of VARVILL and SON.
>
> All orders with which they may be favoured will be executed with dispatch: Quality not to be excelled by any other House, either for well-seasoned wood, or superior workmanship.

Quote 1. From the Yorkshire Gazette, *1st August, 1829.*

Summers Varvill, Michael's eldest son (whose maternal grandmother was Susannah Summers) distinguished himself as a planemaker as well as a plane-iron and edge tool maker. He established his own business at the Ebor Works by North Street Postern, just outside the City wall, in 1840 when the trade announcement in Figure 3 appeared in White's *Directory of York*.

SUMMERS VARVILL,

EBOR WORKS, YORK,

MANUFACTURER OF

EDGE TOOLS, PLANES, JOINERS' TOOLS,

SKATES,

Brace-Bits, Augurs, Gimblets, &c. &c.

S. V. begs to return his most sincere thanks for the extensive support he received during his Partnership with his Father, in the manufacture of Planes, and for the general preference given to Articles of their Manufacture, wherever they have been introduced; and at the same time he respectfully announces that he is now Manufacturing all the above-named Articles on his own account; and, by making EDGE TOOLS, &c. from the best of Steel, and employing superior workmen, he can furnish those Articles so as to give every satisfaction, both as regards Quality and Price.

York, May 1st, 1840.

WILLIAM FORD, PRINTER, YORK-STREET, SHEFFIELD.

Fig. 4. Advertisement from the Historical Gazeteer & Directory for East and North Ridings of Yorkshire, *published by William White, 1840.*

Fig. 5. Advertisement from York Directory *of 1843, published by W. H. Smith of Hull.*

The Ebor Works by North Street Postern seem quite impressive from the illustration which appeared in a trade announcement of 1843. (Fig. 4.)

The Crimean War brought a large order for several thousand planes and other woodworking tools to Summers Varvill's Ebor Works in 1856. In the same year he inserted in the *Yorkshire Gazette* the announcement quoted verbatim in Quote 2.

In addition to the competition from about seven other planemaking firms in York at that time it seems he was most concerned with that encountered from his father's firm.

In 1859 Summers Varvill renewed his lease of the Ebor Works and the following

CAUTION
TO JOINERS, CABINET MAKERS, IRONMONGERS & ETC
SUMMERS VARVILL, of the EBOR WORKS, YORK, PLANE and EDGE TOOL MANUFACTURER to HER MAJESTY'S HON. BOARD of ORDINANCE and WHOLESALE IRONMONGER, having discovered that an Inferior Article in PLANES is made in this City, and stamped
VARVILL & SON
YORK

In a similar manner to those made by him, consider it his duty to Caution the Public against this Imposition.

The PLANES, which have for so many years met with such marked approval, can now only be had at THE EBOR WORKS, where also will be found A WELL SELECTED STOCK OF IRONMONGERY, at such Prices as cannot fail to give satisfaction.

Parties residing in the County are respectfully requested to be particular in advising in full.

'SUMMERS VARVILL, EBOR WORKS, YORK'

Quote 2. From the Yorkshire Gazette, *16th February, 1856.*

Renewed to Summers Varvill of the City of York Planemaker a lease of *All that* piece or parcel of land or ground situate and being without North Street Postern outside the walls of the City of York and entirely surrounded with public ways or roads and whereon the said Summers Varvill hath lately erected certain workshops Engine house warehouses and buildings and also all those buildings lately consisting of cottages and tenements standing and being there and now converted into warehouses and where formerly stood a messuage and tenement commonly called the Tyle houses and which said piece or parcel of land or ground workshops Engine house warehouse cottages and tenement on the block or ground plan thereof are particularly shewn and delineated on the map or plan drawn on these presents all which said premises are now in the tenure or occupation of the said Summers Varvill *Together* with the appurtenances To hold for 40 years from 1st June1850 Reserved Rent £100 and two fat hens – Fine £200.0s.0d.

Quote 3. Extract from lease for Ebor Works, 1859.

extract from the lease granted to him by the Vicars Choral of York Minster again suggests how extensive his planemaking premises were. (Quote 3.)

When Lendal Bridge was built in 1862, hard by the Ebor Works, none of Summers Varvill's planemaking premises were affected. The Ebor Works have, however, disappeared long since.

After Summers Varvill's death in 1862 the lease of the Ebor Works was put up for auction. The lease does not appear to have been reassigned at the time, however, as Summers Varvill's wife, Mary is listed in Frances White's *York Directories* of 1863-67 as the planemaker at the Ebor Works.

The advertisement for the auction which appeared in the *Yorkshire Gazette* of 23rd August, 1862 is quoted and reminds us of the size of the plane and tool works

SUMMERS VARVILL

EBOR WORK, near the Railway Station, York,

(RESIDENCE, 34, TANNER ROW,)

Manufacturer of Edge Tools, Planes, Joiners' Tools, Files, Skates, Brace Bits, Augers, Gimblets, &c. &c.

Please to address, "SUMMERS VARVILL, EBOR WORKS, YORK."

BENCH PLANES

	Single s.	d.	*Double* s.	d.
Smoothing Plane	2	2	3	6
Ditto, 2¼ Irons	2	4	3	8
Ditto, 2⅜ ditto	2	6	3	10
Ditto 2½ ditto	2	8	4	0
Smooth, with plated sole	0	0	7	0
Jack Plane, with 2-inch Irons	2	6	4	6
Ditto, 2⅛ ditto	2	6	4	6
Ditto, 2¼ ditto	2	8	4	8
Spout Plane	4	0	6	0
Pannel Plane	3	0	5	0
Ditto, with slip	3	8	5	8
Trying Plane, 22 inches	4	0	5	10
Ditto, 24 ditto	4	9	6	6
Long Trying, 26 ditto	4	9	6	6
Jointer ditto 28 ditto	5	2	7	4
Ditto 30 ditto	5	6	7	9
Warranted Cast-steel Irons, each for Smooth and Jack extra	0	3	0	3
Ditto, for Trying and Long	0	4	0	4
Ditto, for Jointer	0	5	0	5
Smoothing, 2 inches and 2⅛ Irons *(on the Birmingham Plan)*	0	0	2	10
Jack Planes, 2 inch and 2⅛ Irons *(Ditto)*	0	0	3	10
Trying Planes, 22 inches long, with 2½ Irons *(Ditto)*	0	0	4	9
Compass Plane	2	4	3	9
Ditto, plated sole	5	9	7	3
Ditto, with wood stop	3	0	4	9
Ditto, with brass screw top	5	0	7	0
Toothing ditto	2	9	3	10
Forkstaff ditto	3	0	5	3
Badger Plane	4	6	6	6
Smooth Raising	5	2	7	3
Ditto, full-grooved	5	8	7	8
Ditto, with 2¾ Cast-steel Irons for planted mouldings	0	0	9	0
Jack Raising, with Tooth	6	8	8	10
Ditto, full-grooved with 2¾ Cast-steel Irons, for planted mouldings			10	6
Cove Raising Planes with 3½ Cast-steel Irons			15	0
Stower Planes, to round 3 inch, with handles			7	6
Facia Planes			5	10
Mitre Plane, common			3	9
Ditto, best, with box front			6	6
Ditto, iron, with steel face			26	0
Ditto, Brass, with steel face			30	0
Jack Grooving, per pair, to 1 inch			8	6
Ditto, 1¼			8	9
Ditto, 1½			9	0
Ditto, iron tenon			10	0
Moving Fences, extra			2	0
Gentlemen's Smoothing, 1½ inch single Irons			1	9

COOPERS' JOINTERS

	Ft.	In.	*Single* s.	d.	*Double* s.	d.
Cooper's Jointers	4	0	13	9	16	9
Ditto	4	6	15	3	18	0
Ditto	5	0	15	9	19	0
Ditto	6	0	17	0	19	0
Ditto, one single and one double iron	5	0	11	0	24	0
Ditto	5	6	ditto		25	0
Ditto	6	0	ditto		25	0
Ditto	6	0	2 dble irons		27	0
Coopers' Brace, one boss					3	6
Coopers' Groze 13 inches					5	0
Ditto 14 inches					5	6
Ditto 17 inches					6	6
Coachmakers' Jarvise Planes, plated with iron					8	6

A

	s.	d.
Astragals, to ¾ inch inclusive	2	4
Ditto, solid box mouldings, to ⅝ inch	3	2
Ditto, for every ⅛ above	0	2
Astragal and Hollow Sash	3	0
Ditto with quirk and box'd	3	6
Ditto, ditto, to stick and rabbet	5	4
Ditto, with handles, extra	1	0
Lamb Tongue Sash Planes	3	0
Gothic ditto	3	0
Grecian box'd ditto	3	6
Rustic Sash	3	0
Ditto to stick and rabbet	5	0
Ditto, ditto, with handles	6	0
Circular Sash Planes, extra	1	0

B

	s.	d.
Bead Planes, to ⅝ inch inclusive	2	8
Bead Planes, slip'd, to ⅝	3	0
Beads, thick box'd to ⅝	3	2
Ditto, each ⅛ above, extra	0	2
Ditto dovetail box'd extra	1	0
Sliped extra	0	4
Cock Beads, box'd	2	8
Ditto ditto double	3	4
Bookcase Shelf Planes	5	6
Ditto ditto, with slips	6	0

C

	s.	d.
Cove and Beads, to ¾ inclusive	3	3
Ditto, with double fillets	3	7
Ditto, for every ⅛ above	0	2
Chair-foot Plane	3	0
Chair-splat Plane	4	6
Cylinder Plane, box'd	3	6
Curl'd Shaving Plane	3	0

D

	s.	d.
Dove-tail Plane	2	6
Ditto, solid box, moulding	3	0

F

	s.	d.
Filisters, standing	2	4
Ditto, for drawers	2	10
Ditto, for cock beads	3	10
Ditto trenching plane way, with wood stop	4	10

Ditto, with brass stop 6 10
Moving Filisters, common 4 8
Ditto, wood stop, box'd 5 2
Ditto, brass slip stop, ditto 5 2
Ditto, brass screw, stop and tooth 6 6
Ditto, shoulder'd box'd and ditto. 7 0
Ditto, thumb-stop, wedge-tooth, and improved fence 10 0
Sash Filisters, common 6 6
Ditto, brass top 10 0
Ditto, single-hoop'd 11 6
Ditto, double-hoop'd 13 0
Ditto, ditto, left-hand wedge-tooth, and shoulder'd box 16 0
Ditto, ditto, dove-tail, box'd 17 0
Ditto, with screw stems, extra 3 0
Best left-hand Sash Filisters, box screw stems, box fence, and extra stop 21 0
Fluting Plane, with handle 3 0

G

Grooving Planes, per pair, to ¾ .. 5 6
Ditto, for every ⅛ above, extra, per pair 0 4
Ditto, with open eye 5 9
Ditto, with loose fences 7 6
Grooving Plane for drawer bottoms, box'd 2 8

H

Hollows and Rounds, per pair to No. 12 .... 4 4
Ditto ditto, each pair above 4 6
Ditto, skew-eyed, extra 0 2
Ditto, shoulder box'd to No. 4 .... 6 6
Hand-rail Plane, moving fences, like smoothing 4 6
Ditto ditto, double iron 6 6
Ditto, Hollow, ditto 5 3
Ditto, Rowter 6 0

N

Neckmould, box'd to ¾ inch inclusive 3 6
Ditto, each ⅛ above extra 0 2

O

Ogees to ¾ inclusive 2 4
Ditto, ditto, slip'd 3 0
Reverse Ogees, to ¾ 3 0
Ditto, with bead at foot 4 6
Ditto, ditto, and double fillet 4 10
Ditto, every ⅛ above, extra 0 2
Quirk Ogees, to ¾ inclusive 3 0
Ditto, slip'd ditto 3 6
Quirk Ogee and Quirk'd beads, to ¾ 4 10
Quirk Ogee and Astragal, to ¾ ... 4 6
Quirk'd Ogee and Beads, to ¾ ... 4 6
Ditto, ditto, every ⅛ above extra. 0 2
Ovolos, to ¾ inclusive 2 5
Ovolo Sash 2 5
Ovolo Sash, to stick and rabbet ... 1 9
Ovolo Sash, with handles, extra .. 1 0
Quirk Ovolos, to ¾ 3 4
Ditto, with three Reeds, to ¾ 6 2
Ditto, for every ⅛ above, extra ... 0 2
Quirk Ovolo and bead to ¾ 4 10
Quirk Ovolo and Astragals, to ¾ . 4 10
Ditto, every ⅛ above, extra 0 2
Grecian Quirk Ovolo, to ¾ inclusive 3 4
Grecian Quirk Ogee, to ¾ inclusive 4 8
Every ⅛ above, extra 0 2
Old Woman's Tooth 1 8
Ditto, Smoothing Plane way 1 8

P

Ploughs common, six bits 9 6
Ditto, best brass stop, eight bits ... 18 0
Ploughs, best brass stop, eight bits, single-hooped 19 0
Ditto, ditto, ditto, double hooped. 20 0
Ditto, ditto, ditto, ivory scal'd stems 21 6
Improved Plough 21 0
Circular Plough, for straight and circular work, 12 bits 36 0
Screw Ploughs, 8 bits 22 6
Screw Plough, box stems 23 6
Bookcase Shelf Planes, box stems. 23 6
Bridge Plough, box stems 30 0
Improved, extra 1 0
Ploughs with handles, extra 2 0
Picture Frame Planes, to ¾ 4 4
Ditto, for every ⅛ above 0 2
Italian Picture Frame, ditto 4 10

Q

Quarter Rounds 2 4

R

Rabbet Planes, square, to 1½ inch 2 4
Ditto each ⅛ above 0 1
Ditto, box'd edges, extra 0 10
Ditto, shoulder'd box, extra 2 0
Skew Rabbet, to 1 inch 2 6
Ditto to 1⅝ inch 2 8
Each ⅛ above 0 1
Ditto, with tooth 3 6
Ditto, ditto, and wood stop 4 6
Reed Plane, one reed, whole box'd 3 4
Ditto, two ditto ditto 4 2
Ditto, three ditto ditto 4 10
Ditto, four ditto ditto 5 8
Ditto, five ditto ditto 6 6
Ditto, dove-tail'd, box'd, for each dove-tail extra 1 0
Improved Reeds 4 9
Reed and Guide 4 2

S

Snipe's bill 2
Ditto shoulder'd box 3 3
Side-Snipe, ditto 3 6
Side-Rabbet 2 4
Side-Round 2 6

T

Trenching Plane, wood stop to ¾ 4 6
Ditto, brass stop, to ¾ 6 6
Torus Plane, to ⅝ inclusive 3 0
Ditto, slip'd 3 6
Ditto, for every ⅛ above 0 2
Table Planes, per pair 4 4
Templets, per pair 1 3
Ditto, if screwed 1 6
Whip-makers' Plane, with iron sole 2 9

RUNNERS, &c

Runners, to 1 inch 3 0
Screw Engines 6 0
Ditto, plated with iron 8 0
Ditto, with brass 9 0

SCREWS, &c

Bench Screws, each 3 0
Hand Screws, each 2 6
Dowling Boxes, with 2 pair of slips and collars 7 6
Improved hand wood Dowling Boxes 22 6

MALLETS

Carpenters' and Joiners' Mallets, with square holes
1st size, per dozen 20 0
2nd ditto, ditto 22 0
3rd ditto, ditto 24 0
Tinners' Mallets 6 0

Fig. 5. Reprint of a Summers Varvill price list (not a facsimile).

TO IRON FOUNDERS AND OTHERS
EBOR WORKS, YORK
TO BE SOLD BY AUCTION
By Messrs. HANDS AND SON
At Scawin's Hotel, York on Wednesday the 10th September, 1862
at THREE o'Clock in the Afternoon.

ALL the Extensive Modern and Valuable Business Premises known as the EBOR WORKS situate without North-Street Postern, and near the River Ouse, in York, the property of the late MR. SUMMERS VARVILL, Plane and Edge Tool Manufacturer and General Ironmonger, together with the Engine House, Grinding and Turning Shops Machinery and Trade Fixtures and Fittings.

The property is walled and roaded round, and has an area of about 840 Square Yards. It has every Convenience for carrying on an extensive and Profitable Business.

The property is Leasehold under the Vicars Choral in York, for a term of 40 years from 1st of June, 1859, and is renewable every 14 years on payment of a fine.

The STOCK-IN-TRADE can be taken at a Valuation if wished. Early Possession of the Premises can be given.

The Premises can be Viewed and further Information obtained on Application to MR. ROBERT VARVILL, Ironmonger, Bridge Street, York, or MR. MICHAEL VARVII.L, Lead Merchant, of Railway-Street, York and of York.

19th August, 1862. Messrs LEEMAN AND CLARK
Solicitors

Quote 4. The advertisement for the auction from the Yorkshire Gazette, *23rd August, 1862.*

which once stood alongside the River Ouse. (Shown in Quote 4.)

Summers Varvill had been the eldest of five brothers (and four sisters). Robert was a planemaker, tool maker and ironmonger; Michael Varvill was an important lead and glass merchant; John Varvill was an ironmonger and Fraser Varvill, the youngest, a planemaker. All the Varvills seemed to be involved in tool making and it is interesting to note from the *York Apprenticeship Register* that Robert Varvill and Mary Varvill (presumably Summer Varvill's widow) together had a planemaker apprenticed to them in July, 1865.

The plane and tool making firm of Varvill and Sons later operated from Robert Varvill's (Summers Varvill's brother) workshops in North Street. These were erected in 1873 and were also known as the Ebor Works.

Although it tells us little about the new building it is interesting to read the following report (Quote 5) which appeared in the *Yorkshire Gazette* of 20th September, 1873 on completion of the works.

In 1879 at the York Fine Arts and Industrial Fair, R(obert) Varvill and Sons gained a medal for the excellence of the workmanship and material of their planes. At that time their impressive shop premises by Ouse Bridge, re-built in 1853, were featured on their invoices. (Fig. 6.)

Robert Varvill died in 1885 and his sons John and Michael (grandsons of Michael Varvill the Elder and first planemaker of the family) carried on the business until a Receiver was appointed in 1900. It appears that the firm eventually closed in 1904, a sad ending having regard to the success enjoyed by the firm over so

NEW BUILDINGS IN YORK

On Monday afternoon last, Mr. Roe's large 'bus and live cabs conveyed to Acomb the men employed in the erection of the new works for Messrs. Varvill and Son, situate in North-Street, for the purpose of being entertained to supper. The proprietors and contractors joined in affording the workmen this treat, and Mr Flower, landlord of the Britannia Inn, Acomb, proved himself a capital caterer. As usual on such occasions the health of the employees and prosperity to the undertaking followed the supper as well as songs and other toasts, the time previous to the supper was spent in cricket, running, and other recreations. The vehicles with their thankful occupants, returned at a reasonable hour, all being greatly pleased with the good feeling and generosity shown on the occasion. The contractors for the work were, Mr. John Holmes for the joiner's work; Mr. Henry Swann, for the brick, stone, and plaster work; under the supervision of Mr. Timothy Taylor, clerk of Works.

Quote 5. From the Yorkshire Gazette, *20th September, 1873.*

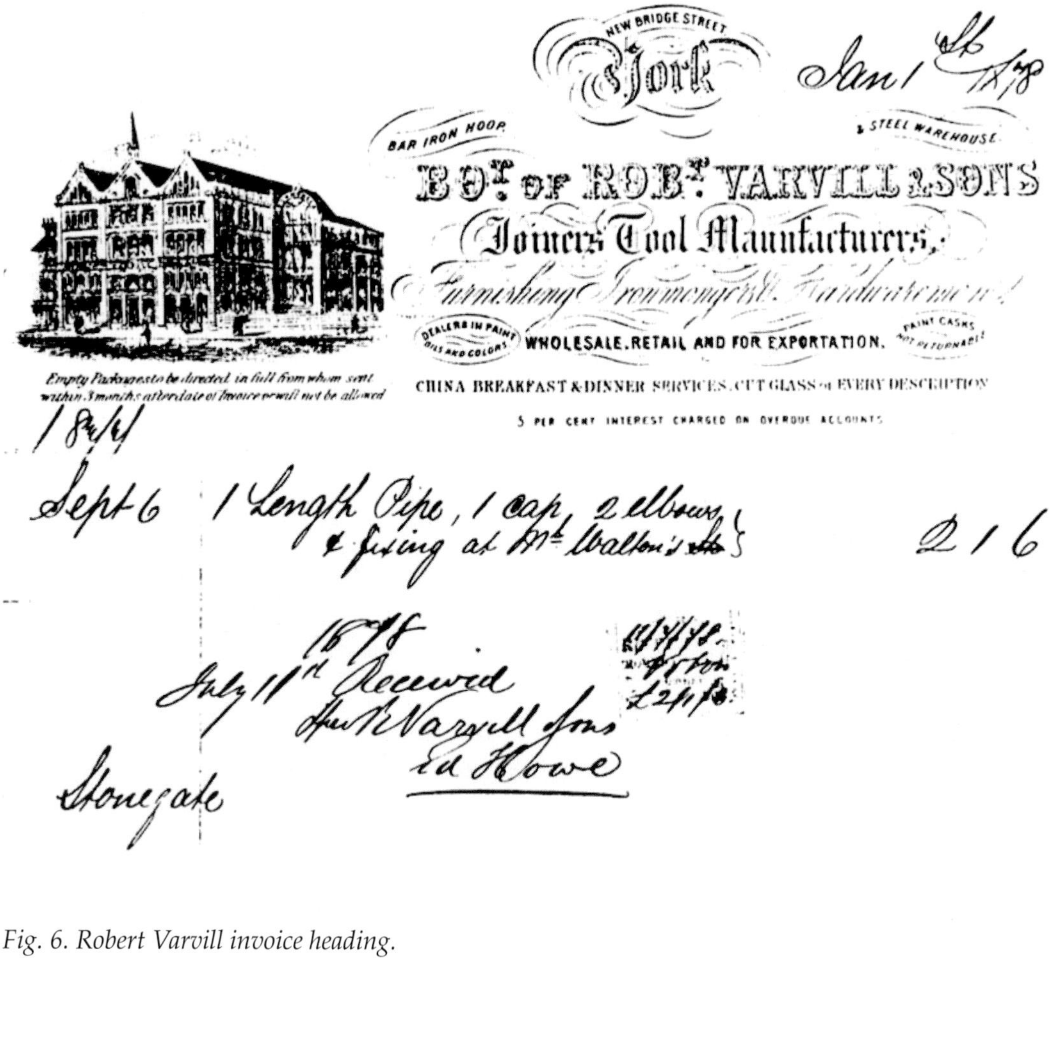

NEW BRIDGE STREET
York
Jan 1st 1878
BAR IRON HOOP & STEEL WAREHOUSE
BOt OF ROBt VARVILL & SONS
Joiners' Tool Manufacturers,
WHOLESALE, RETAIL AND FOR EXPORTATION.
CHINA BREAKFAST & DINNER SERVICES, CUT GLASS of EVERY DESCRIPTION
5 PER CENT INTEREST CHARGED ON OVERDUE ACCOUNTS

1877
Sept 6 1 Length Pipe, 1 cap, 2 elbows & fixing at Mr Walton's 2 1 6

1878
July 11th Received
for R Varvill & Sons
Ed Howe

Stonegate

Fig. 6. Robert Varvill invoice heading.

ROBERT VARVILL & SONS, WHOLESALE IRONMONGERS, PLANE MANUFACTURERS, AND DEALERS IN ALL KINDS OF JOINER'S, COACH BUILDERS', SMITHS', AND ENGINEERS' TOOLS, Bridge Street, York. – This eminent house was founded as far back as the year 1820 by the late Mr. Robert Varvill and his brother John, and is now controlled by the former gentleman's two sons, Messrs. John and Michael Varvill. The concern is now the largest of its kind in the district of York, and its headquarters in Bridge Street are very extensive, adjoining the river Ouse, and occupying a commanding position on Ouse Bridge. These fine premises are no less than seven storeys in height, and have a frontage of a hundred feet, with a rearward extension of ninety-five feet. They rank among the handsomest and most imposing commercial structures in the City.

A more complete or more carefully-assorted stock of ironmongery of every kind, useful, artistic, and decorative, is not to be found within the borders of the "Premier County". The whole place proclaims the character and influence of the firm, and speaks for the magnitude of their trade in its every interesting department; and the latest conveniences contribute to the smooth working and satisfactory progress of the business. These handsome premises are built in what is termed the "gallery style" an opening or "well", 15 feet by 7 feet, being carried from the basement clear up to the roof. Messrs. Varvill keep four travellers "on the road" in all parts of Yorkshire, and also in some quarters of the adjacent counties. These representatives travel in rather a unique way, each being provided with a horse and trap, enabling him to take in all the small towns and villages, as well as the larger centres on his route. This distinguished firm are proprietors of the far-famed Ebor Works, where they engage in the manufacture of planes and high-class edge tools upon a most extensive scale. The history of these celebrated works dates from the year 1793, and they are the largest and most important of their kind in the north of England. The substantial five-storey premises of the Ebor Works constitute an industrial establishment of which the proprietors are justly proud, and one which affords unsurpassed facilities for every department of the trade engaged in. Upwards of eighty hands are employed here, and the speciality of the works consists in planes, for which Messrs. Varvill have a worldwide and unexcelled reputation. The ironmongery establishment and the Ebor Works are within fifty yards of each other, and both have telephone communication. They stand among the most notable spheres of commercial and industrial activity in the City of York, and are worthy, in all respects, of the eminent firm and the trade to whose service they are devoted. Both the principals of this house are widely known and greatly respected throughout the City and district, enjoying the esteem of all with whom they have dealings in business or private life.

Quote 6. From The Industries of Yorkshire, *1890.*

many years as is evidenced by the extract from *The Industries of Yorkshire* published as late as 1890. (Quote 6.)

Planes under the well-known Varvill name, however, continued to be produced as the trade announcement (Quote 7) which appeared in the *Yorkshire Gazette* of 11th March, 1905 – testifies.Many of the planes made by the Varvills are still around. The abridged "Family Tree" (Fig. 8) may help to identify some of the marks used by this famous family of planemakers.

Fig. 7. VARVILL & SONS *"Mitre device" (in use 1860 onwards), a Varvill trade- mark*

MENNELL BROS.
MANUFACTURERS OF "VARVILL'S" CELEBRATED PLANES
JOINERS' TOOLS, AND All KINDS OF WOOD HANDLES AND
GENERAL WOOD TURNERY IRON,
HARDWARE AND TIMBER MERCHANTS

OUR WORKS ARE NOW SPECIALLY EQUIPPED WITH
MACHINERY FOR SAW SHARPENING AND GRINDING OF EVERY
DESCRIPTION. WRINGING MACHINE ROLLERS FITTED AND
TURNED TO CUSTOMERS SPINDLES AT LOWEST PRICES
THE TRADE SUPPLIED

EBOR WORKS, NORTH-STREET, YORK

Quote 7. Trade announcement from the Yorkshire Gazette, *11th March, 1905.*

Fig. 8. Family tree of planemaker Varvills, with imprints from toes of their planes.

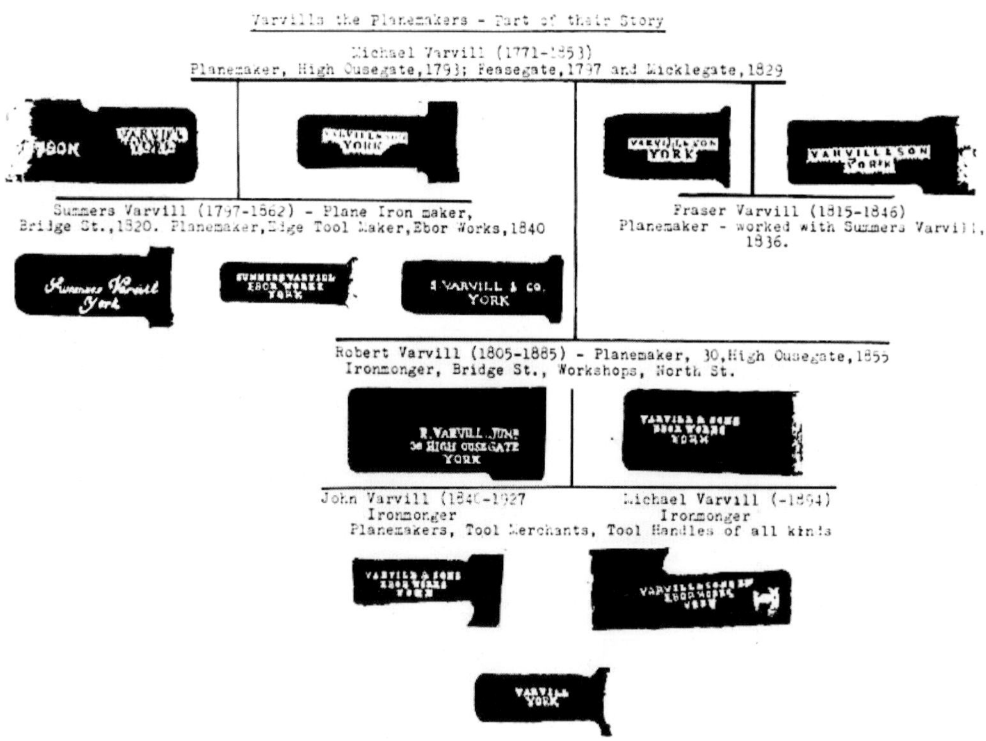

THE Partnership between, JOHN GREEN and PHINEAS TURNER, of this City, Plane Makers, being now dissolved, all Persons having any Demands on, or stand indebted to, the said Partnership are desired to send in their Accounts, and pay their respective Debts, to John Green in Coney-street or Phineas Turner in Feasegate, in order that such Accounts may be settled as soon as possible.

JOHN GREEN
PHINEAS TURNER

The above Business is now carried on separately viz, by John Green at the old shop at Coney-street, and by Phineas Turner at his shop in Spurriergate. They each return thanks for past favours, and hope for a Continuance thereof.

Quote 7. From the York Courant*, 15th January, 1771.*

JOHNGREEN,PLANEMAKERinConey-street,York,returnshismostgratefulAcknowledgements to his friends for past Favours, and hopes for a continuance thereof. He also begs leave to inform all Joiners and others, that they may be supplied with Planes. and every other Article in the Tool Way of the London. Birmingham, Sheffield, and Liverpool Make. As good Materials will recommend themselves he has, and will always endeavour to have, a sufficient Stock of well-seasoned Wood; so that those who please to favour him with their Commands may depend on being served with the best of Goods, and on the shortest Notice.

☞GENTLEMAN'S CHESTS neatly fitted up from 15s to 10£ etc .

Quote 8. From the York Courant, *5th October, 1773.*

John Green

An earlier and well-known planemaking family was that of John Green of Coney Street who was in business prior to 1768 when his son, John, was apprenticed to him. In 1771 it is learned from the *York Courant* of 15th January, that his planemaking partnership with Phineas Turner was dissolved. (Quote 7.)

An interesting advertisement –shown in Quote 8 – appeared in two issues of the *York Courant* of 21st September and 5th October, 1773.

After completing his apprenticeship, John Green the Younger worked with his father until commencing business on his own account in Micklegate in 1798. It was his premises on the corner of Trinity Lane which were subsequently taken over by William Ferrand and Robert Wilkinson in 1808 and afterwards, in 1829 by Michael Varvill the Elder. John Green the Younger died in 1808, aged 54. He is buried in Holy Trinity churchyard, Micklegate, his grave being not 50 yards from his workshop. His tombstone is inscribed "In memory of John Green of this City, Planemaker".

Following his death John Green's Micklegate property was put up for sale, and the advertisement which appeared at the time, which gives us a good idea of the situation and size of his premises, is re-produced in Quote 9.

Fig. 9. The inscription on John Green's gravestone.

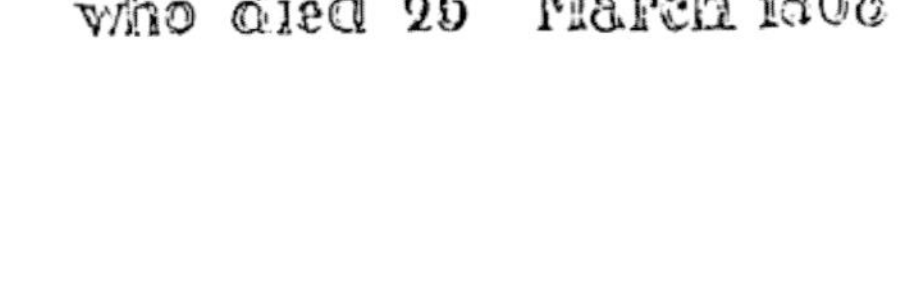

TO PLANEMAKERS, IRONMONGERS and OTHERS
TO BE SOLD
ALL those FREEHOLD PREMISES

lately the Property of Mr. JOHN GREEN, Planemaker deceased, consisting of TWO Messuages or Dwelling-Houses, fronting Micklegate, in the City of York, with the Yard and Outbuildings thereunto respectively belonging one of them late in the possession of the said JOHN GREEN, and now of Mrs. GREEN, and the other of Mr CLEASBY, Grocer.

Also the commodious Workshops, Warehouse, Stable, and spacious Yard, situate at a convenient distance behind the said Messuages, with an entrance from the same, and a Carriage Road from St. Martin's Lane, on which the shops adjoin, and wherein the business of Planemaker hath been successfully carried on upwards of 20 years by the said John Green, and will be continued by his Executors until disposed of.

The Premises are worthy of the attention of a Planemaker, or any person desirous of embarking in that business, being furnished with Sawing and Grinding Machines, worked by a Horse-Mill, and every other requisites for carrying on a considerable Manufactory.

The Stock-in-Trade &c. including a large quantity of dry Beechwood, may be had by the Purchaser at a fair valuation; and part of the Purchase-Money may remain on security of the Premises.

To be viewed, and further particulars known, by applying to Mr. Samuel Green, at the Premises, or to Mr. Thomas Wolstenholme Gillygate, York, the Executors IN TRUST ol the said John Green, to whom all persons having demands on the Estate of the said John Green, are desired to apply for payment of the same. and to whom all persons who stand indebted to the said Estate are requested to pay their respective debts.

Quote 9. The advertisement for the sale of John Green's Micklegate premises.

Ferrand and Wilkinson

The premises advertised above were acquired by William Ferrand and Robert Wilkinson who were already in business independently as planemakers in nearby Bishophill. William Ferrand was in fact John Green's cousin and had been apprenticed to his father in 1776, 32 years previously. On his death in 1799 John Green Snr. left his nephew, Wm. Ferrand, a bequest of £5.

Ferrand and Wilkinson announced their succession to John Green's business in the *York Courant* of 6th June, 1808 as shown in Quote 10.

Ferrand and Wilkinson remained in business together until 1821 when Robert Wilkinson assigned his interest in the firm to trustees. William Ferrand carried on business as a planemaker until 1830.

FERRAND and WILKINSON
PLANEMAKERS
(SUCCESSORS to the late JOHN GREEN)
YORK

RESPECTFULLY inform their Friends and the Public, that they have purchased the PROPERTY with the entire STOCK in TRADE and MACHINERY of the late Mr. Green, and humbly hope, from their long knowledge of business with Mr. Green (the former being with him thirty years, the latter upwards of twenty) to receive a continuance of public patronage, and to merit that esteem for which the above Manufactory has been so much distinguished for its Articles.

Orders to any extent, carefully and expeditiously attended to.

York, June 1st, 1808

Quote 10. Announcement from the York Courant, *6th June 1808.*

NOTICE TO THE PUBLIC

A REPORT having been industriously circulated that JOHN DYSON of the City of York had declined business which might tend to his prejudice, he thinks it necessary to inform the Public, that it is totally void of all foundation, and that the Business will be carried on, in its various branches of Planemaking in Fetter Lane, where all orders will be executed with the utmost despatch, and on the most reasonable terms.

York, 2nd August, 1806

Quote 11. Notice from the York Courant, *14th August, 1806.*

Benjamin Dyson, John Dyson and John Middleton

Another case of the son being apprenticed to his father was John Dyson whose seven year apprenticeship to Benjamin Dyson and his co-partner, John Middleton, commenced on 27th October, 1792. Benjamin Dyson is recorded making planes in Fetter Lane, York in 1772, and, with John Green Senior and the Nelsons (see below), is thought to be the oldest known York planemakers whose planes still survive.

John Dyson inserted the notice, shown in Quote 11, in the *York Courant* of 14th August, 1806.

Shortly afterwards it is thought John Dyson may have moved to London or Manchester.

Nelsons

The Nelson brothers, Thomas and William, were the sons of Richard Nelson of Helperby. Following the death of their father the two brothers set up in business as planemakers in Coppergate, York. They announced their intention in the *York Courant* of 21st September, 1773 (it was in this issue that John Green's advertisement appeared) in the terms as shown in Quote 12.

Although "NELSONS" planes still survive it is not known how long the firm itself survived in Coppergate. It may well have had small beginnings judging from the following extract from the Praisement taken of Richard Nelson's Goods and Cattle following his death in 1773. The executor was John Green Snr., planemaker of York.

> "Shop and Wood and Tools made by them... £27"

George Eastwood

Another distinguished planemaker to come on the scene later was George Eastwood of Walmgate near St. Denys' Church. He had the distinction of being awarded a medal at the Great Exhibition of 1851 "for his invention and manufacture of a panel plane to answer the purpose of panel and mitre."

RICHARD NELSON late of Helperby, planemaker, being deceased, this Business will be continued by his Sons, for the greatest Convenience of such as please to favour them with their orders, have taken a shop in Coppergate (late Phineas Turner's) where all Joiners and others may depend on being served with the best of Goods, they having got the finest Wood in the County, and that they will use their utmost Endeavours to give Satisfaction to those who employ them, whose orders shall be executed in the best Manner, and with the utmost Expedition by

Their humble Servants
THOMAS and WILLIAM NELSON

Quote 12. Notice from the York Courant, *21st September 1773.*

GEORGE EASTWOOD
Plane Maker, 31 Walmgate, York
Is in need of Two or Three good Plane Makers. Constant Employment and the best Prices will be given. None but First Rate Workmen need apply.

Quote 13. Advertisement in the Yorkshire Gazette.

GEORGE EASTWOOD
PLANE MANUFACTURER, WHOLESALE and RETAIL,
31, WALMGATE, YORK.

BEGS leave to inform his friends that he has commenced the above Business in all its Branches, having at considerable expense fitted up every convenience together with his intention to employ none but the best Workmen, he can with confidence state that he will be enabled to supply an article equal, if not superior, to any in the trade, for which he earnestly solicits a trial, as the best proof. All kinds of IRON and BRASS PLANES made on the most improved principles, and the most reasonable terms.

JOINER'S and CABINET MAKER'S TOOLS of every description.
N. B. Workshops down the adjoining Yard

Quote 14. Advertisement from the Yorkshire Gazette, *14th June, 1851.*

Fig. 10. Advertisement from Melville& Coy's 1855 Directory of York and the East Riding.

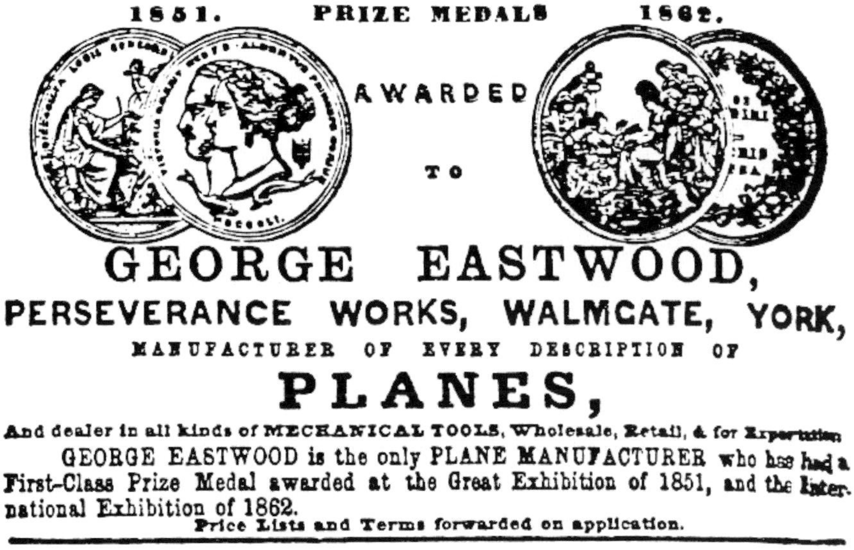

Fig. 11. George Eastwood's advertisement from Slater's Directory, *1865*

It seems George Eastwood's award at the Great Exhibition resulted in increased business as afterwards the advertisement, shown in Quote 13, appeared in the *Yorkshire Gazette.*

On 14th June, 1851 George Eastwood put the advertisement in the *Yorkshire Gazette,* shown in Quote 14.

George Eastwood's firm later moved to the Perseverance Works at 52, Walmgate, York, immediately opposite St. Denys' Church. In 1865 the advertisement, shown in Figure 11, appeared in Slater's *Directory of York.*

Mr. Eastwood also gained a medal at the York Fine Art and Industrial Exhibition of 1866 – "for the superiority of workmanship of his planes and for the general excellence of his assortment of tools."

"The name of Eastwood is now as well known as that of many of the highest firms ..." to quote from a contemporary report from the *Yorkshire Herald* of the York Exhibition which took place in July, 1866. (Quote 15.)

Fig. 12. George Eastwood's advertisement, after 1879.

> "in connection with the manufacture of joiners' and cabinet makers' tools in York, is now about as well known in the country as that of many of the highest firms in the kingdom in this particular line of business. Mr. George Eastwood of Walmgate, was on exhibition at the Exhibition of 1851 and 1852 and on both those occasions earned some honour for his native place by carrying off first class prizes for the cases of articles which he had furnished for competition. It is, therefor, scarcely surprising to find him represented in our Exhibition at home. Here, Mr. Eastwood's case consists of planes with modern improvements, and tools of a variety of descriptions suitable for joiners, cabinet makers and others. The quality of articles usually turned out by this exhibitor has become a proverb for their excellence, whilst to the eye of the visitor their appearance as they stand in the case before them is remarkable for their finish and general adaptability of form and manufacture for the purposes to which they are intended".

Quote 15. Report in the Yorkshire Herald.

George Eastwood gained another medal at the York Exhibition of 1879 where he exhibited planes and tools suitable for joiners, cabinet makers, coachbuilders and wheelwrights etc. This medal is referred to in later advertisements. Also indicated is the firm's move to Railway Street, York in 1889.

The planes

Many of the old woodworking planes still exist although these tend to be those of the larger manufacturers. Some wooden planes continued to be made as recently as the 1960s but not of course in the many forms which were available in the past. An idea of some of the hundreds of types produced in earlier days may be seen from an advertisement for the auction sale held when Mr. F. W. Dibb, son of William Dibb, ceased business in 1860. The advertisement, shown in Quote 16, also gives an idea of the equipment used in the planemaking factory and suggests that a delivery service was available!

The overall shape of the planes, as well as the products of different makers throughout the country varied hardly at all over the years. Invariably the name of the maker appeared on the front end or "toe" of the plane as may be seen from Figure 16.

Fig. 13. George Eastwood's advertisement, after 1889.

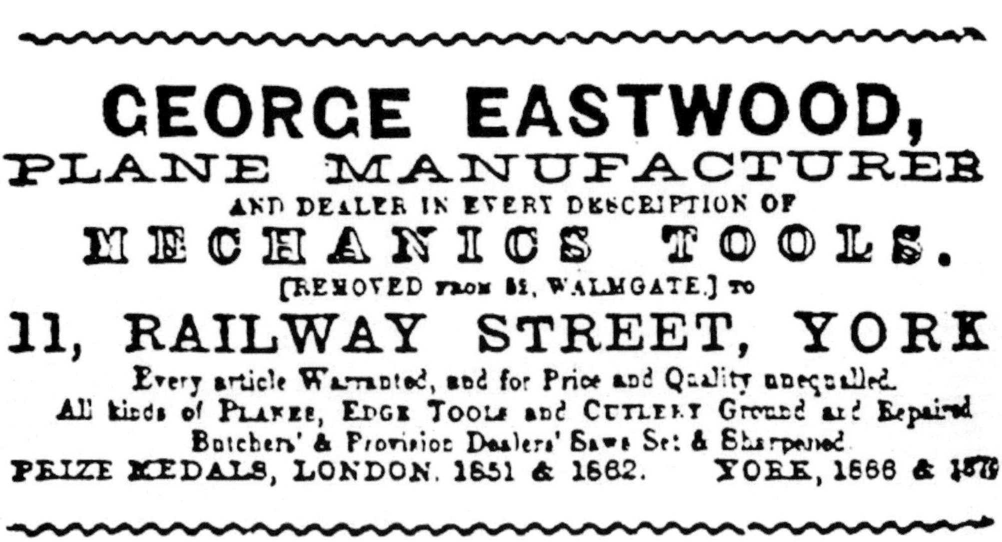

No. 12 NORTH-STREET
TO PLANE MANUFACTURERS, JOINERS, WOOD TURNERS & ETC.
Sale of the Stock-in-Trade and Trade Plant of a Plane Manufacturer

MR. GEORGE ACTON has been favoured with Instructions from Mr. Dibb, Plane Manufacturer, to SELL BY AUCTION, on the Premises, North Street as above, on TUESDAY, JULY 31st, 1860, the whole of the STOCK-IN-TRADE, comprising Sets of Hollows and Round, Lambs Tongue Sash, Ovalo Sash, Grecian Quirk Ovalo, Beads, Reeds, Common O.G., Reverse O.G., Quirk O.G., Reverse O.G. Astragals, Quirked O.G. Astragals, Grecian O.G., Quirked O.G. and Beads, Neckmoulds, Picture Frame, Cove Astragals, Common Ovalo, Quirk Ovalo and Astragal, Cod, Grooving, Wood Boxing, Side Round, Quarter Rounds, Quirk Ovalo, Astragals, Grecian Ovalo, Astragal and Hollow, Gothic Sash, and a variety of other Sets; also Smoothing, Trying and Jack Planes, Plane Irons, Files, Brass Castings Iron Nuts, Packing Nails, Plane Stocks from 17 inches to 30 inches. Moulding Plane Stocks, Smoothing ditto., Plough Stocks & etc.

Amongst the TRADE PLANT will be found 9 Benches, 12 Pairs of Vice, 9 Vice Benches, 2 Anvils, 2 Stoves and Piping, Pair of Bellows and Forge, Crow Bars, Cant Dogs, Knife Wedges and Mell, Screw Hammers, Hand Spokes, Laithe and Tools, Two Circular Saws and Benches, One-horse Mill with Strapping complete; superior Grindstone 4 feet 6 inches diameter, with Frame and Ironwork complete; Grindstone to work with power; Top iron steel, Hoop iron, Planks and Quarters, Tool Chests, Packing Boxes, 3 Wood Rollers and Transome, Ladders, a quantity of Boxwood; 2 large Shades with Tiled Roofs; several Thousand Pieces of Wood, suitable for Wood Turners, Last Makers & etc.

A One-horse Phaeton, Set of Harness, and a Set of Cart Gearing.

Sale to commence at ELEVEN o'Clock

Ebor Rooms, 2 Low Ousegate, York.
July 21st, 1860.

Quote 16. The advertisement for the auction sale held when William Dibb ceased trading in 1860.

Fig. 14. Part of an exhibition which the author mounted in York in his continuing quest for information about the city's erstwhile planemaking industry.

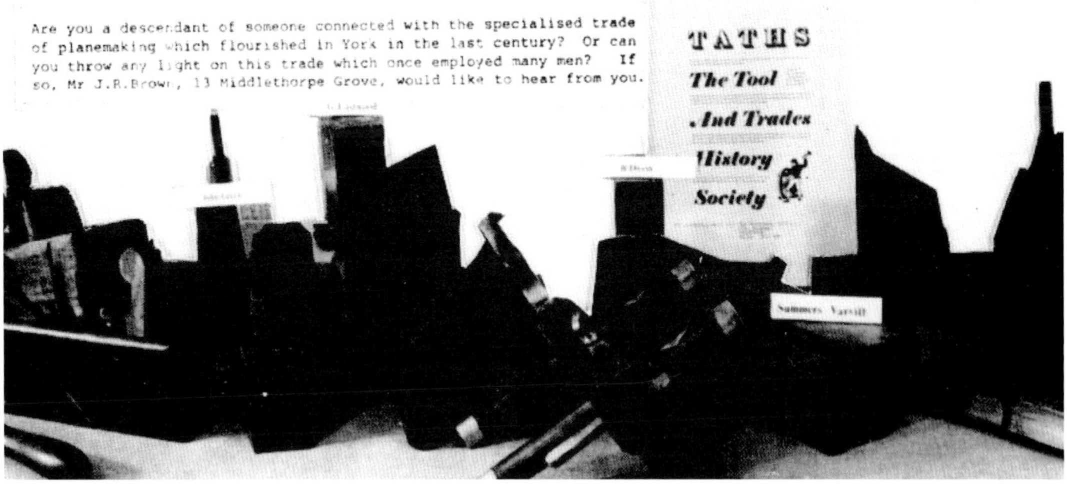

Fig. 15. Some typical planes: a No. 10 round by George Eastwood (1851–99): two sash ovolos and a common ovolo by William Dibb (1800–43)

Acknowledgments

Grateful acknowledgment is made to:

Mrs. Jill Batey, for the reproduction of the Robt. Varvill & Sons' invoice.

W. L. Goodman, author of *British Planemakers from 1700* (2nd ed. 1978).

Hugh Murray: "Murray's York Pedigrees" MS in York City Library.

D. R. Thomas, for the reproduction of the Summers Varvill price list.

Borthwick Institute of Historical Research: Wills.

Minster Library, York: Lease Records.

North Yorkshire Reference Library, York: City Directories and Newspapers.

York City Archives: Register of Apprentices.

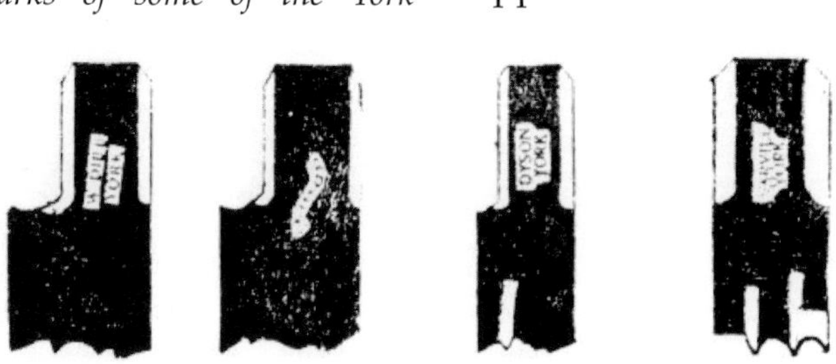

Fig. 16. The marks of some of the York planemakers.

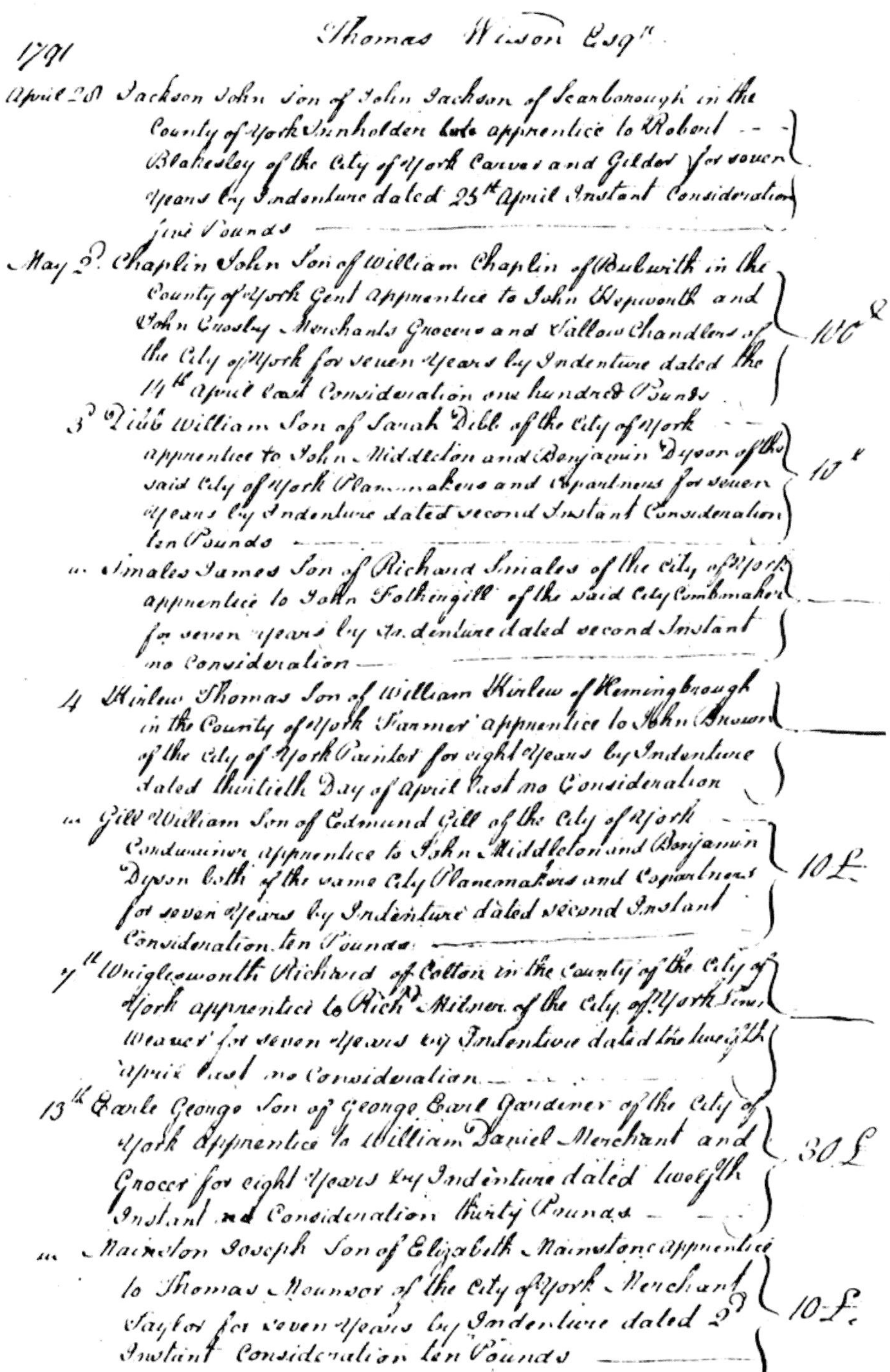
1791 Thomas Wilson Esqr.

April 28 Jackson John Son of John Jackson of Scarborough in the County of York Innholder late apprentice to Robert Blakesley of the City of York Carver and Gilder for seven Years by Indenture dated 25th April Instant Consideration five Pounds —

May 2d. Chaplin John Son of William Chaplin of Bubwith in the County of York Gent apprentice to John Hepworth and John Crosby Merchants Grocers and Tallow Chandlers of the City of York for seven Years by Indenture dated the 14th April last Consideration one hundred Pounds — 100£

3d Dibb William Son of Sarah Dibb of the City of York apprentice to John Middleton and Benjamin Dyson of the said City of York Planemakers and Copartners for seven Years by Indenture dated second Instant Consideration ten Pounds — 10£

" Smales James Son of Richard Smales of the City of York apprentice to John Fothergill of the said City Combmaker for seven years by Indenture dated second Instant no Consideration —

4 Kirlew Thomas Son of William Kirlew of Hemingbrough in the County of York Farmer apprentice to John Brown of the City of York Painter for eight Years by Indenture dated thirtieth Day of April last no Consideration

" Gill William Son of Edmund Gill of the City of York Cordwainer apprentice to John Middleton and Benjamin Dyson both of the same City Planemakers and Copartners for seven Years by Indenture dated second Instant Consideration ten Pounds — 10£

7th Wrigglesworth Richard of Cotton in the County of the City of York apprentice to Richd Milner of the City of York Linen Weaver for seven Years by Indenture dated the twelfth April last no Consideration —

13th Earle George Son of George Earl Gardener of the City of York Apprentice to William Daniel Merchant and Grocer for eight Years by Indenture dated twelfth Instant no Consideration thirty Pounds — 30£

" Nainston Joseph Son of Elizabeth Nainstone apprentice to Thomas Mounsey of the City of York Merchant Taylor for seven Years by Indenture dated 2d Instant Consideration ten Pounds — 10£

Fig. 17. Extract from the Apprentice Indenture Roll *for 1791 showing two planemaker apprentices, Dibb and Gill, with one carver and gilder, one tallow chandler, one comb maker, one painter, one weaver, one merchant and grocer and one merchant taylor.*

The whetstone

Eric Baker

Newsletter No. 5: Spring 1985

For success in woodworking, sharp tools are essential. The worker in any branch of woodwork needs a whetstone, which may be lubricated with water or with oil. Of these, the oilstone is the most important and has been with us at least since Greek and Roman times. Several have been found at Roman sites, in this country, in Germany, Italy and France. Presumably the carpenters' chests in the Mary Rose contained them as one from the same century was found complete in its hollowed-out box in 1871 when the abandoned stores of the Novaya Zembla expedition of 1597 were discovered. This Dutch expedition had been wrecked in trying to find a way through the North East passage to China and had spent the winter on the ice, returning to Holland in the spring.

Stones to be used for sharpening have to contain quartz or silica. Some in fact have been almost pure quartz, and in others siliceous matter is closely mixed with calcareous or aluminous matter. Other materials sometimes present are particles of garnet and magnetite, which also help the cutting action.

The woodworkers of the 18th century had, in the main, two types of stone available to them: Turkey stone, and Charnley Forest or Whittle Hill stones. Turkey stone came from Asia Minor via Smyrna. It was found only in small pieces and was seldom flawless. Few woodworkers possessed Turkey stones as they were expensive and difficult to obtain. Their analysis gives 70 to 75% fine silica closely blended with 20 to 25% calcite. Charnley Forest stone was more common. It resembled slate, was very slow cutting and varied in quality. The possessor of a good stone was therefore envied by his mates.

The general use of both these stones came to a fairly abrupt end in 1889 with the import of a stone discovered in the State of Arkansas in the U.S.A. As these stones were quarried in the area of the Washita River they were called Washita stones. An even better quality quarried later was called Arkansas. The analysis of these stones is 98% silica with small proportions of alumina, potash, soda, and minute traces of iron, lime, magnesia and fluorine – a series of excellent cutting agents.

The impact of this import is best told by Walter Rose in his book *The Village Carpenter*: "In the year 1889 the Washita, an imported stone, appeared on the English market and was hailed with delight by all wood-workers, who straightaway discarded their Charnley Forests forever. One old stone that had until then been considered of supreme merit and priceless value, was then hawked around the workshop where I was serving a term of improvership, and failed to find a purchaser at the proffered price of sixpence. On my week-end visit home, I carried a new stone to show my brother, who insisted on keeping it. It created a minor sensation in my father's workshop, where its undreamed of quality of sharpening captivated my father's men, each of whom speedily obtained one."

A few years later, in about 1900, two artificially manufactured stones appeared. The Indiana, now known as the India, and the Carborundum. Each was manufactured in three grades: fine, medium and coarse. The debut of these stones on the English market does not seem to have been anyway as dramatic as the Washita was. R. A. Salaman, in his *Dictionary of Tools*, quotes how "The late Mr. Arthur Collier (a Brixton ironmonger) related that when first trying to sell artificial oilstones in 1901, carpenters would not take them. So he used to throw one of the stones against a wall, and when the carpenter saw that it did not break he sometimes agreed to try one." I find this a little hard to believe, in view of the number of broken pieces I have come across!

The oil traditionally used with oilstones was neatsfoot oil. This comes from the feet of oxen, sheep and horses. It is an excellent lubricant that is long-lasting and stays on the surface of the stone because of its high viscosity. However, if it is left in a cold shed or workplace it will turn to a gell and cannot be used until it is warmed again. As its function in nature is to provide a buffer between the ground and the animal's foot in cold winter weather this is not surprising.

Water stones have also been available and they are having a renewed popularity as imports from Japan. I find that both the European, which is at least 70 years old, and the two grades of Japanese, are better as finishing stones, as they polish more than they cut.

I hope that collectors of tools who come across stones, especially the natural ones, will keep them even if they are not in their chosen field of collection. These stones have played a part in the high quality craftsmanship that shows itself in the products of cabinet making, coopering, wheelwrighting, turning and all the other trades that we admire so much – not excluding the making of tools themselves.

Let Moxon have the last word. In his *Mechanick Exercises*, published in 1683, he says "Spit on it". One can only assume that he had a water stone!

Dyke fieing in East Anglia

Michael Field

Tools and Trades Volume 4: 1987

Almost all the varied landscapes of Britain are a result of the influence of man. Some, for example, the moonscape of china clay tips near St. Austell in Cornwall, are obviously man-made but other large and apparently natural areas such as the grouse moors of the Borders are just as much the product of a long period of management by man. The fenland areas of East Anglia are no exception. (Fig. 1.)

On entering the area from Cambridgeshire, the first impression is of utter desolation as one gazes down from the road built on top of an embankment across thousands of acres of fenland which, several centuries before, was anything up to 20 ft. below sea level before being reclaimed by means of drainage ditches or dykes. And, having crossed into Norfolk and passed through Norwich, it is only a few minutes drive before the heart of the Norfolk Broads and marshlands is reached, another area which, in the past, was beneath the sea. If it was not for the continual draining of this land by means of dykes it would not be long before the sea reclaimed what had been taken from it.

In every language there are words originating from other countries, now incorporated and in general usage. Some have been brought by invaders, others by visitors or refugees. In East Anglia, one such source of words was the Flemish weavers who settled in Suffolk to escape persecution. Another was the Dutch who came to Norfolk to teach the local inhabitants how to drain the land. It was they who helped to create the world famous Norfolk Broads which were originally shallow peat diggings that later became flooded to form what we now call the Broads.

The Dutch left behind another legacy of their visit in the form of their word DIJK meaning "a shield of the land" (i.e. an embankment), which has now been incorporated into the East Anglian dialect as Dyke (pronounced almost identically as in the Dutch) and which, to date, is the only Dutch word I have found in daily use in Norfolk.

Virtually all traditional hand crafts today have been superseded by mechanisation, dyke cleaning being no exception. This work is now undertaken by mechanical excavators which, although doing an efficient job, do not create for the onlooker the aesthetic appeal of the traditional method. Although many centuries old crafts are now but a memory it is still possible, if one asks around, to find the occasional man who spent his working life "fieing out" the dykes.

The dykes dug in the Fens and Norfolk can be likened to the blood circulation of the body, with capillaries, veins and arteries. Similarly, there were three sizes of dyke. The smallest was 9 ft. wide at the top, 4 ft. wide at the bottom and 4 ft. deep. In addition to being the primary source of drainage from the marshes, they also separated one marsh from the next. Sometimes the only indication of their existence from even close by is a strip of reed showing proud above the

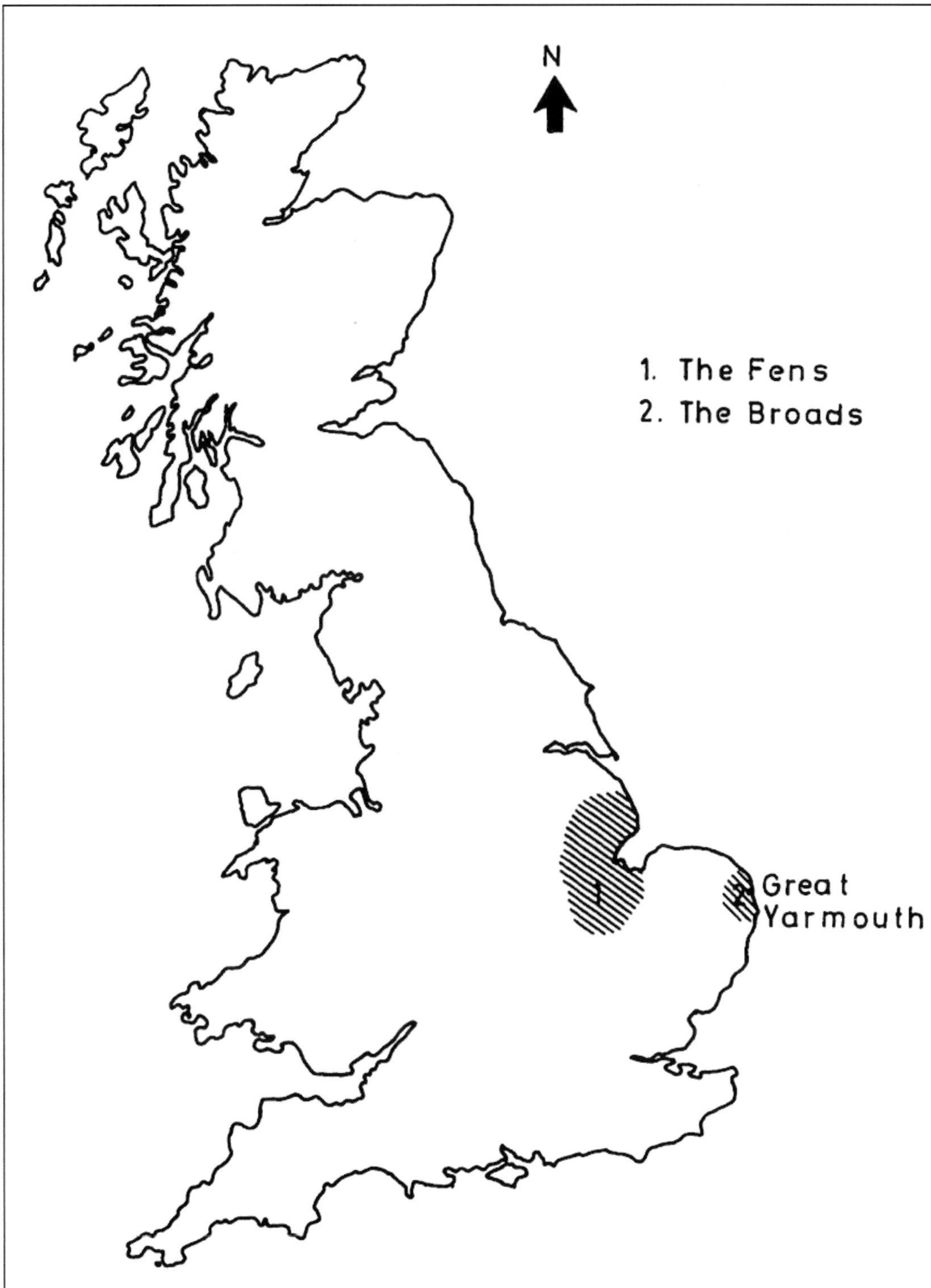

Fig. 1. Location map of the Cambridgeshire Fens and the Norfolk Broads.

surrounding marshes. Norfolk marshes were often only narrow strips of land, sometimes as small as 5 acres in size, and the dykes could be as little as 30 ft. apart.

Next were the veins of the drainage system. These were dug 10 ft. wide at the top, 4 ft. at the bottom and 4 ft. deep. This extra foot in width might not appear to be very much but the extra amount of water this size of dyke carried was considerable when one considers the number of smaller dykes which fed into them. In turn these middle sized dykes fed into the largest of the dykes, often referred to as "roadways."

"Roadways" were dug 12 to 16 ft. wide at the top, 6 to 7 ft. at the bottom and 5 to 6 ft. deep. These roadways ran through thousands of acres of Cambridgeshire fens or Norfolk marshes until they reached a river. Here, as the land would be several feet below sea level, it was usual to find a marsh pump which would lift the water from the dyke into the river. These pumps would originally have been wind powered, appearing as miniature windmills along the river banks. About the turn of the century they were converted to steam power and finally to electricity. It is only when looking at a map (Fig. 2) that it can be seen how the dykes were laid out and the full extent of their network be appreciated.

In the old days it would be the marshman who "fied" out his stretch of dykes in addition to looking after the

Fig. 2. Map of area of marshes between Acle and Great Yarmouth showing the system of dykes still in use.

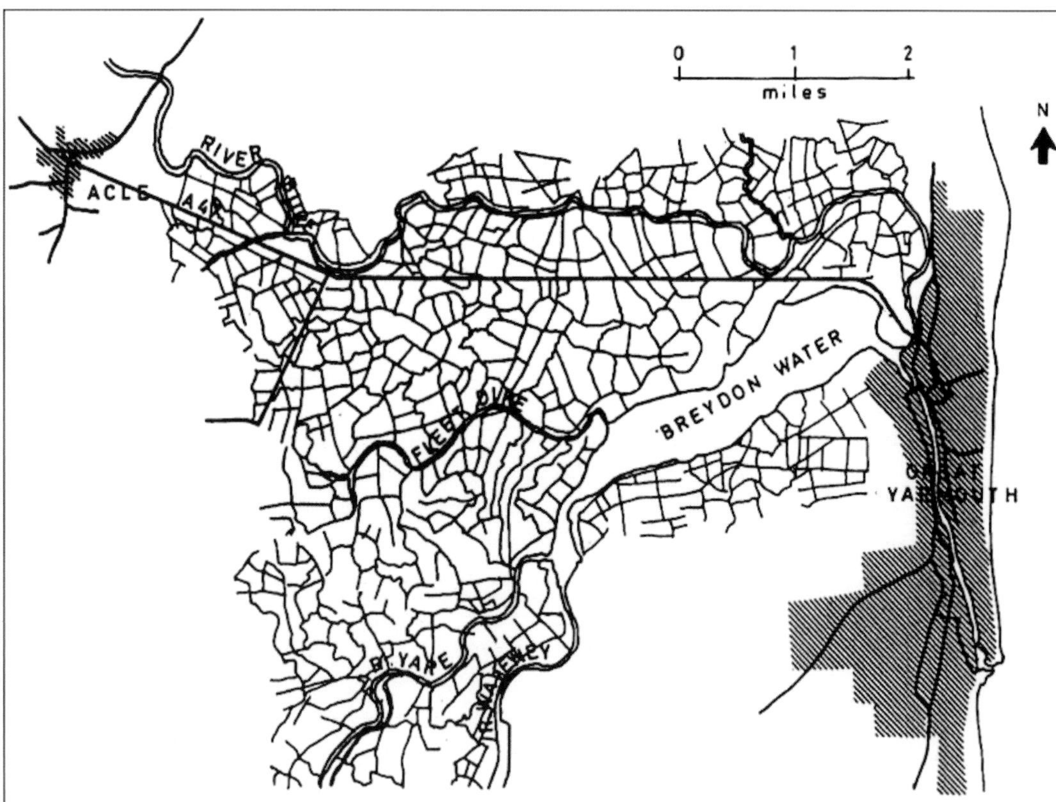

Fig. 3. A "meg", a form of long-handled scythe for cutting weeds under water.

cattle under his care. Later, when the number of pumps had increased until they were less than a mile apart, the man who looked after the pump for a section of dykes would also keep those dykes clear. He often sub-contracted out this work to fishermen who had been paid off at the end of the fishing season and were looking for employment. The maintenance of the dykes was paid for by the owner of the land through which they ran. The wages for the work would have been slightly more than the wages of a farm labourer.

The clothing worn was simple: normal everyday wear, together with thigh boots which were needed when digging out the mud. However the tools that were used were a different matter. Many an old craft only requires the minimum of tools, often adapted from other tools; and so it was with the tools needed to clean out the dykes.

There were two distinct operations which could be carried out when cleaning out a dyke, depending on the time of year and the wishes of the farmer who owned that particular dyke. One was known as "drawing the dykes" and consisted of cutting back the weeds to open up the waterway to enable the cattle to drink. The other was known as "fieing out" when the dykes were drained and the mud removed.

If a dyke was to be "drawn" this would be done between July and November using a punt, three types of scythe and a special rake. First the top banks would be scythed to leave them clear for when the weeds were "chromed" out. Then a second scythe, the "drawing cutter" would be used to "draw" or cut the weed growing along the sides before the bottom of the dyke was cleared of weed using yet another scythe known as a "meg" (Fig. 3). Because of the need to reach the full way down the sides when cutting and raking out, all the adapted tools would be attached to 14 ft. long shafts so that, if the weeds under the water could not be reached from the bank, they could be cut whilst standing in a double-ended punt before being pulled out using the "chrome." (Fig. 4.) Having "drawn" one side of a dyke there were two ways that one could use to cross to the other side, either by a "ligger", a plank laid across a dyke, or, as in the old days, by pole vaulting across using one of the long-shafted tools.

Every three to four years a dyke would be "fied out", that is have the accumulated mud removed. This would be done between January and April when the weeds were dead. For this work another set of specialised tools would be used; a set of "dammin" boards, a wooden beetle with which to knock them in, a "drain cutter" which was adapted from a hay knife, (Fig. 5) and a "mud scuppit." (Fig. 6.)

First, the sides would usually have to be reshaped as, since the previous occasion four years earlier, cattle would have broken the banks down as they slid down to drink. Often it would be found that the dyke was down to a width of only a foot or two, which necessitated having to cut the bank back three or four feet either side using the adapted hay knife. This would have been altered by the blacksmith who straightened the handle by heating and then fitted it with a 14 ft. shaft. Reshaping was done by cutting down using a sawing motion and then pulling out the sods with a "chrome". These sods would sometimes have then been used to dam off the dyke. One advantage for the worker was that, being winter time, there was no growth of weeds to have to cut back.

Having reshaped the sides, the dyke would then be dammed off at the end. This was done by using either the sods from the freshly shaped banks or

Fig. 4. Two "chromes" (shown without their long handles) used for pulling the cut weed from the water.

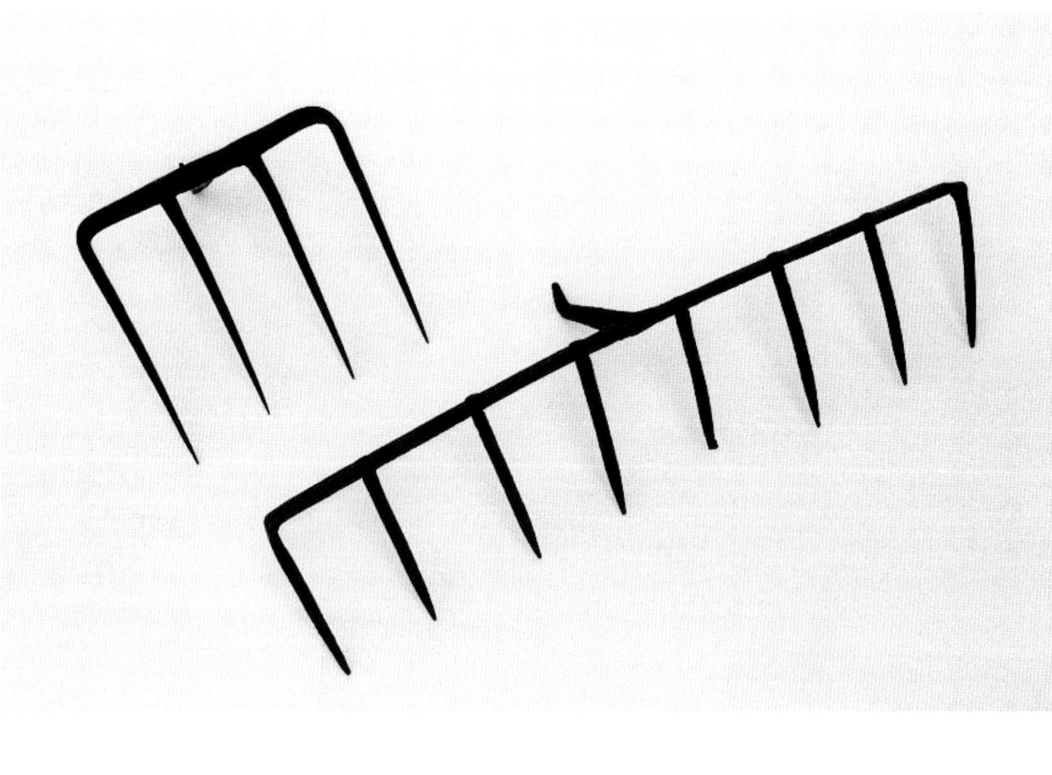

Fig. 5. A "drain cutter", adapted from a hay knife, used for cutting back the dyke banks.

with "dammin boards" working back upstream. (Fig. 7.) If there was only one man working, he would place his boards a "chain" apart, (1 chain = 22 yards) as this was as much as he could clear in a day. However, if there was a team of 5 or 6 men, then the boards would be set several chains apart.

There was an art in fitting a set of "dammin boards" as they needed to be watertight. For this reason the wood used was usually deal which swells in water. First a cross bar would be wedged across the dyke downstream so that when the boards were hammered in with the beetle they were held by the bar against the pressure of the water. The middle board could be up to 6 ft. in length whilst

Fig. 6. A "mud scuppit", an iron-tipped, wooden spade fitted with a leather cowl to retain the mud when lifted.

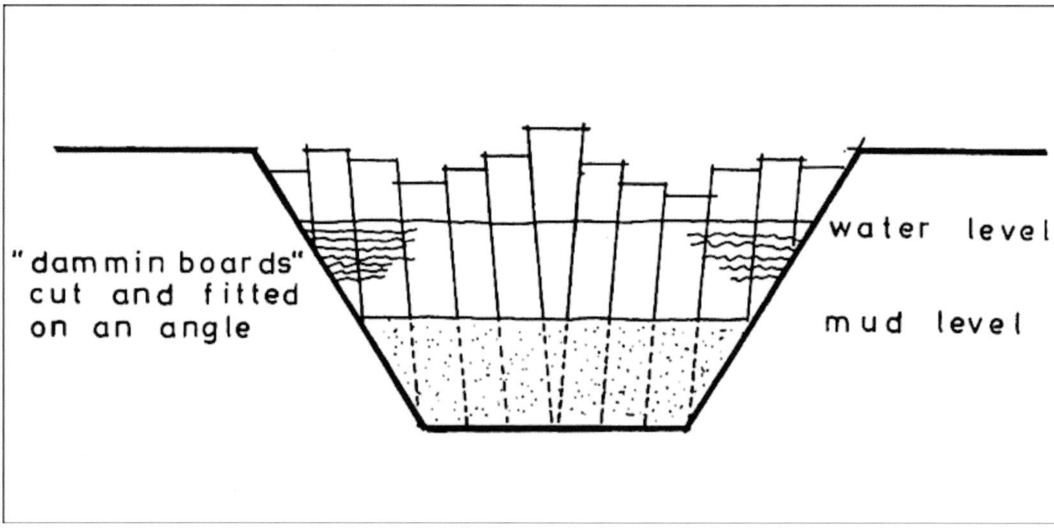

Fig. 7. Cross section of a dyke showing the "dammin boards" in position before "fieing out."

those on either edge might be as little as 3 ft. They were cut on the "huh" (at an angle) so that they would lock tight when hammered in.

Having dammed the dyke the water would then be removed from the first section using either a bucket or the "mud scuppit" till the mud was reached. This could vary in depth according to how fast the current ran. If the current was slow the mud would have had a chance to settle, harden and would be thick. Generally however, it was likely to be between one and a half and two feet in depth. To remove this mud a tool, which can only be described as unique, would be used, namely the "mud scuppit." This consisted of a spade made from a single piece of willow, fitted with a T-handle and having the base of the blade fitted with a leather cowl. The function of this cowl was that, having dug out a shovel full of mud, the "fier" could "hull" (throw) it up onto the bank without the contents falling off and covering his head and shoulders!

Having dug the mud out, the "fier" usually came to a clay base but very occasionally the mud would continue for anything up to 20 ft. or more. When confronted with this problem he would have to stand on boards to dig out as much as was reasonable. The last thing a good "fier" would do before the water was let, in again would be to walk backwards, scraping the clay to erase his footprints. This was because once the water had been let in and settled it, would be so clear that any marks would show up.

Having completed one section, and moving on to "fie out" the second section one of the "dammin boards" would be lifted, the water allowed to flow through, and the dam again made watertight. (Fig. 8.) The mud having been dug out of the second section, the boards would then be fully removed so that when the third section was drained there was more space for the water to flow into.

There was one more unique tool which the "fier" could use, his "dydle" (Fig. 9). This consisted of an iron ring with a blade at the end fitted with a string

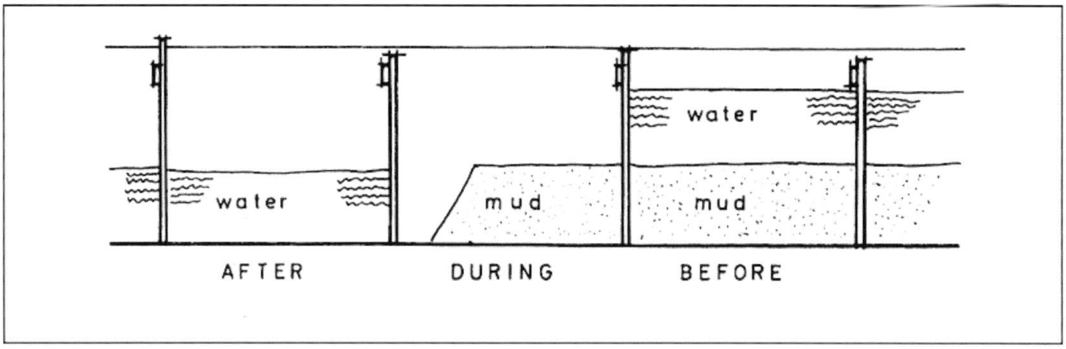

Fig. 8. Diagram of a longitudinal section of dyke showing the sequence of "fieing out."

mesh in the middle. This tool was used in various ways by different "fiers." One man I interviewed (whose set of tools I have in my collection and from which all the illustrations are taken), used his to remove any small weeds which had floated to the surface of the dyke after being cut and which were too small to be raked out by means of the "chrome." Another "fier" who checked the information in this article only used his to scoop out small tools and items which had fallen into the water.

This in essence was the technique of "dyke fieing" as carried out as late as the Second World War in some areas of Norfolk. Today's visitors accept what they see, hardly pausing to consider what was involved and when a meg, chrome or dydle is used to decorate a pub wall in Norfolk they create considerable interest. For me the fascination is in discovering how the tools were used and how they were invented or adapted from other tools to suit the specialist needs of the "bottom fier."

Fig. 9. Two types of "dydle" used for retrieving weed or other items from the dykes.

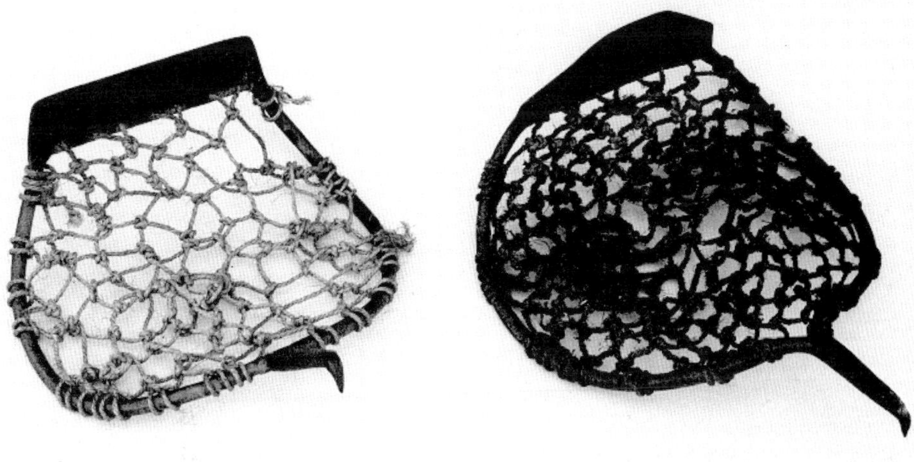

The craft of riving wood

R. C. C. Tabor

Tools & Trades Volume 5: 1988

Preface

When the West-Suffolk woodman who taught me many of his skills came in search of wood to the coppice I work, one of his first actions was to cut a two foot rod of hazel, and rive it perfectly into two pieces using his Suffolk billhook – "to see what it's like." It was an action performed with deceptive ease, frustratingly difficult to emulate. Indeed some men never master the art of riving wood, becoming the butt of disdainful comment, from true woodmen.

Traditional woodmen were craftsmen of enormous knowledge and skill; knowledge of the essential characteristics of different woods; knowledge of how to get their tools to perform effortlessly; and the skill to produce functional, durable, consistent artefacts from variable material. This wisdom has always been passed verbally from father to son, whilst the skills have been honed by continuous, often harsh, practice in the coppice.

I have been fortunate in knowing woodmen in Suffolk and Kent who have shared their knowledge with me, and I have known the delights of working in the coppice, practising some of their crafts. This may allow me to give readers

RIVING A POLE USING ONLY THE HANDS AND LEGS AFTER STARTING THE SPLIT WITH AN AXE OR BILL HOOK. NOTE HOW THE POLE GOES UNDER THE RIGHT KNEE, AND OVER THE LEFT THIGH SO LEVERAGE CAN BE APPLIED TO KEEP THE SPLIT CENTRAL – AS IN A BREAK.

Fig. 1.

a deeper insight into one facet of English woodmanship – the riving of small wood.

Introduction: History

How early man, struggling to survive in the damp forests of prehistory, first came to rive wood must remain conjecture. Whether he saw a damaged tree split down its stem, or whether a pole split up from the base when being wrenched or cut from a stool, the value of riven small wood must have been quickly realized. Although wooden artefacts do not normally survive long in a moist Atlantic climate, the oldest examples of the craft have been preserved for 6,000 years in the peat of the Somerset Levels, where Neolithic man cut and rent coppice wood to make the hurdles used as trackways. The pioneering work at Butser, in Hampshire, has shown how riven hazel clefts were probably used by iron-age man, whilst perfect oak shingles from the first half-century A.D. have been unearthed at Winchester.

As the Somerset discoveries reveal, cleaving predates metal tools. Wood is riven not by cutting but by leverage, and in small wood once the riving is started, it can be continued and controlled without tools. Even today some craftsmen rive wood up to 2 or 3 ins. in diameter, once started with an edge tool, using solely their hands and legs. (Fig. 1.) A flint will split a green hazel rod as well as a billhook, so small cleft wood has been a major resource since the dawn of human activities: laths and shingles for house roofs and walls; broches and pegs for thatching cottages and ricks; posts and pales for fencing deer parks and gardens; gate and wattle hurdles for folding the sheep that gave England her pre-industrial wealth; and hoops and rods for the barrels and crates needed to transport the output of a growing industrial economy. The 20th century has seen the rapid demise of all but a handful of these crafts, and with them six millennia of accumulated wisdom.

Merits

A process as old as woodmanship itself – indeed fundamental to the craft – must have much to commend it. Riving does; it is fast, ideal for small wood and the resultant clefts have advantages unobtainable by any other process.

Small wood is the raw material for coppice products, it being uncommon to use poles of more than 15 summers. However well stocked the coppice, and however kind the growth, no pole is ever truly straight, making sawn lengths of 6 ft. or more wasteful and better cut from wood grown on a longer cycle. Riving allows the craftsman to cut the coppice at varying ages in response to changing demands, and his seemingly endless ingenuity has developed many subtle methods to incorporate wavy, wound and even forked material into saleable, durable products. And, of course, an edge tool such as the bill or froe creates no kerf and hence no wasteful sawdust, important since coppice products have always commanded low prices, and a good living needs good yields. But speed is also critical; less time spent making up means more wood can be cut and more products made, and for small wood, riving is faster than sawing.

By their very nature, hurdles, wattles, fencing, thatching wood and many other underwood products have a hard life,

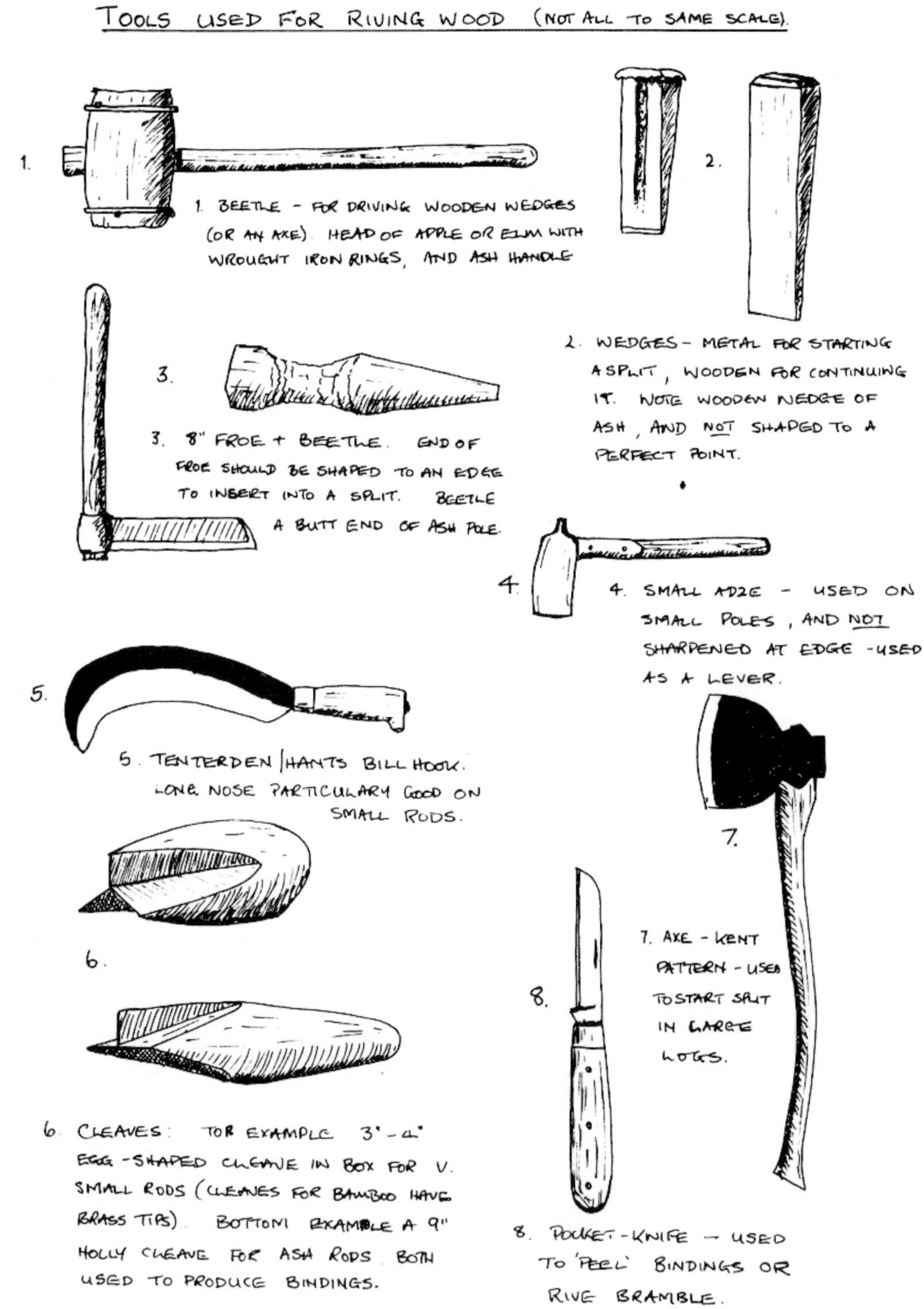
TOOLS USED FOR RIVING WOOD (NOT ALL TO SAME SCALE).
1.
2.
1. BEETLE - FOR DRIVING WOODEN WEDGES (OR AN AXE). HEAD OF APPLE OR ELM WITH WROUGHT IRON RINGS, AND ASH HANDLE
2. WEDGES - METAL FOR STARTING A SPLIT, WOODEN FOR CONTINUING IT. NOTE WOODEN WEDGE OF ASH, AND NOT SHAPED TO A PERFECT POINT.
3.
3. 8" FROE + BEETLE. END OF FROE SHOULD BE SHAPED TO AN EDGE TO INSERT INTO A SPLIT. BEETLE A BUTT END OF ASH POLE.
4.
4. SMALL ADZE - USED ON SMALL POLES, AND NOT SHARPENED AT EDGE - USED AS A LEVER.
5.
5. TENTERDEN/HANTS BILL HOOK. LONG NOSE PARTICULARY GOOD ON SMALL RODS.
7.
7. AXE - KENT PATTERN - USED TO START SPLIT IN LARGE LOGS.
6.
8.
6. CLEAVES: FOR EXAMPLE 3"-4" EGG-SHAPED CLEAVE IN BOX FOR V. SMALL RODS (CLEAVES FOR BAMBOO HAVE BRASS TIPS). BOTTOM EXAMPLE A 9" HOLLY CLEAVE FOR ASH RODS. BOTH USED TO PRODUCE BINDINGS.
8. POCKET-KNIFE - USED TO 'PEEL' BINDINGS OR RIVE BRAMBLE.

Fig. 2.

thumped and humped by man and beast, and exposed to the rain, frost and sun of the English seasons. Durability and strength are thus important assets, and cleft wood has both in greater measure, size for size, than sawn wood. When wood is riven, the fibres are parted from one another along their length. A few are torn, and raised as spears, but the face of a cleft presents a ribbed-rough surface of remarkable continuity, following every curve and fold of the pole's growth, even around knots. Because the wood vessels have not been cut across, exposing their open ends, this surface is uniquely waterproof, and explains why cleft pales in oak or chestnut, have stood – frequently in damp shade – on park banks for over three-quarters of a century.

Hurdles, which may have to be moved and re-sited every day, must combine lightness with strength, and small clefts have a remarkable resilience. Since they follow the natural flow of the grain, rather than cutting across it as do sawn lengths, there are fewer points of weakness where a rod might fracture under stress, and indeed the very process of riving frequently reveals weaknesses that sawing might not. This virtue was appreciated beyond the coppice, particularly where reliable strength was essential; spokes for wooden wheels were always riven, as were axe helves – Welsh miners specifying all hewing-axe handles should be fashioned from cleft ash.

Nomenclature

I was trained firstly by a man of Kent, and then by woodmen of Essex and Suffolk, where I have spent the whole of my life. Inevitably all the "craft" words used in this article are the coinage of these three counties.

One further point; the dictionary defines a cleft as a split or crack; but to woodmen a cleft is the piece of wood resulting from the cleaving/riving process, and I use the word in this sense.

The craft: Principles

Riving always starts at the smaller end of the "stuff", so ensuring any "run-out" occurs towards the thicker end, still leaving usable "clefts." Where possible the stuff is riven into two equal segments. Unequal clefts, needed to maintain yields from larger poles, demand considerably more care since the thinner cleft flexes more than the thicker, and hence tends to run-out.

A split is started by driving either wedge or edge tool into the stuff and is continued by levering the two clefts apart, normally using a froe, adze or bill-hook, (Fig. 2.) although a skilled man can rive a pole by literally pulling it apart. (Fig. 1.) To master this ancient method is to understand the essence of riving; that a split runs true under even pressure, but will always run towards the cleft under greater tension. This knowledge allows a run-out split to be corrected by applying tension to the thicker cleft. Ingenious devices – named locally as "horses" or "breaks" (Fig. 3.) – have been evolved by woodmen to allow pressure to be applied to the clefts most easily, in the same way as the man with no tools uses his knees and legs.

At no time does the woodman cut along the grain – although a particularly intransigent knot may have to be chopped through. A rod riven centrally requires little or no close inspection by an experienced woodman. The clefts separate

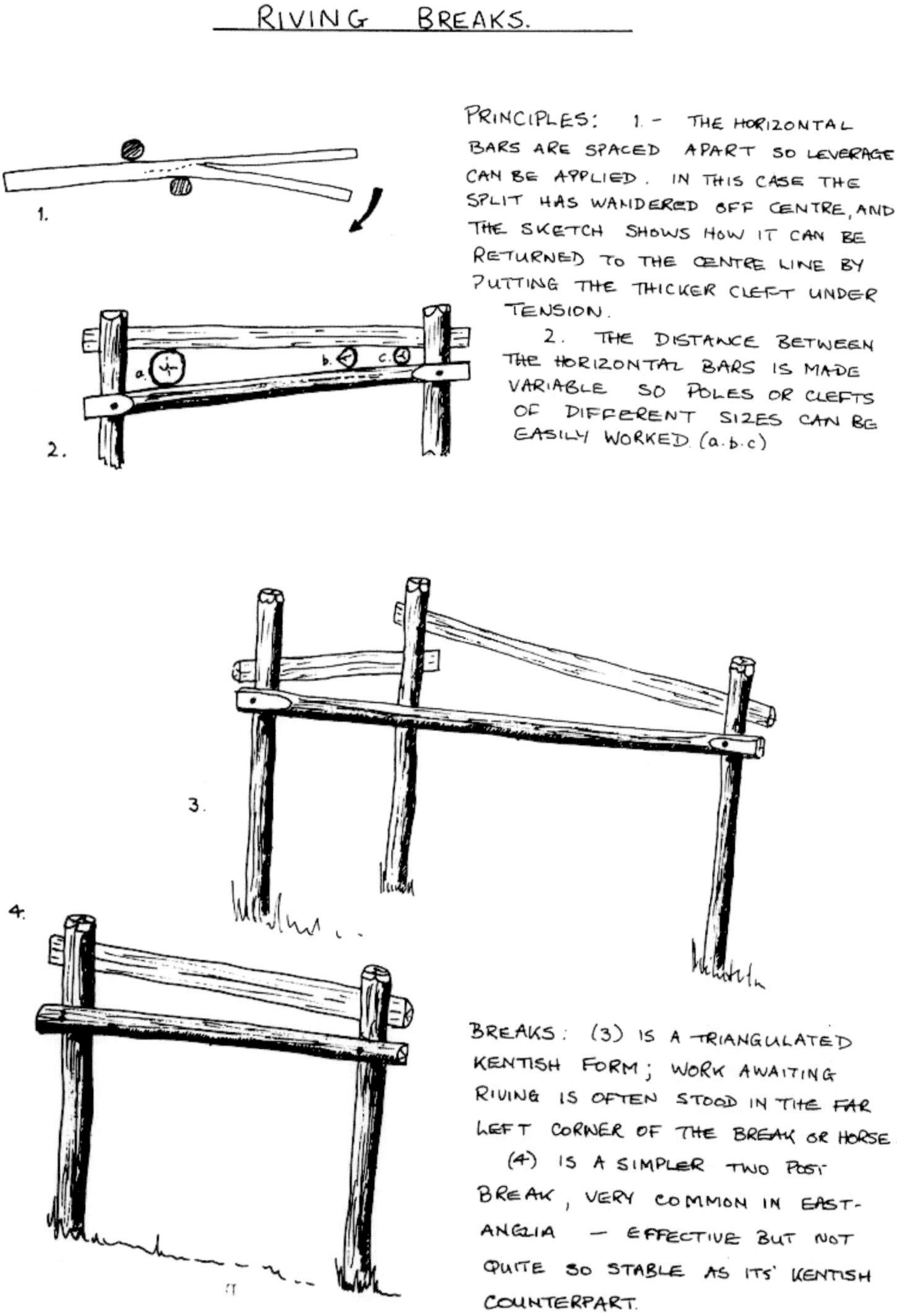
RIVING BREAKS.
PRINCIPLES: 1. - THE HORIZONTAL BARS ARE SPACED APART SO LEVERAGE CAN BE APPLIED. IN THIS CASE THE SPLIT HAS WANDERED OFF CENTRE, AND THE SKETCH SHOWS HOW IT CAN BE RETURNED TO THE CENTRE LINE BY PUTTING THE THICKER CLEFT UNDER TENSION.
2. THE DISTANCE BETWEEN THE HORIZONTAL BARS IS MADE VARIABLE SO POLES OR CLEFTS OF DIFFERENT SIZES CAN BE EASILY WORKED. (a. b. c)
1.
2.
a.
b.
c.
3.
4.
BREAKS: (3) IS A TRIANGULATED KENTISH FORM; WORK AWAITING RIVING IS OFTEN STOOD IN THE FAR LEFT CORNER OF THE BREAK OR HORSE.
(4) IS A SIMPLER TWO POST BREAK, VERY COMMON IN EAST-ANGLIA - EFFECTIVE BUT NOT QUITE SO STABLE AS ITS' KENTISH COUNTERPART.

Fig. 3

with a crisp, clear, unmistakable cra-a-ck, whilst the hands sense the similar resistance of even clefts, and the sharp separation of cleanly riven surfaces. This experience allows skilled woodmen to rive accurately at remarkable speed, my mentor producing 1600 "broches" in a good day!

Material

Not all wood rives well. In addition to differences between species are those resulting from the site, the genetic make-up of the tree, and even the way it has been managed. Wood from hedgerows or exposed sites at the edge of a coppice rarely makes a good product, its grain "winding" as a result of the constant rotating movement of the crown to the prevailing winds. Suffolk woodmen often speak of "pink" or "red" ash which, apart from a blush of colour described by the name, possesses a "stringy" grain resistant to riving. It is locally prized for making rake heads since it does not split when the teeth are driven in.

Ash, hazel, willow and sweet chestnut all rive superbly in a variety of sizes, and are the backbone of the cleft-wood trades. Oak, when grown fast and clean as coppice, also rives beautifully. Elm, renowned for its resistance to splitting, will, when grown as coppice, rive cleanly and in Suffolk gate hurdles made from these clefts can be found.

However, the best material from a favoured site can still be useless to a skilled craftsman if it is not in the right condition. Wood for riving must have the right degree of moisture, "greenness", resilience and toughness. Hazel rods cut after January – when the sap has started rising – are too green to make broches straight from the stool since the split frequently runs out, and as a result they are stored for 4 to 6 weeks before riving. Similarly ash poles for gate hurdles are stored after felling until the summer to "toughen up". Conversely "sere" wood, having lost its resilience, is useless, breaking under tension. When hazel rods are to be stored for wattle or crate making, they are "riddled" – an inch or two of the small twigs left on – for if they are "knotted" or "budded" flush and any bark is removed, that area will dry in the wind and sun of early summer, and then break when riven or wound.

Uses

What follows is a list of the main artefacts produced in the coppice from cleft wood. It is not exhaustive:

Fencing:	stakes; pale and wire; feather edged pales; gate hurdles; wattle hurdles; rails
Thatching:	broches; liggers; sways
Miscellaneous:	barrel hoops; tent pegs; besom bindings

Techniques: Large poles

Poles greater in diameter than about 6 ins. are difficult to rive with a froe in a break. The beetle is rarely heavy enough to force the froe in across a wide face; the weight of the pole makes it difficult to manage; and the clefts are too thick to bend in the break to control the direction of the split.

It is normal therefore, when making "spites" – which should be about 3½ ins. diameter or face – to rive the poles using wedges. After "rinding", the pole is laid on the coppice floor, usually with its thicker end against a stool or a short post firmly

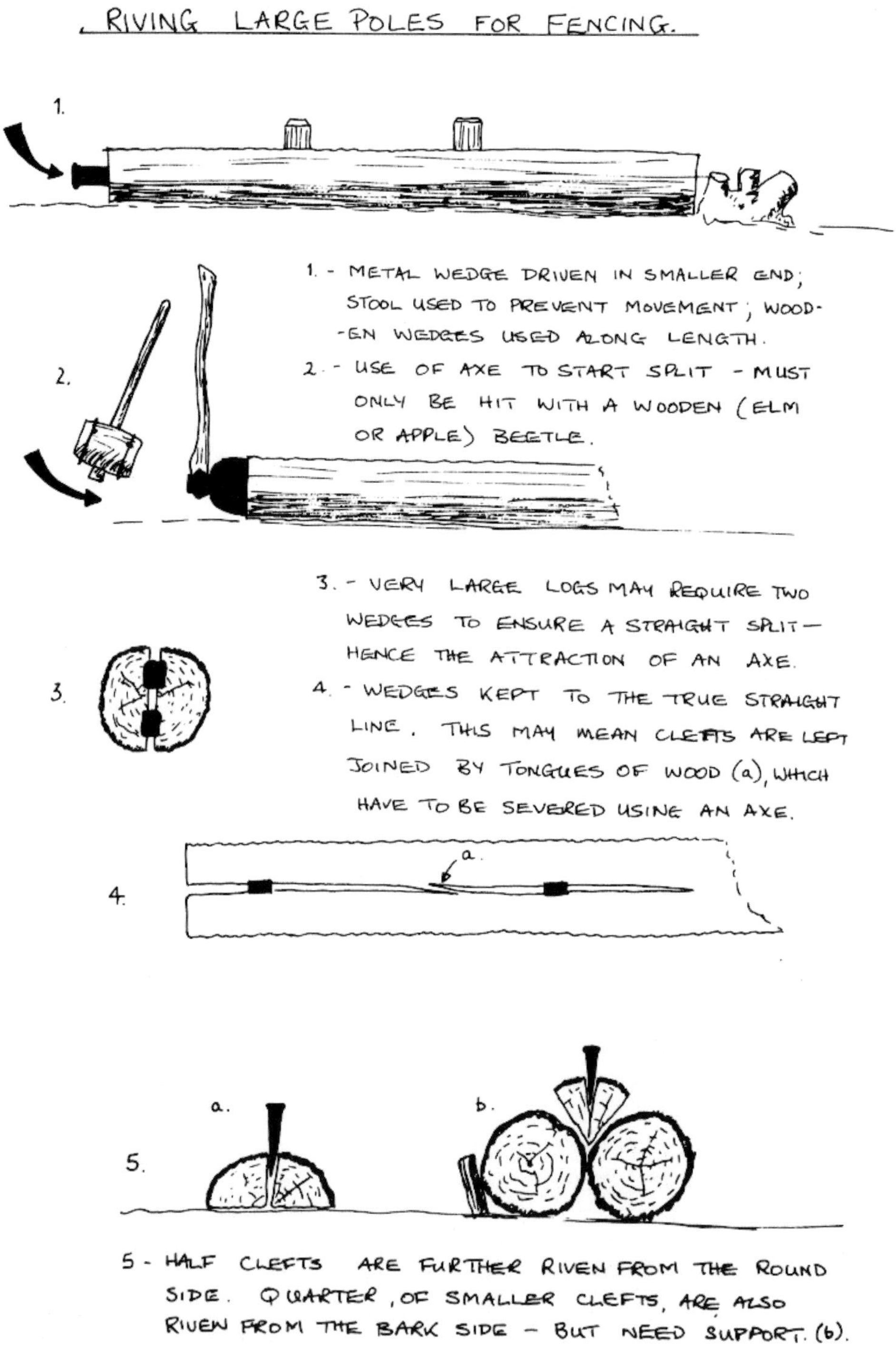

RIVING LARGE POLES FOR FENCING.
1.
1. - METAL WEDGE DRIVEN IN SMALLER END; STOOL USED TO PREVENT MOVEMENT; WOOD-
-EN WEDGES USED ALONG LENGTH.
2. - USE OF AXE TO START SPLIT - MUST ONLY BE HIT WITH A WOODEN (ELM OR APPLE) BEETLE.
2.
3. - VERY LARGE LOGS MAY REQUIRE TWO WEDGES TO ENSURE A STRAIGHT SPLIT— HENCE THE ATTRACTION OF AN AXE.
4. - WEDGES KEPT TO THE TRUE STRAIGHT LINE. THIS MAY MEAN CLEFTS ARE LEFT JOINED BY TONGUES OF WOOD (a), WHICH HAVE TO BE SEVERED USING AN AXE.
3.
4.
a.
5.
a.
b.
5 - HALF CLEFTS ARE FURTHER RIVEN FROM THE ROUND SIDE. QUARTER, OF SMALLER CLEFTS, ARE ALSO RIVEN FROM THE BARK SIDE - BUT NEED SUPPORT. (b).

Fig. 4.

driven into the ground. Riving starts by driving a metal wedge centrally into the smaller end with a sledge-hammer. (Fig. 4.) An axe may be used to start the split, and although a woodman is accurate enough to bed his axe in the centre of a pole to start the split, most avoid swinging the razor sharp edge so close to the ground with its often unseen snags, preferring to use it as a wedge, holding it against the end of the pole and smiting the poll with a wooden beetle.

Once a split has been started, it is continued along the length of the pole using further wedges, and woodmen who care use hardwood wedges –driven by an elm beetle – since they do not leave unsightly torn fibres, bruising, and with oak alone, a characteristic blue-black stain, that results from an interaction between iron and tannin. Wooden wedges are best sawn from the resilient yet tough wood found in butts of ash; and woodmen always hit wood with wood, since even the best ash cannot withstand the unyielding power of the sledge-hammer.

If the split starts to wander too far from the centre line, another wedge may have to be driven in along the correct line. This leaves the clefts joined by tongues of wood that must be severed with the axe – another good reason for using wooden wedges – and cleaned off with a side-axe. Large poles can be repeatedly split until the clefts are the size required, or are small enough for further conversion using a froe – for feather edge palings for example. Clefts of a quarter girth or smaller need the support of two parallel poles, preferably restrained, so that wedges may be driven vertically downwards from the circumference. (Fig. 4.)

Small poles

Millions of gate hurdles and miles of pale and wire fencing have been made from cleft poles 10 or 15 summers old. At 2 to 4 ins. in diameter this material is light, fast and easy to work. A "riving break" is always used, the form of which is the subject of regional variation and individual preference. The Kentish "horse" is particularly good, being stable and handling a range of wood sizes easily and effectively. Poles are held at an angle in the break, butt on the ground (Fig. 5), whilst the froe is driven into the end. Levering the froe to left and right progressively extends the split along the length of the pole – the tool not cutting unless a big knot needs severing. Sweet, kind poles, easy to rive, require little pressure, and the froe is frequently held under the pole so no uneven stress is placed on either cleft to force the split off-centre; should this happen, however, the spaced horizontal frame of the break allows the thicker cleft to be put under tension, which will centralize the split.

Halving poles to make gate hurdles is relatively easy. Maximizing the yield of chestnut pales from poles of varying sizes requires more skill however. A half pole may have to be split into three, or a cleft riven tangentially – processes requiring a subtlety and sensitivity perhaps not evident in the rugged finished product. (Fig. 5.)

Rods

In Sussex, Hampshire and Wiltshire, hazel rods grow dense and "suent" in the copses; and it is here that men became uniquely skilled in cleaving them to produce wattle hurdles, hoops and thatching wood.

USE OF THE FROE
1. DRIVING THE FROE INTO THE END OF A POLE USING A BEETLE. THE 'HORSE' OR 'BREAK' SUPPORTS THE POLE, THE END OF WHICH IS ON THE GROUND.
2. LEVERING WITH THE FROE TO EXTEND THE SPLIT, WHILE THE POLE IS HELD IN THE BREAK. NOTE HOW PRESSURE APPLIED BY FREE HAND TO CONTROL DIRECTION OF SPLIT AS NEEDED.

Fig. 5.

3.

4.

3- WHEN THE POLE IS RIVING CLEANLY WITH THE SPLIT CENTRAL, IT IS NORMAL TO KEEP THE SPLIT VERTICAL RATHER THAN HORIZONTAL SO NO UNDUE PRESSURE IS APPLIED TO EITHER CLEFT.

4 - FREQUENTLY LARGE KNOTS CANNOT BE LEVERED APART WITHOUT RUINING THE CLEFTS : THEY HAVE TO BE CUT THROUGH – SMITING THE FROE WITH A BEETLE AS SHOWN.

5.

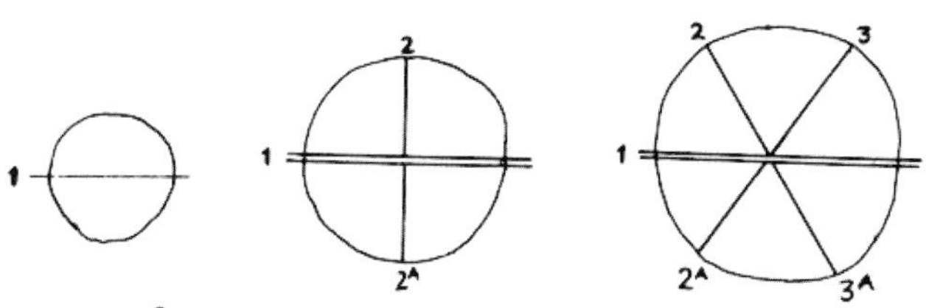

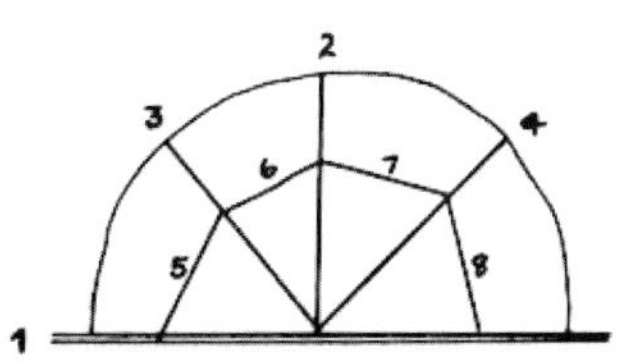

5. PATTERNS OF RIVING. WHERE VARIABLE MATERIAL IS USED TO PRODUCE A UNIFORM PRODUCT (CHESTNUT PALES) THE PATTERN OF RIVING IS ADJUST-ED ACCORDINGLY. THE NUMBERS REFER TO THE SEQUENCE OF SPL-ITTING EACH POLE.

Fig. 5 cont.

Wattles are made, in the main, of cleft rods 8 ft. or more long and 1½ ins. or less butt diameter. The simplest method requires solely a billhook, with which the hurdle-maker cuts into the rod about 1 foot from the crown end, penetrating as close to the centre of the rod as possible. (Fig. 6.) A simple twist of the hook, pressing the blade face to the rod, opens a split which is quickly run down the rod by continuing to twist the hook left and right and pressing gently forward to follow the other hand to the butt. More pressure with the back of the hook on either cleft controls the direction of the split., which is prevented from running too far by a firm grip on the rod. Strong wrists and the experience to feel and hear the clefts parting along the narrow central pith are pre-requisites to this deceptively difficult job, particularly since the billhook blade is used close up to the handle where it offers little leverage.

Some hurdle-makers prefer to use a riving post – a 2½ to 3 in. stake driven into the ground with a small peg to support the clefts driven through 2 or 3 ins. below the top. (Fig. 6.) The end of the rod is placed on top of the post, and a billhook chopped into it to start the split, which is then opened so that one cleft passes on each side of the post, supported by the peg. Hurdle-makers always use long nosed billhooks of the Tenterden, Hampshire or Spar hook pattern, which, when inserted into the split from below are ideal for levering the clefts apart as the rod is moved forward around the post. In Hampshire and Suffolk a small adze is often used in place of the billhook. (Fig. 6.) Again the tool is chopped down into the end of the rod to start the split, which is progressed by backwards and forwards leverage on the adze. I have never seen this tool sharpened at the side, as described by some writers. There is no need, for it is solely leverage that separates the clefts, knots being dealt with by replacing the rod on top of the post, and chopping down, using the tool's normal cutting edge. Many woodmen believe this is the finest way to rive hazel, the highly polished patina on their tools testifying to their almost continuous use.

Rick-pegs – no longer used since the demise of hay and corn ricks – and broches were required in thousands by thatchers every year. Broches – still used to fix thatch – vary in length regionally from 2 ft. 2 ins. to 2 ft. 6 ins., and have a cleft face of about ½ in. Knot-free hazel rods are first cut to the length required before riving begins. Sitting on a faggot in the warmth of the coppice using only a Hampshire bill or a Spar hook to rive the rods is one of the pleasures of woodmanship. The hook, twisting to and fro, is worked along the rod towards the woodman. In Suffolk a small horse with a "V" shaped vertical post at the front was used. (Fig. 7.) This post forced the clefts – separated initially by a small adze – to pass either side, extending the split, whilst running out was avoided by the hand twisting or applying lateral pressure to the rod.

Small rods

As wire became more generally available it drove the craft of producing besom bindings from natural material into decline. It is very rare today to find craftsmen able to produce the flat clefts of ash or hazel – fine enough to bind without being wound, yet with the immense strength of unbroken fibres – with which to bind a

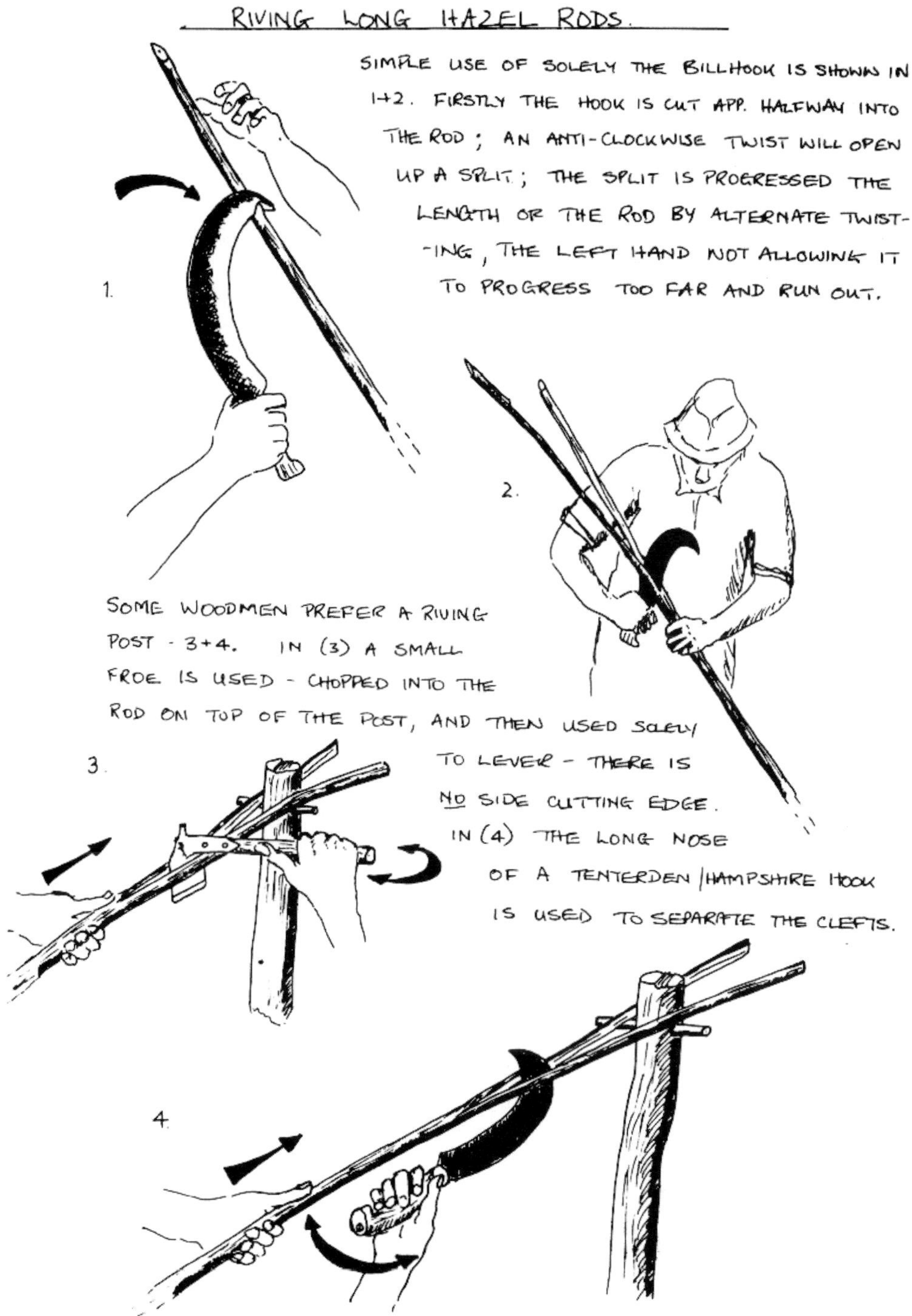
RIVING LONG HAZEL RODS.
SIMPLE USE OF SOLELY THE BILLHOOK IS SHOWN IN 1+2. FIRSTLY THE HOOK IS CUT APP. HALFWAY INTO THE ROD; AN ANTI-CLOCKWISE TWIST WILL OPEN UP A SPLIT; THE SPLIT IS PROGRESSED THE LENGTH OF THE ROD BY ALTERNATE TWIST-ING, THE LEFT HAND NOT ALLOWING IT TO PROGRESS TOO FAR AND RUN OUT.
1.
2.
SOME WOODMEN PREFER A RIVING POST - 3+4. IN (3) A SMALL FROE IS USED - CHOPPED INTO THE ROD ON TOP OF THE POST, AND THEN USED SOLELY TO LEVER - THERE IS NO SIDE CUTTING EDGE.
3.
IN (4) THE LONG NOSE OF A TENTERDEN/HAMPSHIRE HOOK IS USED TO SEPARATE THE CLEFTS.
4.

Fig. 6.

RIVING SHORT HAZEL RODS FOR BROCHES.

1.

2.

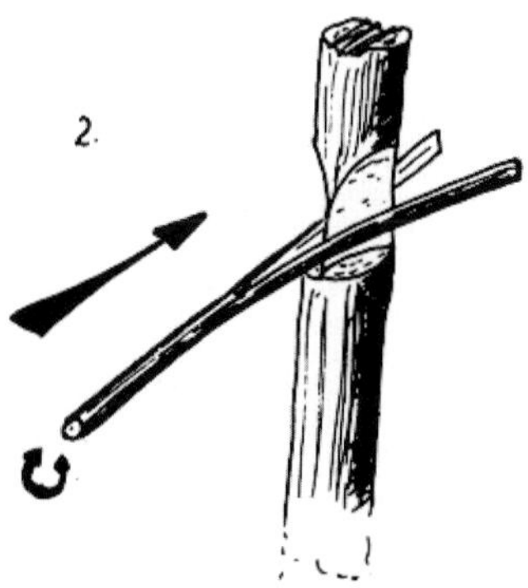

ALTHOUGH SOME WOODMEN USE THE METHOD ALREADY DESCRIBED FOR LONG RODS, IN SUFFOLK A SPECIAL HORSE (1) IS USED WITH A SHAPED POST (2). ONCE THE SPLIT IS STARTED BY BILL HOOK OR ADZE, IT CAN BE CONTINUED BY STEADY FORE-WARD PRESSURE. DIRECTION OF THE SPLIT CAN BE CONTROLLED BY TWISTING THE ROD TO PUT ONE SIDE UNDER TENSION.

BROCHES CAN ALSO BE RIVEN USING A SMALL 'SPAR' HOOK (3). THE CLEAVING IS ACCOMPLISHED BY THE LEVERAGE EXERTED WHEN THE HOOK IS TWISTED. DIFFERENTIAL PRESSURE IN THE WAY THE HOOK IS TWIST-ED CONTROLS THE DIRECTION; THE LEFT HAND (HOLDING THE ROD) IS PULLED TIGHT IN TO THE SIDE OF THE BODY TO GIVE MORE CONTROL AND EXERT MORE LEVERAGE.

3

Fig. 7.

fistful of birch twigs securely. To produce three fine, even clefts from a inch hazel rod requires a cleave – a three edged wedge of box or holly wood about the size of an egg. Even these dense woods cannot sever a knot, so the rods used have to be clean and knot-free. Firm pressure is needed to start the riving process, which is progressed by pulling or pushing the cleave down through the rod, and adjusting the centrality of the split by lateral pressure when needed. (Fig. 8.)

Triangular clefts, however small, are no use for besom bindings until the centre of the cleft is shaved away to leave a flat, flexible band of wood that can bend round a besom without cracking. A method that seeks to produce this flat band of wood without wasteful shaving involves the "peeling" of clefts. Starting with a ½ in. triangular cleft produced using a large 9 in. cleave, a penknife is inserted at the end, and a thin (1/16 in.) cleft lifted. Once this fine cleft has been lifted back 6 ins. or so, the end of the thicker cleft is held in the jaws of a horse, astride which the besom maker sits, and the thinner cleft is carefully pulled away from the thicker. The thickness of the fine cleft is determined by controlled bending of the thicker cleft; too little and the fine cleft will run-out; too much and the fine cleft will become thicker. (Fig. 8.)

This technique can also be used to produce clefts from round hazel rods – a far older craft than those already described, and probably no longer practised. In this case a cleft is lifted by cutting into the side of a rod 6 ins. or so from the end with a pen-knife, and is extended to the 4 ft. needed for a besom tie by bending the rod as required and levering with the knife – but never cutting. (Fig. 8.)

Both methods produce very thin, ½ in. wide bands of white wood that look so well against the dark birch twigs of the besom, and – when properly bound – tighten their grip as they dry.

Bramble

To most woodmen bramble is a nuisance; it impedes spring from fresh-cut stools; it is a danger when swinging axe or billhook; and it hinders movement about the cant. But the very toughness that makes it a nuisance also produces an excellent binding material, frequently used the past by besom makers.

After "shrieing" the thorns off with a stoutly gloved hand, a pen-knife is used to split the end of the stem centrally, and by twisting it to and fro – in the same way as the billhook in a hazel rod – continue the split along the entire length. (Fig. 8.) It is essential, in common with all riving, that the longitudinal fibres are kept intact to avoid points of weakness at which the binding will break. After riving and subsequently removing the pith, a really strong binding is produced, capable of holding a besom together for its working life.

Postscript

In the last 40 years woods, woodmen and the craft of woodmanship have declined at a rate unparalleled in their 3,000 year history. Mass production has little place for variable raw materials whose effective conversion needs skill, judgement and adaptability. Another generation could see most woodland crafts relegated to the history book.

Of the three woodmen who have

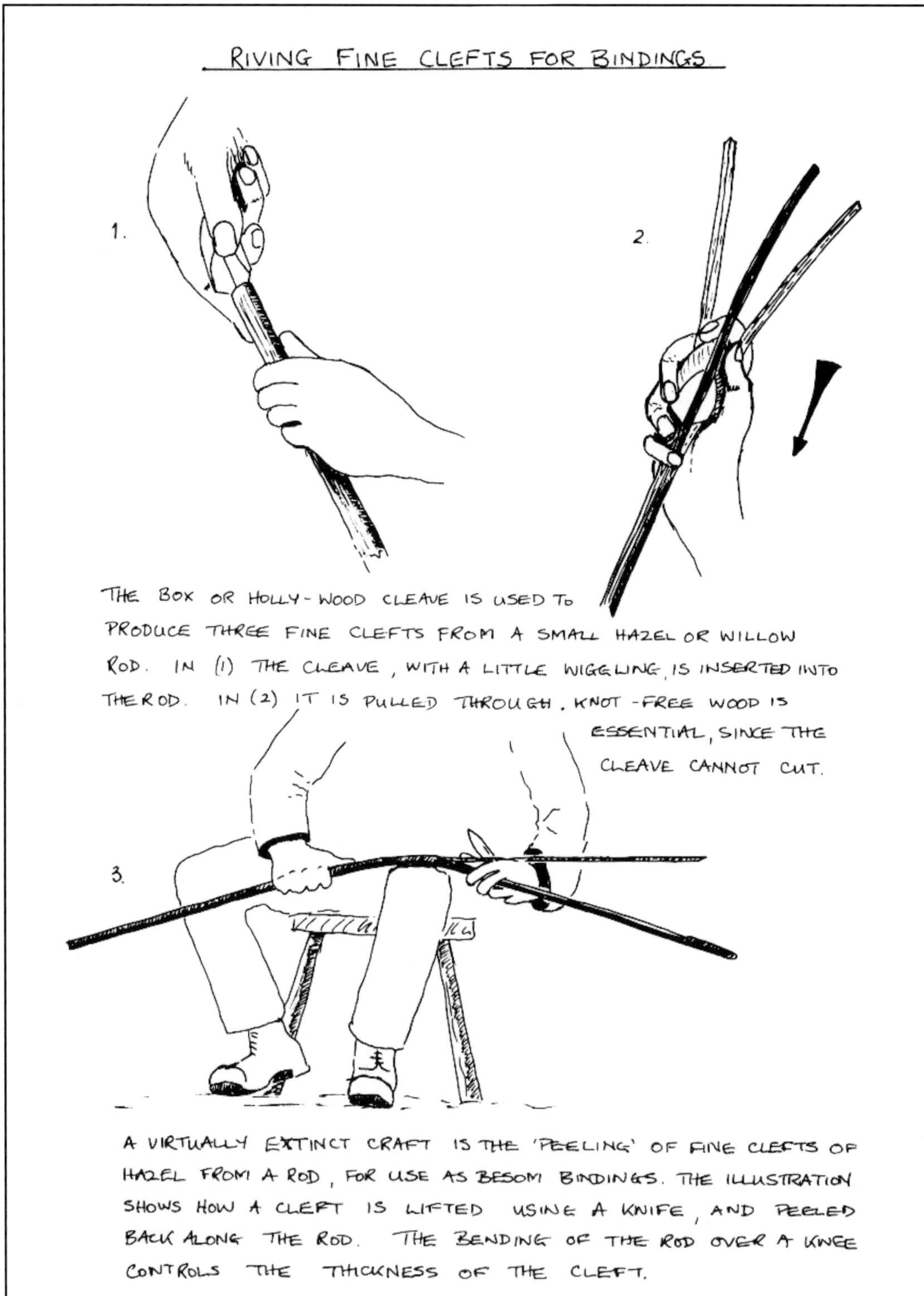
RIVING FINE CLEFTS FOR BINDINGS
1.
2.
THE BOX OR HOLLY-WOOD CLEAVE IS USED TO PRODUCE THREE FINE CLEFTS FROM A SMALL HAZEL OR WILLOW ROD. IN (1) THE CLEAVE, WITH A LITTLE WIGGLING, IS INSERTED INTO THE ROD. IN (2) IT IS PULLED THROUGH. KNOT-FREE WOOD IS ESSENTIAL, SINCE THE CLEAVE CANNOT CUT.
3.
A VIRTUALLY EXTINCT CRAFT IS THE 'PEELING' OF FINE CLEFTS OF HAZEL FROM A ROD, FOR USE AS BESOM BINDINGS. THE ILLUSTRATION SHOWS HOW A CLEFT IS LIFTED USING A KNIFE, AND PEELED BACK ALONG THE ROD. THE BENDING OF THE ROD OVER A KNEE CONTROLS THE THICKNESS OF THE CLEFT.

Fig. 8.

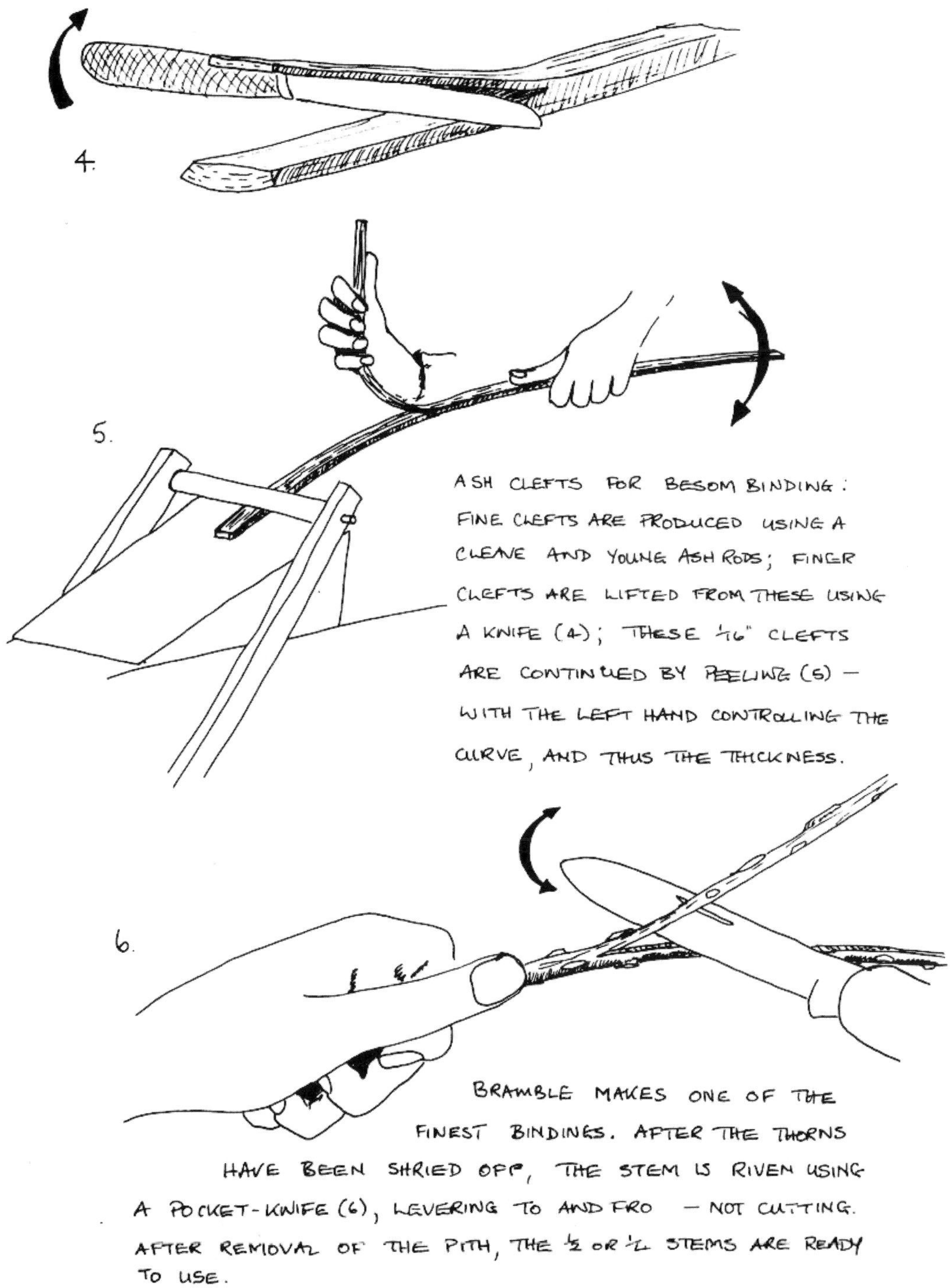
4.
5.
ASH CLEFTS FOR BESOM BINDING: FINE CLEFTS ARE PRODUCED USING A CLEAVE AND YOUNG ASH RODS; FINER CLEFTS ARE LIFTED FROM THESE USING A KNIFE (4); THESE 1/16" CLEFTS ARE CONTINUED BY PEELING (5) — WITH THE LEFT HAND CONTROLLING THE CURVE, AND THUS THE THICKNESS.
6.
BRAMBLE MAKES ONE OF THE FINEST BINDINGS. AFTER THE THORNS HAVE BEEN SHRIED OFF, THE STEM IS RIVEN USING A POCKET-KNIFE (6), LEVERING TO AND FRO — NOT CUTTING. AFTER REMOVAL OF THE PITH, THE ½ OR ¼ STEMS ARE READY TO USE.

Fig. 8 cont.

taught me their craft, and whose skills I have tried to reproduce faithfully here, only one is still at work in a Suffolk wood. One has since died, and the third retired, neither having been replaced by a younger man.

Glossary

Broche: a 30 in. length of cleft hazel twisted to a hairpin shape and used to hold thatch on a roof.

Wound wood: wood with a twisted grain.

Stuff: poles waiting to be worked up.

To run out: split that comes out at the side of a pole rather than running the full length.

Sere wood: dry brittle wood with no sap.

To rid: to remove the side branches from a pole leaving 1 in. or so projecting.

To knot or bud: to remove all the side branches and buds from a pole flush with the bark.

Liggers and sways: left hazel 5 ft. to 8 ft. long used to secure thatch.

Spiles: Kentish name for fencing stakes.

Rinding: removing the bark from a pole.

Silent: kind, easy to use, smooth.

To shrie: to remove thorns from a bramble by passing them through a gloved hand.

A carpenter's rule from the *Mary Rose*

Richard Knight

Tools and Trades Volume 6: 1990

Among the tools recovered from the wreck of the *Mary Rose* is a carpenter's rule having a line of timber measure of the kind first described in print by Leonard Digges in 1556. It is probably the earliest known example of such a rule and it gives substance to Digges' criticism of the accuracy of contemporary timber lines as well as pointing to his definitive set of tables from which rules could be made. Since it must have been made before 1545, when the *Mary Rose* went down in Portsmouth harbour, it also confirms that publication of these tables was the purpose Digges had in mind and not, as some writers have suggested, the announcement of an invention of his own.

Description of the rule

Figs. 1 and 2 show photographs of the two faces of the rule and Fig. 3 is a copy of a full-size drawing (reduced for publication). The rule, made of oak, is 24 in. long, 2 in. wide and approximately ½ in. thick.[1] It is graduated on both faces, in each case on either side of a central line inscribed along the length from end to end.

On Face A, the central line separates two distinct measures, a line of timber measure or "timber line" and a line of inches which is further subdivided into halves and quarters and which extends only to 12 in. with no graduations beyond. The whole-inch marks on this divided foot are designated by crude Arabic numerals, variously oriented as if drawn by an illiterate hand; the halves and quarters are distinguished, in familiar fashion, by marks of different lengths. (Apparently, few artificer's rules known to be from this period bear numerals). However, the most curious feature of this divided foot is its position. It is so placed that the zero is about a quarter of an inch from the end of the rule and unmarked; the 12 in. mark is the same distance beyond the midpoint, though it coincides with the 12 in. square mark on the timber line, as it should on a rule which has been correctly divided. Doubt is thus immediately cast on the accuracy of the timber line, even before any serious measurements have been made.

The timber line is otherwise notable only for the absence of numerals or other distinguishing marks, save at 13 in. square and an ingenious guide to the eye at the end where the lines are closest together.

Fig. 1. Face A.

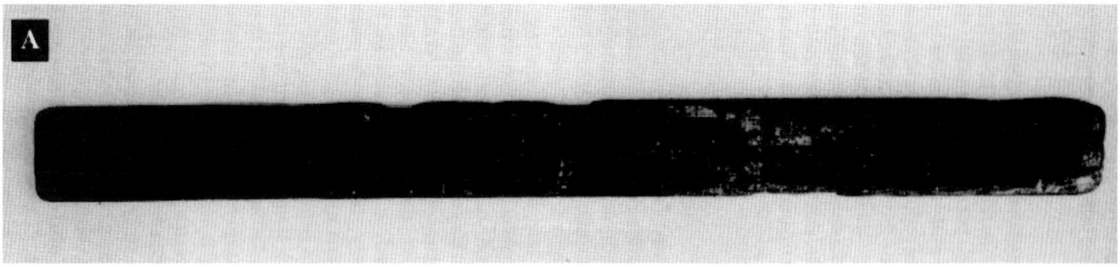

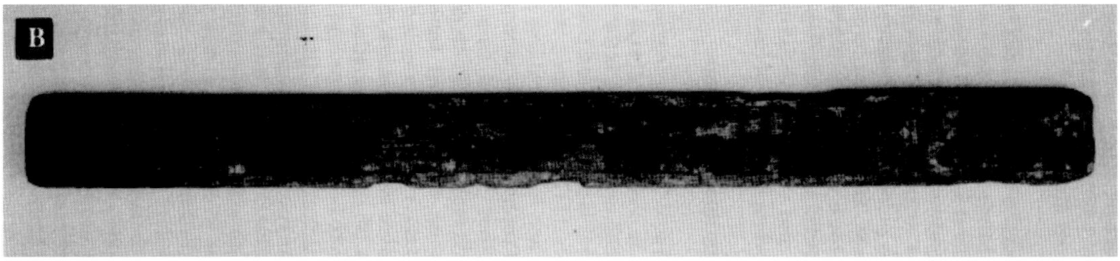

Fig. 2. Face B.

Here the marks for 20 in., 24 in. and 30 in. square are made longer than the others and from the tips of these elongated markers are drawn sloping lines at which the intermediate marks are terminated. The meaning of the strange symbol at 14 in. square is not clear. The largest cross-section the timber line can accommodate is 36 in. square, though there is a hint of one mark beyond that.

Face B is divided in inches across its full width from end to end, but without distinguishing numerals. The one-foot station is identified by a ¾ in. circle centred on the mid-line and the half- and quarter-foot stations by crude semicircles of similar diameter. These simple guides to the eye are not uncommonly seen on 16th century rules; there are three other examples on the *Mary Rose*.

The inches are further divided in halves by marks which extend from the centre line towards one edge in the first foot and towards the other edge in the second. Thus the rule has a curious parity whereby the finer divisions at the free end are towards the user when he holds it in his right hand and away from him when in his left hand, *whichever way he picks it up*. Another example from the *Mary Rose*, a simple 2-foot rule, has the terminal 5½ in. at both ends divided into quarters and disposed in exactly this fashion, while the middle portion is divided no finer than whole inches.[2] It would be interesting to hear of other examples of this disposition of marks and to know whether the arrangement holds any significance for historians of workshop practice.

A major part of the interest of the rule lies in its timber line, which can be examined quantitatively only in terms of the unit of length – the inch – to which the rule itself conforms. If the inch marks

Fig. 3. The rule.

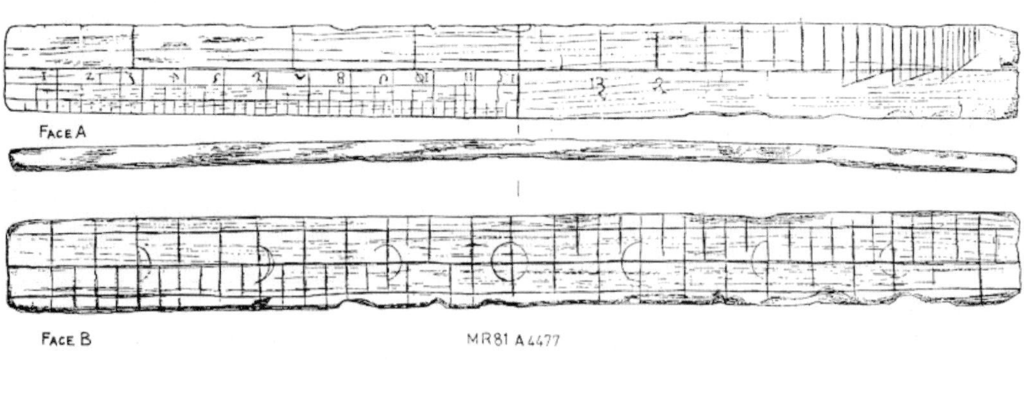

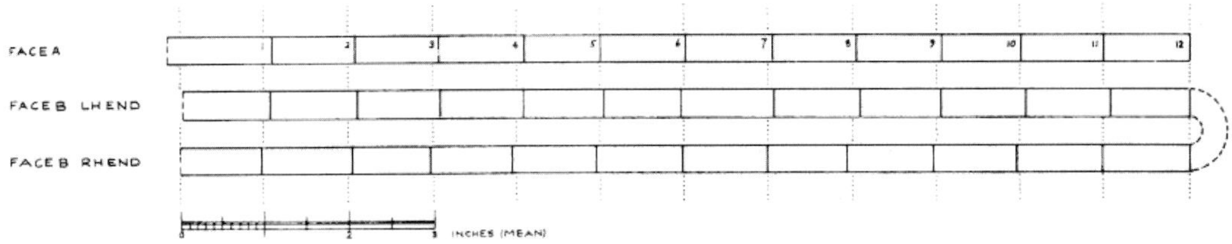

Fig. 4. The three divided feet.

were all the same distance apart this would be easy, but a mere glance shows that they are not. Consequently all the inches on the rule have to be measured in order to discover the standard by which the marker was trying to divide it.

The line of inches

Measurements have been made on a slightly enlarged copy (x 1.025) of the accurate full-size drawing from which Fig. 3 was also taken, recording the positions of all the marks on a millimetre scale. It was judged wise to exclude the three "inches" at the ends of the rule, partly because the ends cannot be observed with the same precision as can the marks on the faces and partly because of the possibility that the rule might have been shortened by wear. The first unit on Face A, of course, is not even nominally an inch.

Four sets of readings yielded 72 independent values of the mean length of six inches, from which is calculated a mean inch of 26.00 ±0.12mm *on the copy*. This is in very good agreement with the simple average of 26.04 mm obtained by dividing 24 into the overall length of 625 mm and, in the event, the rule appears to have suffered no significant shortening. Fig. 4 shows the positions of all the inch marks on both faces against a grid of dotted lines which are separated by the mean inch. For the purpose of comparison the 12 in. marks have all been brought into line and the right-hand half of Face B has been turned through 180°. The hatched lines serve as a reminder that the ends have played no part in the calculations.

The lengths of the 33 "internal" inches have also been found from the same data, each as the mean of four observations. Fig. 5 shows their distribution about the mean, with the deviations expressed as a percentage of it. The extreme range is from –7.8% to +8.8% of the mean and 73% of the values lie within one standard deviation, which is 3.8%. The distribu-

Fig. 5. Distribution of inches.

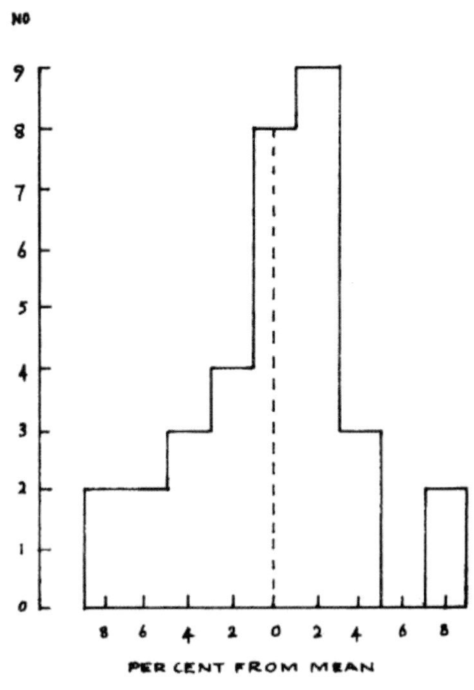

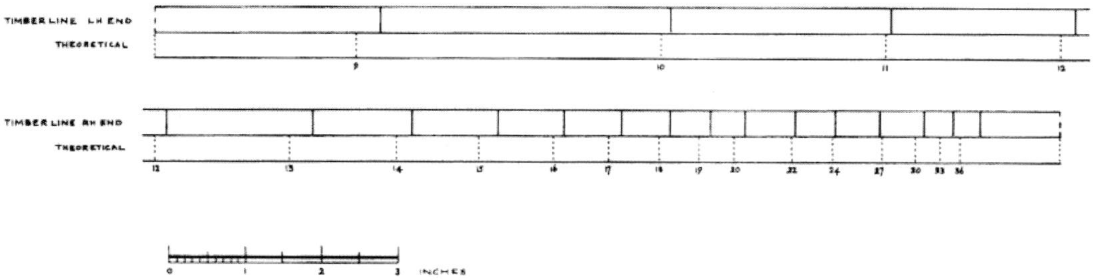

Fig. 6. The timber line.

tion is sufficiently skewed for there to be no obvious value for the "true" inch because, in theory, the mode may have as much to commend it as the mean and a choice between them cannot be made on statistical grounds alone. However, the close agreement between the accurate mean derived from detailed measurements along the whole rule and the simple one based on the overall length, though of a different order of precision, tips the balance in favour of the mean. In the absence of any other compelling consideration, this is the best that can be done and the length of the inch on the copy is taken as 26.00 mm. This reduces to 25.37 mm on the original drawing and on the rule itself, in good agreement with the modern inch, 25.40 mm.

The line of timber measure

Before proceeding to the measurements, it may be useful to recapitulate the function of timber lines in general. Their purpose was to enable the cubic content of square-section timber to be calculated from its dimensions without the use of arithmetic. Such devices were necessary because at that time few artificers knew how to multiply or divide. On the timber line, the distance of each mark from the end of the rule is the length required to make a cubic foot of timber having the square cross-section which that mark represents. This unit length could then be stepped out along the piece, using compasses or otherwise, counting a cubic foot for every step. For example, the mark labelled 13 in Fig. 3 refers to timber 13 in. square in section and its distance from the right-hand end of the rule (Fig. 3.) should theoretically be: 1728/13 x 13 = 10.22 in., the length of 13 in. square material to make 1728 cubic inches or one cubic foot.

The positions of all the marks on the timber line have been recorded and the results are displayed in Fig 6. For the sake of compactness, the line is broken in two at the middle and the right-hand half is placed, without rotation, under the left-hand half. Alongside for comparison is a theoretical timber line scaled to the same overall length. To avoid confusion from overlapping at the right-hand end where the marks are closest together, only a selection of them appears on the diagram. The selected marks are those which, by convention, came to be the standard set drawn on timber lines of the 17th and 18th centuries.

With several of the marks more than half a centimetre from their proper positions, the timber line is obviously inaccurate. In practice, of course, the absolute error in the position of a mark ought to be less important than the

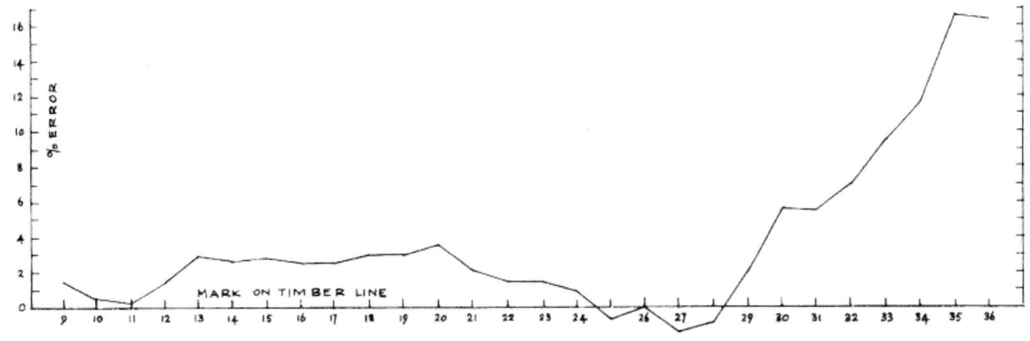

Fig. 7.

percentage error in its distance from the end of the rule from which the unit length is reckoned, but errors were probably never thought of in such terms in the 16th century. The percentage errors have nevertheless been worked out and are displayed in Fig. 7. From 9 in. square to 29 in. square the error in the length of a cubic foot nowhere exceeds 4%. From 30 in. square upwards the errors rise from 5.5% to more than 16%. With four exceptions, every mark lies to the right of its proper distance from the right-hand end of the rule, giving advantage to a seller rather than to a buyer. The errors would be much reduced in size and more evenly distributed about zero if it could be said that the rule had lost about a quarter of an inch from its right-hand end, but that suggestion has no other evidence to support it and must be discarded.

Discussion

With discrepancies up to 8% or so in the lengths of individual inches, it might be thought that as a measuring device the rule would be worthless. But there are some operations in which errors in detail are not necessarily a serious handicap. For example, in the bulk buying of timber, approximate answers may be good enough where there is a tradition of making agreed "allowances" to compensate for uncertainties of measurement which are acknowledged in principle by both parties to a transaction. The possibility that this particular rule was intended for exclusive use in the buying and selling of timber is strengthened by an overall coarseness of division which implies an accepted lack of precision quite separate from errors due to the faulty placing of marks.

There is also a simple technical principle which pervades all craft and in terms of which a rule like this, with all its inaccuracies, would not be disqualified from use "at the bench." Where precise contact is required between two components of a structure, for the sake either of appearance or of strength, methods which employ gauging and scribing are always preferred to those which depend on the precise repetition of a measured length. In these circumstances, the rule has only to measure a workpiece which is sufficiently over-size without being wasteful, and for this "rough" purpose modest inaccuracies are not important. Considerations such as these, taken in relation to the sizes of timber commonly used in a particular trade, are a potential source of interest to those who study the history and evolution of techniques and there may well be clues here to the methods used by shipwrights.

It would be wrong to leave this technical discussion without saying a little more about the strange position of the single divided foot on Face A, with its initial quarter-inch almost half an inch long and with its 12 in. mark against the wrongly placed 12 in. square mark on the timber line. The most plausible explanation of these oddities is that the line was a later addition to a rule which originally had only a line of inches and half-inches on one face and a timber line on the other. In its original form, devoid of divisions finer than half-inches of linear measure and whole inches of timber measure, such a rule would certainly have been used solely for the buying and selling of timber. Whether the addition was made for the sole purpose of adding quarter-inches to a rule otherwise ill-designed for detailed work, is very much open to question. On the one hand is the suggestion that a ship's carpenter might have been a shipwright on land.[3] The shipwright's essential timber line (for buying stock), though taken aboard in his tool chest, would be redundant at sea unless provided with fine divisions for detailed work. On the other hand, a divided line intended for use in measurement would surely have had its zero at the end of the rule.

More probably, the marking was begun at 12 in. to link it with the timber line and then found to fall short because the timber line was wrong in the first place. There is a curious hesitancy about the marks in the region of 2 in. to 3 in. which lends support to this view. If these speculations are correct, it can only be further supposed that the motive was to attempt an improvement in the precision with which the timber line could be used in the region between 9 in. and 12 in. square; a region, perhaps, of special interest to the man who made the addition. In that case, the addition relates rather to his shipwright's than to his ship's carpenter's role.

Historical content

The importance of this rule lies in the fact that it pre-dates, by at least eleven years, the first written account of a line of timber measure, that of Leonard Digges, published in 1556.[4] But it differs from the rule described by Digges in two interesting respects. In the first place, it cannot measure timber smaller in cross-section than about 8½ in. because, below that size, greater lengths than two feet are needed to make a cubic foot. Digges overcame this difficulty by having the missing lengths written on the face of the rule, each one against the number of inches of cross-section to which it refers. Indeed, Digges' rule is only 12 in. long and has a written length for each unit of cross-section below 12 in. square. (In the 17th and 18th centuries, instead of being distributed along the whole length of the rule, this information was concentrated in a small table at the end). There is no such written information on the *Mary Rose* rule, which may indicate that shipwrights, as distinct from house carpenters, had no use for the smaller sizes of timber. It may also mean that Digges was not only an important link between the crude measuring devices used by artificers and the precise work of skilled instrument makers such as his contemporary Humphrey Cole, but also that he began the subsequent long tradition of displaying information in tabular form on rules of all kinds.

The second interesting difference is that the rule described by Digges has not only a timber line, but also a "board line" which gave, in comparable fashion, the length to make a square foot of board of given width. There is no such line on this rule, nor, apparently, anywhere else on the *Mary Rose*. Hence arises the question of whether the Tudor shipwrights had no use for boards or planks bought by the square foot or, rather improbably, whether board lines were invented after this rule was made.

Although he made no such claim, Digges has often been credited with the invention of the timber line, notably by Richard More, a remarkably articulate carpenter with a passion for geometry, who wrote in 1602: "The ordinarie Rule which Carpenters, Shipwrights and others doe use to measure timber withall, was invented and published by Master Leonard Digges."[5] Digges, on the other hand, implied that it already existed when he wrote "... the ruler of tymber measure which the most part of them hath is not made by right arte ..." Evidently More's intention was to credit Digges, not with inventing the principle, but with producing a set of tables from which rules could be made, for the first time with complete confidence. The *Mary Rose* sank in 1545 and the presence of this rule aboard her not only sets a new date before which timber lines can be said with certainty to have been in use, it also confirms these interpretations of the role of Leonard Digges in their history.

The rule also gives substance to the errors mentioned by Digges and about which Richard More was still complaining half a century later. More attributes their persistence to repeated copying: "... ordinarily men make (rules) one by another, whereof hath grown the former error." Of their ubiquity he says: "... hardly shall you see two rules that do everywhere agree. Neither is this error insensible and not to be respected; but apparently grosse and therefore not to be tollerated"; and of their magnitude that he has seen rules which "... in some of their divisions have erred from the truth and from one another after the rate of sixe foote in an hundreth of Boorde and after foure foote in a lode of Timber."

A load of sawn timber contained 50 cubic feet, so "foure foote in a lode" was 8%, a figure exceeded on the *Mary Rose* rule only beyond about 32 in. square. In any case, that end of a timber line is fraught with problems, even when it is correctly marked, on account of the small length of a cubic foot when breadth and thickness are large. More recommended terminating timber lines at 30 in. or even 24 in. square because "the oft drawing of that (short) length upon the timber cannot but breede apparent error." (His method was to use the half cross-section of thick material "and then accoumpt every foote for foure foote").

It is to be concluded, therefore, that this important rule, inaccurate though it is, is no more than typically so for the period of its making. A buyer of timber up to 30 in. square would not have lost more than two cubic feet in a load and for the most part less. Whether that would have been "tollerated" is not clear, nor is it clear whether Richard More was thinking in fractional terms at all. Such was the state of 16th century arithmetic, for the most part without the advantage of decimal fractions as we know them, that he was probably saying, quite simply, that four cubic feet of timber was too much for a man to lose, regardless of how small a percentage of some total it might have been.

Acknowledgements
It is a pleasure to thank Dr. Margaret Rule and the officers of the *Mary Rose* Trust for their generous provision of the drawings and photographs on which this study is based and for their permission to publish the conclusions.[6] Dr. Rule and Mr. David Kendall-Carpenter have read the penultimate draft and kindly made helpful suggestions.

References and notes

1. Catalogue Number MR 81 A4477
2. Catalogue Number MR 82 A2265
3. M. Rule, personal communication.
4. Digges, Leonard,. *Tectonicon*, London, 1562, 1st ed. 1556.
5. More, Richard, *The Carpenters Rule*, London, 1602.
6. The copyright of Figs. 1, 2 and 3 remains with the *Mary Rose* Trust.

Stanley Anderson

R. J. E. Inglis

Tools & Trades Volume 6: 1990

Stanley Anderson, who lived from 1884 to 1966, is unique as the only artist ever to have achieved election as a Royal Academician (in 1941) principally on the strength of his line engravings.[1] He is especially significant to TATHS because some of his later engravings, from the 1930s to early 1950s, record working craftsmen at a time when demand for their products was declining, some to vanishing point. To the author, a tool collector with special interest in how tools are actually used and in the people who used them, his portraits of individual craftsmen are fascinating. His personal interest in Anderson's work dates from 1944 when he acquired his first engraving, "The Hedger" (one of a series of agricultural activities). Contact was maintained for several years thereafter during which time the writer collected several more line engravings.

After serving a seven year apprenticeship as a heraldic engraver under his father in Bristol, Stanley Anderson decided to become an artist and published his first work in 1908.[2] He achieved his early reputation with the public on the strength of his etchings and drypoints of topographical subjects, mostly in Germany, Spain and France, with strong emphasis on architecture.

Anderson, as was quite common at that time, practised in a wide range of media; for example he painted in oil, watercolours and tempera and produced woodcuts and mezzotints. This article, however, concentrates on only one aspect of his life's work, his studies of craftsmen, and the reason why he came to produce these portraits.[3]

In about 1930, his compassion for the less fortunate elements of society, such as tramps and poor people in urban surroundings, began to be reflected in his work. Also at this time, when the market for landscapes was declining, he changed almost exclusively to line engraving and began to record rural activities, always with a strong human interest. These were based on subjects in the Cotswolds and in the Oxfordshire countryside near the village of Towersey about 3 miles from Thame. He had an old house there to which he moved permanently in 1941 after being bombed out of London. Many of his subjects were agricultural workers carrying out simple tasks such as clamping potatoes, sheep shearing and ditching in the countryside near his home. However, as time went on he began more and more to record craftsmen.

Industrial mechanization, coupled with the social and economic environment that prevailed from the depression of the 1930s until well after World War II led to the virtual extinction of the crafts that Anderson portrayed. People had little appreciation of traditionally made articles and society had no sympathy with the idea that making everyday things by hand could provide a living as well as a fulfilling way of life. Anderson was among the few of his contemporaries who thought the ever increasing pace of industrialisation and the adverse effect on the quality of people's lives was

Fig. 1. Dorcas Ing, lacemaker.

utterly distasteful.[4] Many of his letters reflected these passionately held beliefs in outbursts of bitter social comment, although only one of his engravings did so.[5]

It is understandable that, being a

craftsman himself, and a very stern critic of his own work, Anderson should clearly recognise the personal qualities of integrity and discipline which governed the lives of his subjects, the sort of attributes which set apart the real craftsmen from people with occupations giving no scope for self expression. It is quite evident from his letters that he thought of "his craftsmen" with deep affection; to him they were the salt of the earth and he counted all of them his friends.[6] He was a shy and modest man and always thought of himself as their equal and this feeling comes across in these portraits of people who were all characters in their own right.

In his pictures each individual is meticulously depicted in accurate detail working and concentrating on the job, not posed as in a conventional portrait. Their tools lie around in their own working environment with all the shavings and typical craftsman's clutter, but the detail is not overdone and not all the tradesman's tools are necessarily shown. Four portraits, not previously widely published, have been selected for study in this article.

Dorcas Ing, lacemaker

Dorcas Ing (Fig. 1.) was the artist's only female subject in this series of portraits. She was 87 when the preliminary drawings were made in 1939 and sadly died before the engraving was published the next year.

Lace making was a typical cottage industry and was a popular occupation for women in Long Crendon, about 6 miles from Thame.[7] When Dorcas was young many girls learned lace making and she probably acquired her skills, beginning perhaps as young as eight years old, in a lace making school in the village. Tools were customarily handed down in the family, but sadly none of Dorcas' seem to be in her family now. Although miserably paid, making lace enabled married women to earn a welcome addition to their husband's often poor wages.

It was quite usual for lace makers to sit outside in fine weather, taking advantage of daylight while working and gossiping.

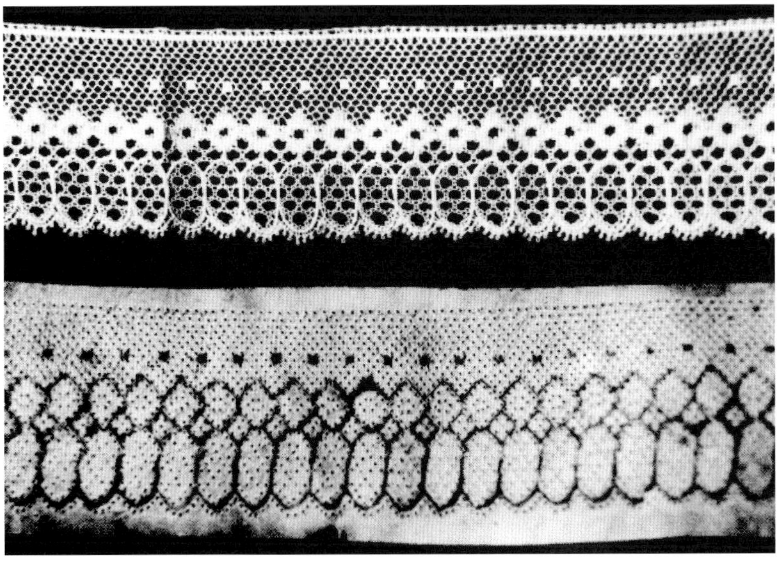

Fig. 2. Top: A piece of Bucks Point Ground Lace. Bottom: The parchment pattern for the lace shown above.

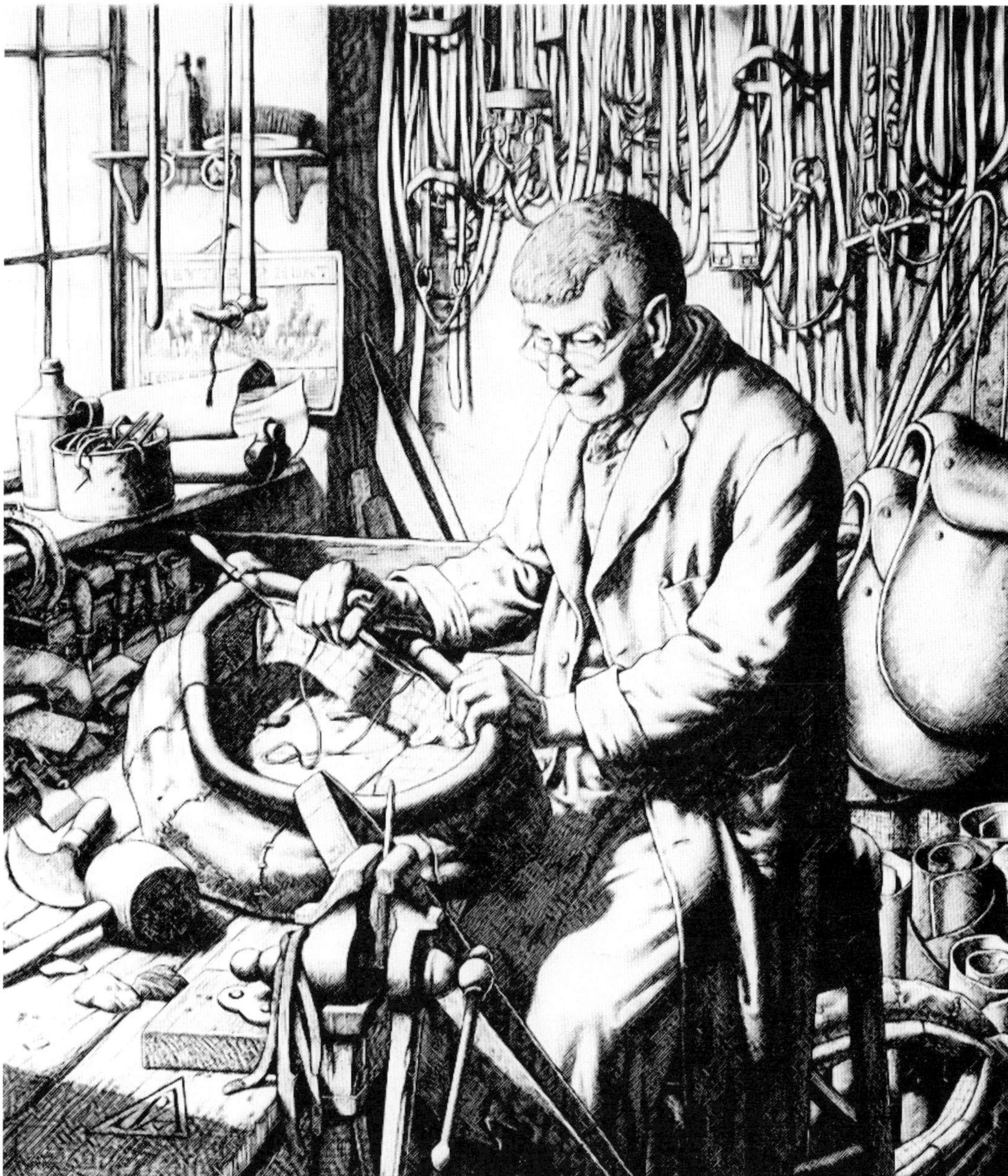

Fig. 3. William Bowl, saddler.

The artist shows her at her pillow tucked into its horse making a piece of Bucks Point Ground lace (Fig. 2, top).[8] The parchment pattern (Fig. 2, bottom), full of pins and pin holes, outlining the design hangs over the pillow, and a drawter keeps the finished lace clean. A set of typical Flemish-style fruitwood bobbins, each weighing enough to maintain the correct tension on its linen thread, lies over the pillow like a fan and each bobbin is positioned so that it can be picked up and its thread twisted swiftly round the appropriate pin with the minimum of movement.[9] Bobbins are manipulated one at a time with alternate hands to create the finished design. It seemed that the artist had some difficulty in drawing her fingers as she said to him, "I'm so sorry. I feel that I must ply my bobbins when I get them in my hands."

Although the development of machine-made lace in the 1850s (around the time Dorcas was born) resulted in the drastic decline of handmade lace, ladies' fashions in late Victorian times and during the first decade of this century ensured that there was still a market for the hand-made article. In Dorcas' time much of the finished lace was sold to retail shops in London, but there were still some private commissions from society ladies. Occasionally the Crendon lace makers went to London to demonstrate their skills. For example, in 1900 Dorcas and two other married ladies, with their bobbins and pillows, had a glorious week sitting in the shop window of Arding and Hobbs at Clapham Junction, where there was an exhibition of lace making.

When this portrait was made, lace making was very far from being a thriving occupation, but in recent years interest has revived strongly and it is now a very popular hobby.

William Bowl, saddler

In the days before the use of motor transport was widespread, the saddler was one of the essential craftsmen of every small country town.

Will Bowl is seen working in 1946 (Fig. 3.) in his shop which was one of the front rooms of his home in Witney Street, Burford, Oxfordshire. He was born at Alvescot about 6 miles away and at 14 was apprenticed to his uncle Henry who owned Henry Wyatt's Saddlery in the High Street at Burford. Will died in 1956, aged 91, a very popular local character, the father of 8 children. Will could remember the days when he repaired the harness of the last team of oxen used for ploughing near Burford.

He is repairing the lining of a horse collar, pushing his needle with his saddler's palm. (Fig. 4.) Making new horse collars and keeping them in repair was an important part of a rural saddler's work. After World War I a new collar for a carthorse cost £5 and "piecing" (repairs) cost 4*s* 6*d* per item, on average.

Although his eldest son, Henry, now 82, was apprenticed to his father for 5 years, the prospects for the trade were very uncertain when he finished his time and he did not continue in the trade. Nevertheless, he still kept his father's tools.[10]

As the apprentice, one of Henry's jobs was to cycle out to the farms in the early morning with three or four of his father's collars of different sizes. He picked up the farmer's collar which needed repair and exchanged it for the loan of one off his back.

Except for his splitting machine and his plough gauge (Fig. 4.), many of the tools used in Will's shop can be seen in the engraving: wooden clamps, mallet, various prickers and a half round knife (used with a rolling action). On the bench by the mallet are two shapeless lumps, the lighter one being beeswax for brown stitching, the other, black wax (made of a mixture of Swedish pitch, resin and grease) for working harness. Will never had a sewing machine; he despised them!

Fig. 4. A splitting machine (top left), a plough gauge (right) and a saddler's palm (bottom left).

All his products were hand sewn in the traditional way, the stitches being of waxed hemp threads which were made up for each job. He reckoned that this method made the most durable saddlery. The spike in the vice was used for pulling round (stretching) the donkey raw-hide thongs lying on the vice, to soften them before greasing.

In the background are two pig skin saddles (calf was never used for saddles). A normal astride saddle took about a fortnight to make, including the time for standing, stretching and drying, and cost £7 10s. Embossing was £2 extra. By contrast a ready-made saddle with machine stitching cost about £5. Side saddles were very seldom called for and were much more expensive. Polished bridles were made from calf with scarfed joints to make up the lengths needed.

Will's greatest leisure pastime was fox hunting with the Heythrop Hunt which he kept up until he was 84. The calendar by the window reminds us of this sport. The artist wrote in a letter of 13th May 1946 "the saddler is a dear old craftsman of 82 who still rides to hounds with ageless zest and has not missed a meet for 63 years." He kept his grey cob in a field at the end of the street.

Will's business came from the members of the various local hunts and of course from the farmers round about Burford. At that time craftsmen and small traders did not advertise and Will was no exception.

Ernest Sims, rakemaker

Rake making was one of the many traditional woodland crafts practised in the Berkshire/Hampshire border area.

The firm of John Sims and Son was

Fig. 5. Ernest Sims, rakemaker.

first set up at Pamber End, 8 miles north of Basingstoke in 1820 and, from small beginnings, became the largest supplier of hay rakes in the south of England in the 1920s and 30s.

Ernie Sims (Fig. 5.) was born in

December 1894 and worked for his father after leaving school at fourteen. When the Great War broke out he was one of the first 300,000 who responded to Kitchener's call for volunteers in August 1914. After four years in the trenches he returned to work for his father in the yard.[11]

Hay rakes were made in quantity by hand methods using simple tools.[12] In common with other woodland products each component had its own clamp or brake for holding it temporarily while one or more hand operations were performed on it. Parts for the rakes were made in batches, but quantities were not related to specific orders for finished rakes unless the order was exceptionally large.

The engraving shows Ernie in the yard in 1948. He is demonstrating how the foot operated clamp held the willow rake head against two stops, whilst he used a home-made brace and spoon bit to bore holes in the head, about 9 in. apart. The angle of the head to the handle is quite critical: if the angle is correct, the optimum amount of hay is gathered at each draw, if incorrect the teeth either dig into the ground or skid over the grass. Each hole Ernie is boring is angled to the rake head so as to receive the splayed ends of the handle. Making these holes looks deceptively simple. Ernie did them purely by eye without any type of jig. The engraving also shows piles of raw and partly processed materials.

Handles were first cut to 6 ft. lengths before two flats were cut with a side axe on opposite sides of one end. Next the bigger humps were shaved off in a brake: Ernie's father is seen doing this in the right-hand background. The handle was then steamed for half an hour, before being rounded with a stail engine (Fig. 6.) while still soft. After hardening an 18 in. slot was sawn in the end of the handle. A stack of these handles is shown behind Ernie.

A piece of ½ in. wide metal cut from a tobacco tin was tacked round the handle just above the slot to prevent splitting and the two ends of the slotted handle were opened by twisting a wooden key (Fig. 7.) in the slot so the ends could be rounded. To assemble the finished rake the handle was splayed open sufficiently for the head to be tapped onto the ends of the handle and finally two nails were hammered through the head to fix the

Fig. 6, left. A stail engine for rounding rake handles.
Fig. 7, right. A key for opening the slot in rake handles.

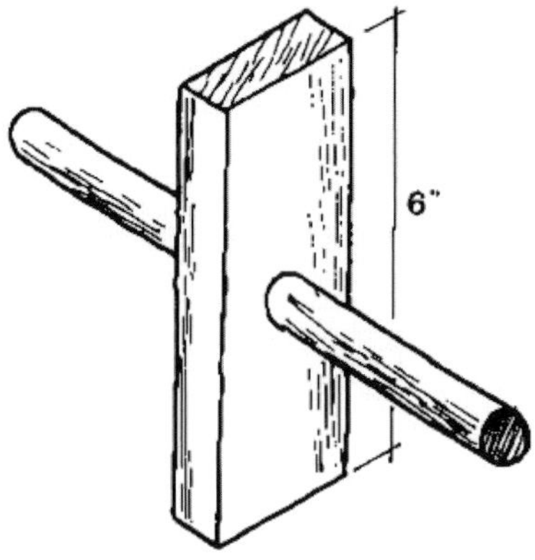

handle before the protruding ends were sawn off.

In the foreground the equipment for making the tines (rake teeth), is shown. The trick was to avoid ruining the mallet by ensuring that it did not touch the cutting iron.

Only one concession was made to modernity: after 1950 an electric drill was used to make the thirteen holes in the head.

Harold, Ernie's elder son, returned to the yard after four and a half years in the Royal Air Force. One of his jobs was to get rakes ready for dispatch by bundling them in dozens, six heads one way and six the other. The firm never advertised. Orders were just received from wholesalers, hardware merchants and seeds-men. One hundred dozen was a very large order and would take the three men in the yard about 10 working days to complete. Rakes were sold wholesale for 2*s* 6*d* to 3*s* 0*d* each and retailed from 4*s* 0*d* to 5*s* 0*d*.

After the war, with increasing farm mechanisation, demand began to fall away steadily. By 1957 the level of orders no longer justified the employment of the boys and they left the yard while Ernie carried on single handed.

He died in July 1983 aged 88 having carried on working until about 6 months before his death. Unfortunately, all the tools, records and materials comprising the business were dispersed immediately after the funeral and today, no trace of the yard remains.

Rupert Timms, farrier and blacksmith

When horses provided virtually all the motive power in the countryside all market towns and many villages had at least one blacksmith/farrier. In this engraving Rupert is depicted making a gate in 1949. (Fig. 8.)

Rupert comes from a long and direct line of farriers, and was born in 1912 at Aston Clinton about 12 miles from Thame.[13] When he was four he moved with the family to Thame where he still lives. On leaving school at fourteen he was apprenticed to his father with whom he continued in partnership until the old man's death in 1960.

Rupert told the author that when he started in the 1920s a set of shoes for a carthorse cost 8*s* 0*d* and took about an hour and a half to make and fit. A lighter set for a hunter in fullered (grooved) iron cost 6*s* 0*d* and a set for a cob (a dual purpose riding and light working horse) cost 5*s* 0*d*. Farriers worked in pairs: one man made the shoes at the forge and fitted them individually while the other stripped and prepared the horse's hooves; then, normally, the first man would nail and clinch up.

Market day was invariably the busiest day of the week. Farmers used to leave their cobs for shoeing on arrival in Thame. No one made appointments. Once a week, Rupert used to visit the stables at the back of local pubs and pick up orders from the ostlers and in the evenings, shoes would be made for stock ready for casual callers.

Up to 1939, there was sufficient shoeing work and small repairs to farm implements to provide a reasonable living for the father and son but the outbreak of war altered everything. Throughout the next four and a half years the two were fortunate to have a steady income from making flat iron horseshoes under contract and according to patterns

Fig. 8. Rupert Timms, farrier and blacksmith.

Fig. 9. Mr. Ralph Timms with the winning gate and the cup.

supplied by the Army. However, in 1945, the Ministry contract ceased. During the war years, the use of horses had of course become drastically reduced so that by 1945 civilian demand was scarce and agricultural repair work could not fill the void. Something had to be done if they were to stay in business.

To foster the revival of rural crafts after the war the Royal Agricultural Society of England instituted a number of annual competitions and the Timms entered the one for blacksmiths which called for the forging of a wrought iron gate. Entries were exhibited and judged at the first post-war Royal Show at Oxford in 1947. Anderson produced the design and the Timms won the cup, shown in Figure 9 together with Mr. Ralph Timms and the winning gate. The next year they won again in York and from then on steadily built up a business as ornamental blacksmiths, executing commissions for gates to Anderson's basic design. Eventually they branched out into other products.

In the portrait, Rupert is forging a traditional joint, part of a garden gate to Anderson's original design which is

Fig. 10, left. The pair of gates, now at 36 - 40 High Street, Thame.
Fig. 11, right. The gates to Elm Park Recreation Ground, Thame.

nailed up behind him (under a design for a hanging pub sign). This particular gate is one of a pair now set up fifty yards away from the forge at "The Crucke", 36-40 High Street, Thame. (Fig. 10.) Among many other commissions they made gates for St. Mary's Church, Thame and the gates for Elm Park Recreation Ground, Thame. (Fig. 11.) In the early 1950s a pair of garden gates cost between £30 and £35 and a 10 ft. high pair of church gates, £90 to £100.

The engraving is a reminder of the time when Rupert was a full-time farrier: carthorse shoes are nailed up on the wall, a box of farrier's hand tools and a tripod are on the ground and a heel cropper for rounding the ends of shoes (Rupert calls it a thief) is under the point of the anvil. (Fig. 12.)[14]

Regarding the tools in the picture, the forge with its anvil and the associated tongs and hammers are the same for a farrier as for an ornamental smith, except that the latter does rather more forging and bending of hot iron and needs an extra pair of tools to do this: a claw for holding the red hot bar steady set into the heel of the anvil and a simple lever to put the required curve in the bar (lying across the anvil). During the 1940s and early 1950s riding, particularly racing, hunting and point-to-pointing gradually revived, and then during the 1960s show jumping, eventing and polo became increasingly popular. After his father died, manhandling large pairs of gates single-handed become too much for Rupert and by 1965, the demand for shoeing enabled him to revert full time to his original trade.

Fig. 12. A heel cropper.

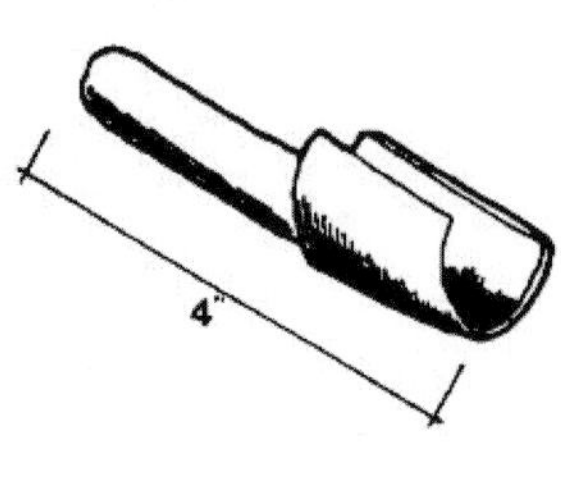

About 10 years ago, Rupert retired and was persuaded to sell the forge, but soon found that he could not abide being idle, so he joined his farrier son and is, in 1990, still very happy working five mornings a week.

Other engravings of craftsmen

Sadly, the series of Anderson's craftsmen portraits is rather small, about 14 in all, the last being published in 1953.[15] Line engraving is very taxing and he only ever produced two or three finished plates in a year. Latterly, when arthritis began to affect his right hand, he concentrated on water colours of agricultural landscapes.

The series is completed by the following engravings.

The brothers Charles and William Chinchen, Purbeck quarry-men of Langton Matravers (1936) finish granite kerbstones.

Herbert Soames, hurdle maker (1937) trims a stake while in the foreground his son Leonard cuts a mortice with a twybil.

George Scott, wheelwright of Sheepscombe (1939) uses a spoke dog to assemble a wagon wheel.

William Youens Fleet, basket maker of Thame (1942) is at his lap board making a half bushel basket.

Jack Goodchild, chairmaker of Naphill (1944) adjusts the back of one of his Windsor chairs.

Arthur Ing (son of Dorcas), thatcher of Long Crendon (1944), uses his bat on the hip of a cottage.

The brothers Owen and Alan Dean,

wood turners (bodgers) (1945) are making chair legs in the woods at Speen.

George Ramsey, cooper of Chesham (1947) drives an iron raising-hoop on a cask.

Clifford Hoing16, violin maker of Holmer Green (1953) shapes the back of an instrument.

The gypsy clothes peg maker (1953) argues with his wife out-side their caravan.

Although some photographers and other artists have recorded craftsmen at work, none in the writer's opinion has managed to produce so many distinctive portraits; the pictorial emphasis has nearly always been on the process and virtually no effort has been made by the artist to identify the craftsmen. Stanley Anderson seems to have created images with a very pleasing blend of his own special skill with the craft of his subjects to make powerful records for posterity. The portraits must surely have given him much personal satisfaction and can be thought of as his homage to craftsmanship, the culmination of his career as an engraver and the justification for his reputation as an artist.

Acknowledgements

The author is particularly indebted to the artist's elder son Mr. Ivan Anderson and his wife for encouragement and much detailed help in the preparation of this paper.

Mr. Ian Lowe provided help and advice both whilst he was a curator at the Ashmolean Museum, Oxford and subsequently. The kind assistance of other people too numerous to mention by name is gratefully acknowledged.

Notes

1. The entry in the *Dictionary of National Biography 1961-1970* contains the salient facts of the artist's life. *The Times* published an obituary on 14th March 1966 followed by a letter from Humphrey Brooke, Secretary of the Royal Academy, on 18th March.
2. In the *Print Collector's Quarterly*, Vol. XX, July 1933, pp. 221-246, Martin Hardie's catalogue raisonné lists Anderson's first etching as "Head Study" published in an edition of fifty-five in 1908. (An edition in this context usually means that only this number of prints will be made after which the plate will be defaced or destroyed.)
3. Anderson produced about 50 engravings between 1930 and 1953. Mr. Ian Lowe, when Curator of Western Art at the Ashmolean Museum, catalogued the museum's collection of Anderson's prints with the help of the artist shortly before he died.
4. Two writers who thought like Stanley Anderson were Hennell, Thomas, *Change in the Farm*, C.U.P., 1943, and Massingham, H. J., *Men of Earth*, Chapman & Hall, 1943.
5. "False Gods", a line engraving published in 1947, expressed these sentiments. An unpublished letter from the artist to a friend explains the significance of the various symbols in this engraving.
6. Two letters to the author of August 1944 and the artist's letter of condolence, 26th May 1966, to Mrs. Timms on the death of Ralph, her husband (Rupert's father).
7. Mr. Jim Ing, Dorcas' eldest grandson and his sister, Miss Dorcas Ing,

kindly supplied much of the information about the family. General historical background was obtained from Donald, Joyce, *Long Crendon, a Short History,* The Long Crendon Preservation Society, 1983, part II, pp. 24 - 25.

8. Mrs. Fudge of Luton Museum and Art Gallery kindly identified the type of lace in the engraving. She also extracted a piece of Bucks Point Ground lace and its corresponding parchment pattern from the Museum's extensive collection and allowed the photograph to be taken.
9. Mrs Fudge said that the bobbins were typically Flemish in appearance.
10. I am indebted to Henry Bowl and Mrs. Cook, the elder son and third daughter respectively of the subject for all the family details and to Henry for the technical details.
11. Harold Sims, Ernie's elder son, and his wife supplied the detailed information about the family working practices in the yard.
12. Jenkins, J. Geraint, "Craft of the Village Rakemaker", *Country Life,* 2nd Jan. 1958. Eight photos of Ernie at work in the yard from the extensive collection in the Museum of English Rural Life, Reading.
13. Rupert Timms provided all the detailed information about himself, the family and his trade during a number of meetings spread over 18 months. Incidentally Rupert is the last survivor of Anderson's craftsmen.
14. The boy standing in the doorway is Brian Edwards, now 52 and still living in Towersey, where Anderson drew him. Children have always been fascinated by blacksmiths working with red hot iron; his inclusion in the engraving is a typical piece of artist's licence.
15. The portraits are to be found in the following publications:
Hennell, Thomas, *British Craftsmen,* Collins, 1946, p.11: Purbeck Quarrymen [Brothers Chinchen], p.21: Wheelwright [George Scott].
Massingham, H. J., *Men of Earth,* C.U.P 1943. Frontispiece: William Youens Fleet at his Lap-Board.
Singer, C., ed., *History of Technology,* Vol. III, C.U.P., 1952. Pl. 6: Wheelwright George Scott, Pl. 7: Cooper [George Ramsey], pp. 123-133, J. Geraint Jenkins and R. A. Salaman discuss their tools.
Mayes, L. H. "Jack Goodchild: Chairmaker", *Woodworker,* March 1957, p. 66. Collis, John Stewart, *The Worm Forgives the Plough*, Barrie and Jenkins, 1988, p.35: Will Bowl, saddler, p.157: Arthur Ing, thatcher.
Lowe, Ian, *Oxford Roundabout*, 1966. (Monthly periodical). January: Making the Gate [Rupert Timms]. February: The Chairmaker [Jack Goodchild]. April: The Wheelwright [George Scott]. June: The Saddler [Will Bowl]. July: The Lacemaker [Dorcas Ing]:. August: [Herbert Soames]. September: The Thatcher [Arthur Ing]. December: The Basketmaker [William Youens Fleet].
16. Clifford Hoing died in July 1989.

An apprenticeship at T. Norris & Sons

W. J. Yarranton

Newsletter No. 29: Spring 1991

Memories of my apprenticeship days working for T. Norris & Son, specialist plane manufacturer, established 1860, written in September 1968.

Next year will be the 50th anniversary of my starting a career in the toolmaking/engineering industry. It was in the year of 1939 that I left school at the immature age of 14. At the start of the school term previous to this I well remember the head master of New Malden West Central School, Mr J. Thomas Crowson, gathering us together one morning in the school hall and warning us that if we didn't do well during the coming term we would leave school at 14 years of age with a poor academic record which would result in us finding difficulty in getting a job and that this in turn would affect the whole of our working lives.

My achievement during the school years was not particularly good, I remember I was delayed in starting school as the school was full and I remember being away from school on various occasions through illness; at one stage I was even sent away to stop with my Auntie Alice in Great Yarmouth because the doctor, Dr. Colonel Pettit, of New Malden, suggested to my parents that my health would improve if I could get some sea air in my lungs. However, the Headmaster made his point on that particular morning and left me worrying about my future. The result was that at the end of the next term, for the first time in my life I came top of the class and actually received a prize for English; it was a book entitled *King Arthur's Knights of the Round Table*.

Looking back over the years, my education on leaving school was very, very limited. I could read, write and do simple arithmetic although I did shine in the practical subjects of woodwork, drawing and gardening. I left school at 14 years of age not really knowing what I wanted to do. My father was a good simple and practical man who thought quite correctly that my working future would have to be in something practical. In those days everyone thought the real achievement was to get a trade behind you and with this in mind, my father almost decided for me that I should try and get a job in toolmaking. Armed with this decision my father and I put on our best suits and went to the labour exchange in Kingston and asked if there were any vacancies in the field of toolmaking. At that point in time nothing suitable was available and we returned home with my father wondering what to do next. I was so inexperienced in life that I didn't understand fully and I was wondering what all the fuss was about.

After about a week had passed, a green Labour exchange card came through our letter box in Fleetwood Road telling me to go to the firm of T. Norris & Sons in Sycamore Grove, New Malden for an interview. My dad and I put on our best suits again and after a lecture from my dad on how to stand and what to say, we arrived at the firm of T. Norris & Son, makers of fine English planes for cabinet makers. We approached the factory entrance down a long driveway covered with loose shingle which made a lot of noise when you walked over it. To the right of the drive was a large Victorian house which was all part of the premises but partly separated by a hedge.

We entered the door at the front of the factory and my dad asked to see the Manager. During the interview, the Manager asked me a few questions about my hobbies, etc. and I do recall being a little shy and my father doing most of the talking for me. Anyway, the Manager decided that he would give me the job and said that the wages would be 12*s* 6*d* per week. I thought this was a very high wage because some of the lads who left school at the same time, and who went to work at the Brush factory in Kingston Road, New Malden, only received 10*s* 0*d* per week (equivalent to 50 pence in today's currency). The manager went on to explain that the hours of work were 48 hours per week and that they started at 7 a.m. and stopped for ½ hr. at 9 a.m. for a breakfast break. I would need to take along each week a clean khaki overall and I remember my mum taking me into Kingston to buy two button-down-the-front khaki overalls which she had to alter on her hand-driven Singer sewing machine. I remember having to walk to work the first week or so because I didn't have a bicycle. After the first couple of weeks we went to the cycle shop in London Road, Kingston and Dad got me a Raleigh roadster on hire purchase. I think the idea was to pay for the bike as quickly as possible and every week I had to go to the shop with 10*s* 0*d* of my wages.

My mother was quite worried about me because she thought that the hours of work would make it a long day for me. The other men in the factory went home for breakfast and for dinner, they lived quite locally to the factory and I well remember being left alone in the factory during meal breaks and feeling quite sorry for myself. The other men in the factory were Mr. Bill Ratcliffe, the working manager, Mr. Bowley, who everyone called Bow, and the other man was called Stan. Stan worked continually on a turret lathe and, as I understood, he was the only one on War work. The director associated with the company was Mrs. Norris, a tall upright lady who must have been in her 80s. Mrs Norris lived in the big Victorian house on the right of the factory. On the odd occasions when I met her she was always very pleasant to me and I remember thinking now nice she was. I sometimes met her on a Friday when she brought the wage packets over from the big house.

Bill Ratcliffe, the manager, was a man of my father's age; he wore big heavy boots and a peaked cap and he rode a large upright cycle and I always called him Mr. Ratcliffe. Bow, who seemed to be his understudy, I thought at the time was rather a cocky person; like the rest of us he wore a brown khaki overall but it was too long and came almost down to his ankles. I never really got on with him from the word go, he always seemed to be finding fault with me, not like Mr. Ratcliffe who seemed to encourage me and teach me. I never really had a lot to do with Stan, the turret lathe operator, he was always quite pleasant and always had a kind word for me. All three of the men in the factory seemed quite old and I would imagine they are no longer with us mortals. I suppose that I am really the only surviving member of that band of merry men.

The factory was rather large for the number of persons working in it. The main building was oblong in shape with a lot of large windows down each side. Stan's turret lathe was positioned just inside the entrance door and benches were positioned down the right hand side against the wall with good daylight from the windows. The vices on the well worn benches, I recall, were the old-fashioned type that went all the way down to the floor.

In the centre of the shop was a large surface table with finished planes placed on it. Right down the other end of the shop was another building or extension to the main shop. At the end of this other workshop was a large power press and just adjacent to the entrance to this shop was the large, "could be 6 ft. diameter" whetstone running through water and driven by a large belt from a countershaft. I particularly remember this whetstone because they had to build me a plinth to stand on because I was too short for grinding the plane irons. Through the side door to the left of this building was a pathway alongside the factory which led to the one and only outside toilet. You were obliged to walk the length of the main factory, past all the windows so that everyone could see where you were going.

My jobs in the factory were varied. I used to sweep up and keep the benches clean but never got involved in making tea. Everyone seemed to take a flask to work with them. I was tried on various aspects of making the now famous Norris planes. I learnt with some accuracy how to use a file and this has stood me in good stead all my working life. The most common plane made at that time was the dove-tailed coffin sided smoother with the sides dovetailed to the sole plate, all of these were filed and fitted by hand which made it essential for accuracy with a file. 1 became particularly proficient at making the rosewood plane handles, these came to the factory rough sawn to shape. I can still smell the rosewood and the subsequent coatings of "sanding sealer" which smelt like the pear drops that we bought at the local sweet shop.

I made quite an impression on the large whetstone in the extension shop, in fact after I had finished grinding the plane irons all that had to be done was a slight rubbing on an oil stone for a final and really keen cutting edge. I remember Mr. Ratcliffe telling me I had a fine eye for concentricity and squareness during the various hand operations I got involved in. Another tedious task on the coffin sided smoothing planes was burnishing the radiused section adjacent to the pivot point of the gun metal lever. I say tedious because it was not a quick operation; it firstly involved filing a perfect radius around the sides in two planes of direction. This then had to be followed by fine filing followed by about three grades of emery and finally by flour paper. During each of these operations of course it was very easy to deform the original shape and make the job second-hand looking. The final operation necessary was the task of burnishing with long straight strokes with a burnishing tool. The burnishing tool was made from a ground-down triangular file with the edges and surfaces oil stoned to a very fine finish. The end result of a perfectly burnished job is that it should look like a chromed finish. During the whole of my engineering career I have never had the occasion to burnish any other job other than the Norris planes.

As my tuition progressed through the various aspects of the metal work it soon became apparent that I had "Rusty Fingers", so called in the engineering trade because one leaves a perfect finger print of rust on steel which if left for any length of time would etch to quite a depth. It is quite common with boys in their teens and is caused by too much acid in their perspiration. Of course, Bow always wiped the jobs over with an oil rag when I had finished them.

As mentioned previously most of the planes made were coffin sided smoothers and the occasional panel plane and gun metal violin planes. I feel that at that stage the company was in a run down state, only three men and one boy employed; probably previous to this the work force was larger. It seemed that it was only the Mrs. Norris, previously mentioned, who was running the operation.

I volunteered for the RAF in April 1943 and came out of the RAF in 1947. By this time I understood the company was no longer in Sycamore Grove and obtained a job nearer my home at High Speed Service Tool Company, still in toolmaking but the type of tools involved here were press tools.

When I was employed by T. Norris and Sons I never took the opportunity of purchasing any of the now sought after Norris planes, and two years ago, getting a little nostalgic in my mature years, I decided to make, in the traditional manner, a 1920 A4 model Norris Coffin Sided Smoother. The result was quite satisfactory and I have been commended on the finished article by cabinet makers and engineers of good standing. (Fig. 1.)

When I left T. Norris & Son, Mrs. Norris gave me a reference which reads:

> William Yarranton has been with us since Oct. 10th 1939 and we have found him most satisfactory in every way, he is a good worker and time keeper.
>
> We are very sorry to part with him.
> Signed H. E. Norris, Director.

I was very proud to have received this testimonial, I stil1 have the original and have tried to live up to it during my working life. I think I have succeeded.

Fig. 1. Mr. Yarranton's Norris plane.

17th century saws at Skoklosters Castle, Sweden

Dr. Bengt Kylsberg

Newsletter No. 31: Autumn 1991

The extensive tool collection at Skoklosters Castle at Balsta in Sweden was formed by the Count Carl Gustav Wrangel who built the castle during the latter part of the 17th century. The collection is particularly interesting as most of it was acquired during this same period including a large order of 200 items of carpenter's tools (mostly planes but also including saws) that was delivered from Amsterdam in February 1664 and, what is of even more significance, the documentation for this order is still with the collection.

This article is based on a general article published in the Swedish periodical "Hemslojden" in June 1986. It attempts to summarise some of the important developments in saw making up to the end of the 17th century and is illustrated with saws in the Skoklosters' collection.

Saws are one of mankind's oldest tools. Four thousand years ago Egyptian carpenters used saws, the oldest of which were made of copper and, later, bronze which was considerably better and easier to forge. Bronze saws and other tools were spread all over the antique world.

About 2,500 years ago the first iron saws were made; however, the metal was still so soft that only very shallow blades could be made and to avoid buckling, the saws had to be used with a pulling action. Also, it was not possible to give saws made of iron a set.

Setting the teeth

About 2,000 years ago the Romans solved the problem of setting the teeth. With a special tool, the teeth of the saw were bent alternately to the left and to the right in relation to the median of the blade. (Fig. 1.)

By this ingenious invention (something that seems self-evident to us today) the saw became considerably more effective. In addition, the teeth could be filed so that the saw could work with a pushing action. Anyone who regularly uses a saw will understand the significance of this improvement! Also, a carpenter no longer had to necessarily use a sawing horse as previously; he could hold the work with his knee or hand against a steady support.

Until then all saws had a relatively long blade with a thin handle fixed to one

Fig. 1. A close-up of a 17th century Dutch handsaw showing the set. A special setting tool and triangular file for sharpening the teeth were included with the saw.

Fig. 2. Two Dutch framed saws made of jacaranda. Saws of this design have been in existence for 2,000 years.

end. The Romans also invented the first frame saws to facilitate the conversion of logs into boards. There were two advantages: the power of two men could now be applied to the saw and the blade did not bend. (Fig. 2.)

The oldest metal saws found in Sweden are about 1,000 years old. They were excavated in 1936 at Mastermyr, on the island of Gotland, together with a considerable number of other carpenter's tools. In appearance, they are very like the, considerably older, Roman ones.

During the Middle Ages different kinds of bow and framed saws were very common although for tree felling the axe was still the most commonly used tool.

During the latter part of the 15th century a new design of saw appeared. It was a long, thin two-man saw with handles fitted at right angles to the blade. It had large "M" shaped teeth which efficiently discharged the sawdust and could saw thick logs and also fell trees. (Fig.3.) This type of saw has been in common use almost until the present day.

The handsaw

For the satisfactory manufacturing of handsaws, two things are neces-

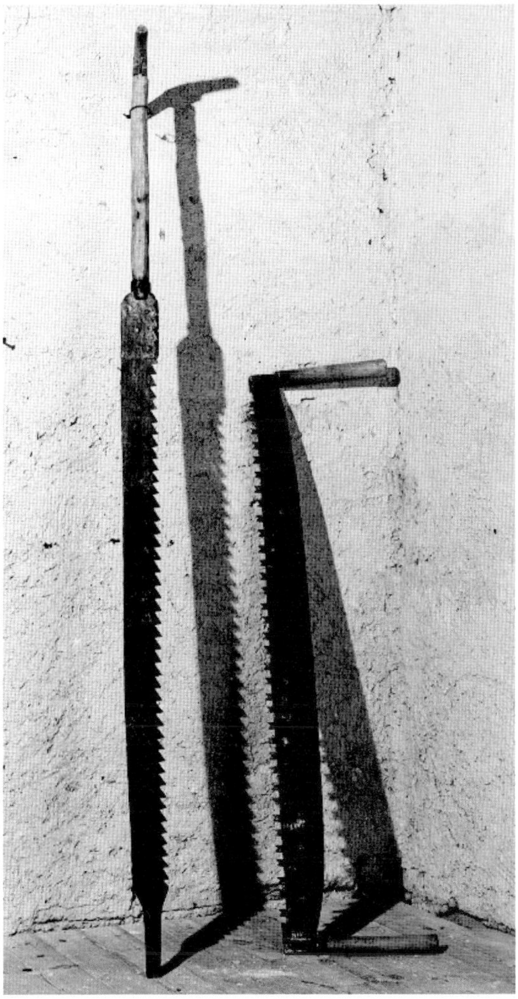

Fig. 3. Saws with M shaped teeth as that shown on the right hand side have appeared in 15th century pictures. The left hand saw was originally used for sawing planks, but was later adapted for ice-sawing. Both probably date from the 17th century and may have been made in Sweden.

Fig. 4. The Dutch handsaws have carved boxwood handles reinforced with a horn ring. Note the beautiful decoration at the toe. The blade of the larger one is 64 cm. long.

sary; firstly, the production of steel and secondly the knowledge to roll sufficiently broad blades. This technology was available both in England and Holland during the 17th century. The two oldest handsaws of the Dutch type found in Europe can be seen at Skoklosters Castle. (Figs. 4 & 5.) Both were part of the order from Amsterdam and are splendid examples of Dutch tool making.

Most tools, up to and including this time, were made by the craftsmen themselves or in close co-operation with a blacksmith. However, it is interesting to realise that, from the 17th century, there were also special tool makers manufacturing a variety of tools for selling to a wide group of customers, *vide* Count

Wrangel's order. Thirty years later, in 1697, the future Tsar, Peter the Great, visited Holland and bought tools which are now in the Hermitage Museum in Leningrad.

Steel in saw blades

The Englishman, Joseph Moxon, wrote in his *Mechanick Exercises*, published in London in 1677, that saws preferably ought to be bought in an ironmonger's shop in Foster Lane, London. At the same time, the reader is advised not to buy saws of iron, but saws of steel which was the new material. (Fig. 6.)

Fig. 5. A close up of the two handles of the saws shown in Fig. 4.

Fig. 6. A Dutch steel saw with a turned handle. The blade is held as in a hack saw. Its most likely use was to saw out small pieces of hard material such as horn or bone.

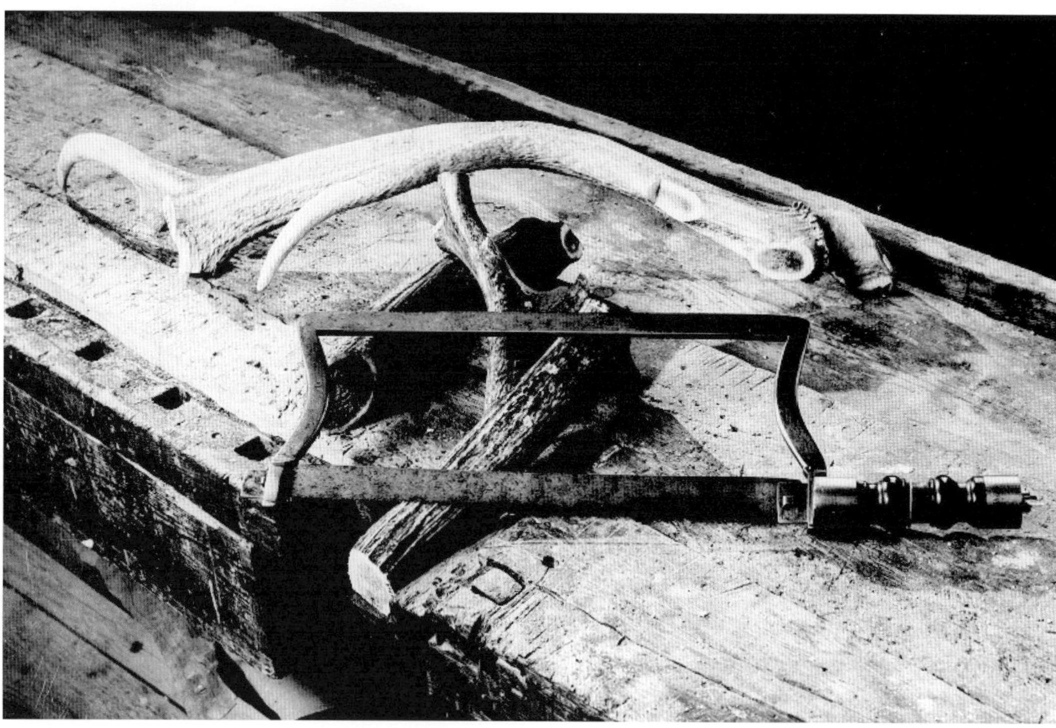

Hart's patent plane

Mark Rees

Tools and Trades Volume 7: 1992

Introduction

English patent planes of any period are uncommon and examples dating from before 1900 particularly so. During the last few years, the author has become aware of three planes, all substantially the same and all marked "Hart's Patent". All three are in private collections.

The basic form of these planes is such that they could be described as stop chamfer planes. Whilst the planes have a strong similarity there are certain differences between all three. The size varies but little, they are all made of beech, they all have a cut-away section to the underside at the rear and a thumb screw operating an adjustable sole in the centre of the plane.

Photograph 1 shows a general view of the three planes and Photograph 2 a view of the undersides. Photograph 3 is a view of the fore-ends showing the marks. No other planes of this pattern either with or without the Hart's patent mark are known to the author.

Description

Plane A (on the left in the photographs): Body: length 304 mm. (12 in.), width 48 mm. (1⅞ in.), depth 70 mm. (2¾ in.). Steel adjustable foot 14 mm. (9/16 in.) wide moved vertically by means of a brass thumbscrew. The front portion of the foot is angled upwards; the rear part is flat (parallel with the axis of the plane) with two plain holes.

Photograph 1: Hart's patent planes. In all the photographs, plane A is on the left, B is in the centre and C is on the right.

Photograph 2. Soles of Hart's patent planes.

Marks: W. GREENSLADE, BRISTOL, EXHIBITION MEDALS, LONDON AND DUBLIN. HART'S PATENT (The exhibition medals listed in the maker's mark suggest a date of manufacture between 1865 and 1880).

Plane B (in the centre in the photographs): This plane differs from A in the following respects. Body: width 41 mm. (1⅝ in.), depth 76 mm. (3 in.). The "V" shape on the sole extends the full width of the plane. Steel adjustable foot 25 mm. (1 in.) wide without holes. The sole operates at angle which is approximately parallel with the an angle of the iron and is operated by a thumb screw within the escapement. There is an upstanding brass strap on the centre line in "handle" area at rear. Two screws are inserted through the handle and into the brass section.

Marks: 42, HART'S PATENT, LONDON.

Plane C (on the right in the photographs): This plane is the same as B except in the following respects. The steel foot has a sliding screw securing the mechanism at the side. The handle area has a wooden block infill (this is not original). Additional stability to this block is effected by a shallow groove in the plane body and a corresponding tongue in the block. Two wood screws secure this insert. The position of the screws is the same as the screws in Plane B.

Marks: HART'S PATENT, 37, NORRIS, LONDON, MAKER.

The patent

A search in the Patents Office produced Patent No. 1291, filed 5 May 1870, issued

Photograph 3. Fore-ends of Hart's patent planes showing marks.

to Frederick Hart of Bourton, Dorset, for the invention of "Improvements in Planes for Chamfering and Moulding and in Means Connected with their Use."

The patent extends to eight pages and the following is a precis and commentary on it.

With the benefit of the photographs and descriptions that are given above, the general arrangement and construction of the plane should be apparent to the reader. Figs. 1, 2 & 3 are the general arrangement drawings given in the patent.

In addition to chamfering, the plane was claimed to be capable of making moulded chamfers by the use of an iron of the desired profile and a matching profiled block secured to the adjustable foot. (Fig. 4.)

The accurate cutting at the ends of the chamfer (the stopped end) is effected by the use of the clamp shown in Fig. 6 which is fixed to the workpiece and controls the start of the cut by the rear of the plane bearing upon it. The method of working for stopped chamfers is shown in Fig. 5.

Fig. 7 shows a further development. This is a plane having two adjustable soles each with interchangeable faces. When used with the sole behind the iron lowered, the plane is said to be suitable for stopped chamfers on cross-grain work and to be able to work up to the stopped end of the chamfer. It will not escape the reader that a plane of such arrangement would be wholly impractical, there being no sole in front of the iron, there is nothing to stop it digging in at least until the last cut when the angles of the chamfer sole would provide some guidance. This plane had angles to the toe and heel to enable use with the clamp guide at either end.

The inventiveness of Mr. Hart did not however finish at this point. Fancy ends to the chamfers are formed by a (metal?)

FIG. 1.

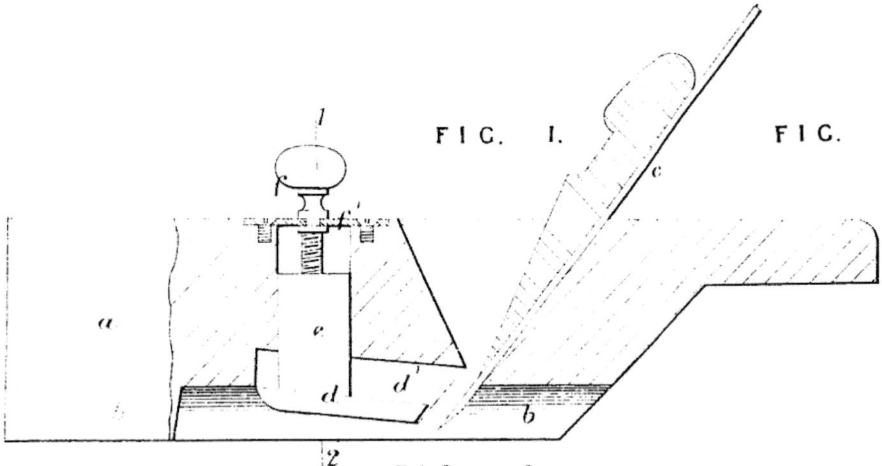

FIG. 2.

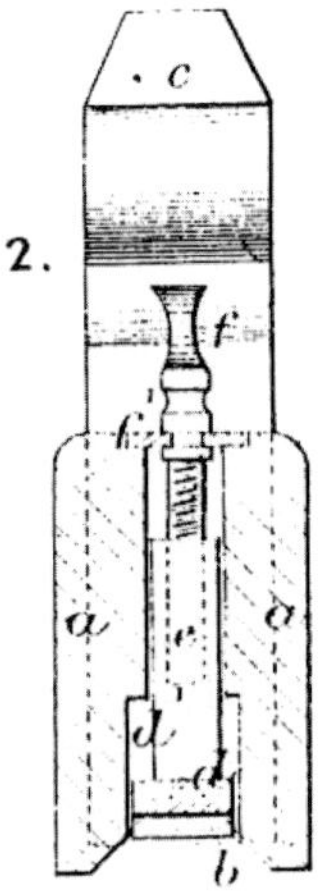

FIG. 3.

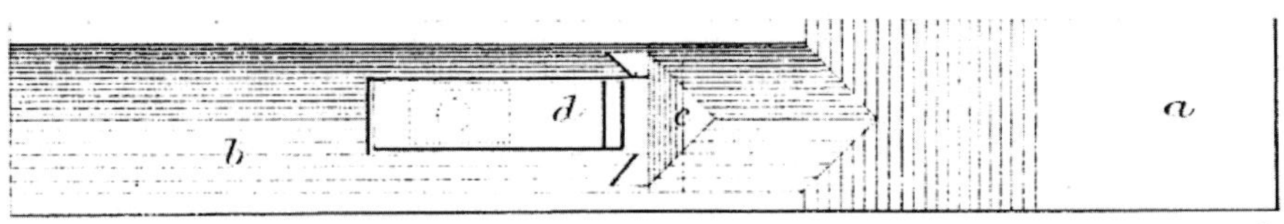

piece fitted to the rear of the plane which would run on a guide of the desired profile (Fig. 8) secured to the workpiece with a clamp similar to Fig. 6 but in addition holding the profile guide. As an alternative method, shaped guides could be fitted to the rear of the plane (Figs. 10 & 11) to form fancy ends to chamfers by running over the clamped guide.

Discussion

To the experienced woodworker the advantages claimed in the patent will seem in the initial claims to be truthful. The planes will undertake chamfering work and although the irons are set by means of a wedge, the screw adjustment to the moving sole would allow adjustment of the cut without re-setting the iron although admittedly also with some adjustment in the size of the chamfer. Although none of the known planes have any of the profiled soles (and indeed only Plane A could ever have had these) there is no reason to suppose that the planes would not work decently when used in this way.

Working the plane either using the plain or ornamental version of the stop

FIG. 4.

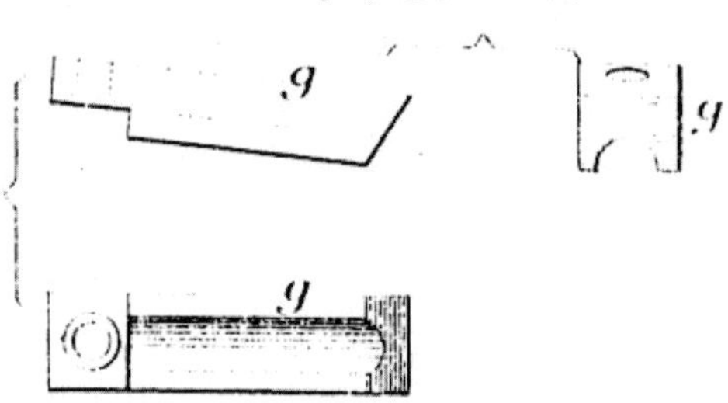

FIG. 6.

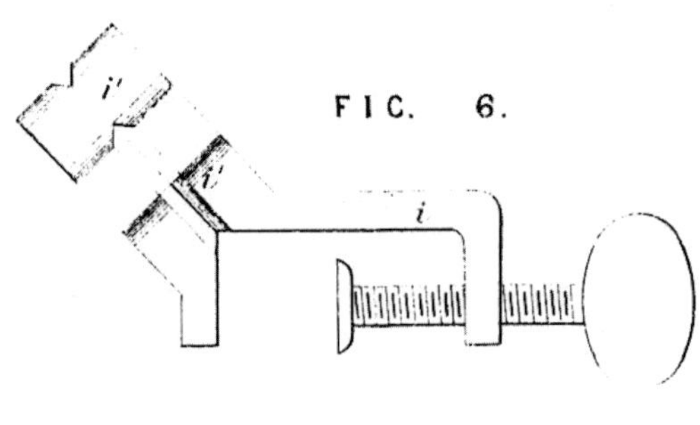

FIG. 5.

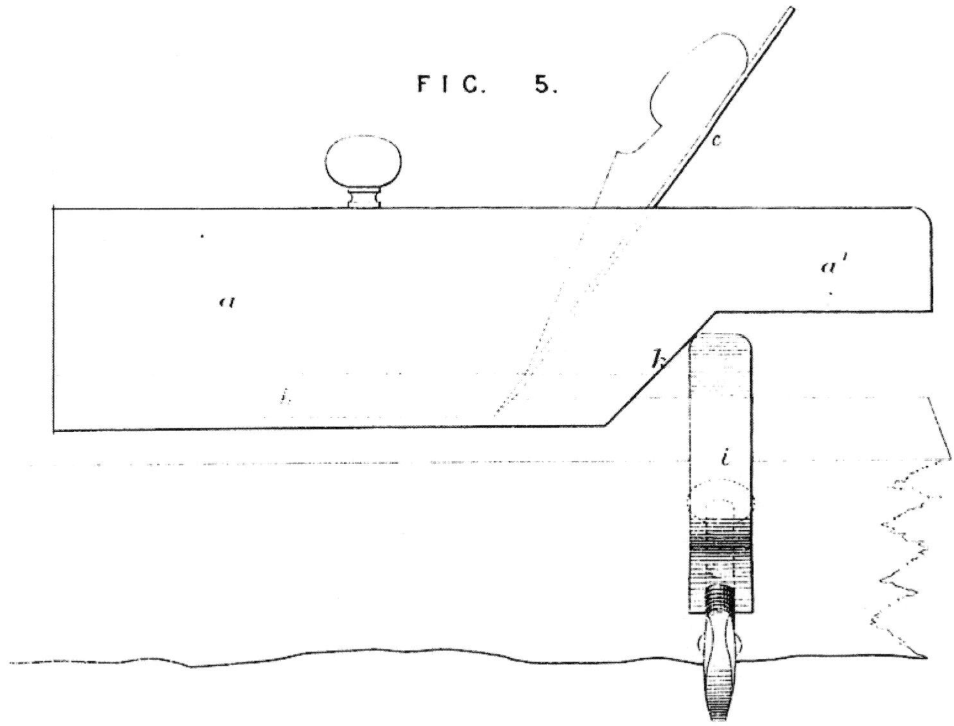

clamp would seem to be difficult, if not impossible, and even if successful would only achieve what could be done in a few seconds using a chisel, gouge or file.

The version shown in Figs. 7, 9, & 10 would seem therefore to have been wholly impractical and be an uneconomic method of achieving something simply done by normal woodworking methods.

The known examples do however present something of an enigma. None of the planes have all the principle features of the patent specification. Plane A allows for the fixing of the supplementary profile soles and has the vertical adjustment of the patent specification but no provision for additional guides at the back.

Planes B and C have the adjustment fitted at an angle but do have provision for guides or at least for something to be fitted at the back. The infill on plane C is conjectural and unlikely to be correct.

Conclusion

An examination of the mark "HART'S PATENT" on the three planes indicates that whilst the word HART appears to have been struck from the same punch on all three planes, the word PATENT on plane A is probably struck using individual letters and certainly is not the mark as on Planes B and C which are almost certainly struck with the same (patent) mark. Thus Norris is likely to have been the maker of B as well as C. It is probable that the number 37 and 42 represent sequential numbering of the production.

The variations indicate a continuing desire to improve the design and it is not surprising that the most impractical parts of the invention remain only as drawings in the patent specification.

FIG. 7.

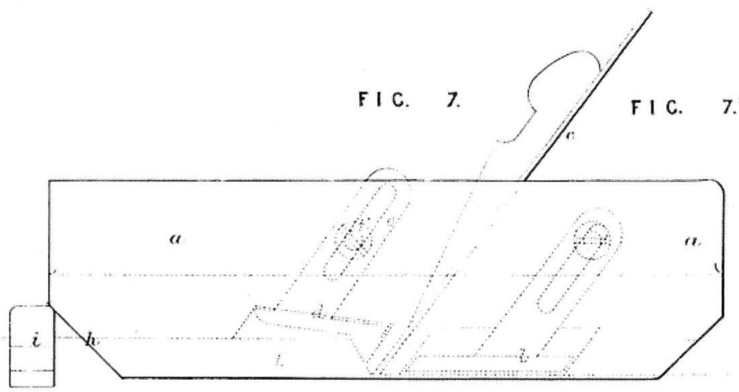

FIG. 7.x

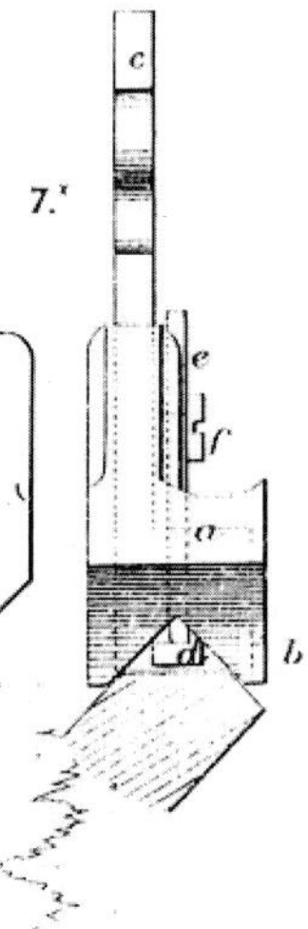

FIG. 8.

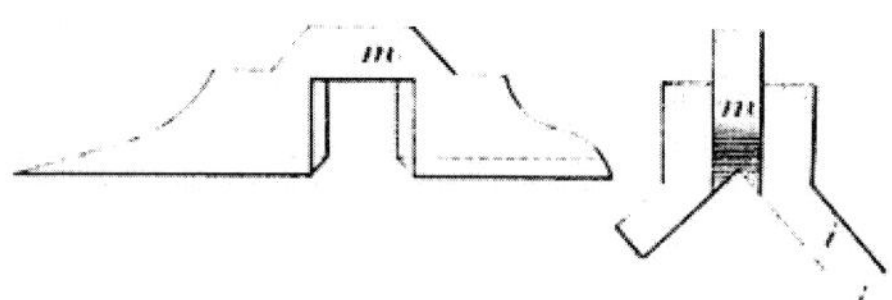

FIG. 9.

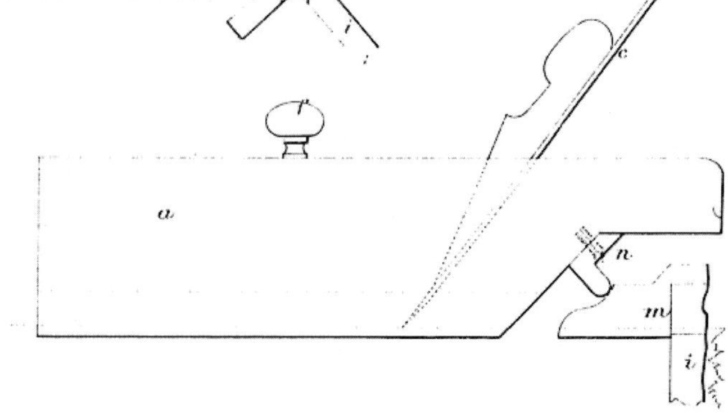

FIG. 10.

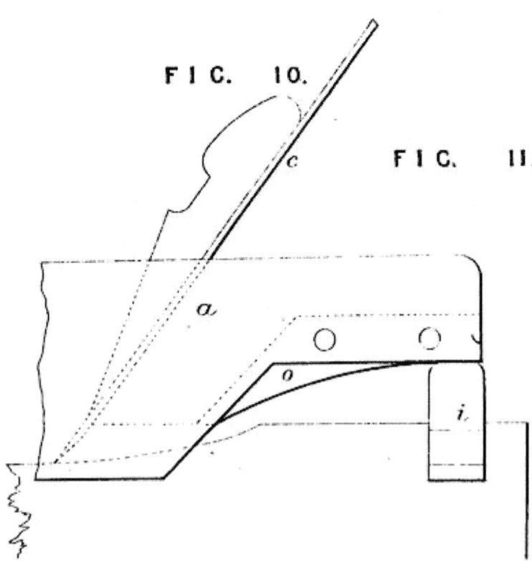

FIG. 11.

The ledgers of John Littlewood, Sheffield edge tool makers, 1900 - 1909

K. W. Hawley

Tools and Trades Volume 7: 1992

Introduction

Occasionally, with a bit of good fortune, interesting documents or artifacts come to light which make one realise how few original such items survive to give a detailed insight into the enterprise from which they originate.

To illustrate the point, a friend recently brought me three books to look at. (Fig. 1.) They are what we would call today purchase and sales ledgers. The pages are beautifully bound with leather spines and corners and marbled endpapers. The books are a credit to the bookbinder's art and would not look out of place in any library of fine books, and no doubt they were "come by". (The ledgers are of a high quality and it seems unlikely that a manufacturer of this size could have afforded them. They were therefore probably acquired or found which also explains the titles bearing no relation to the contents.) However, the main interest lies with-in.

The contents of the pages reveal that the account books belonged to a Sheffield edge tool manufacturer whose main output consisted of axes, adzes, billhooks, and draw knives, amongst a wide range of edge tools. It is clear from the information in the books that the output of the firm was quite significant. For example, in the year 1900 it produced nearly 17,000 edge tools, and these were to have the trade-marks of many of Sheffield's leading tool manufacturers. The books themselves bear no owner's name and the identity of

Fig. 1. The three ledgers.

Fig. 2, right. Ordnance survey map (1:500) of Sheffield 1889, showing the site of Clough Dam and Clough Works.

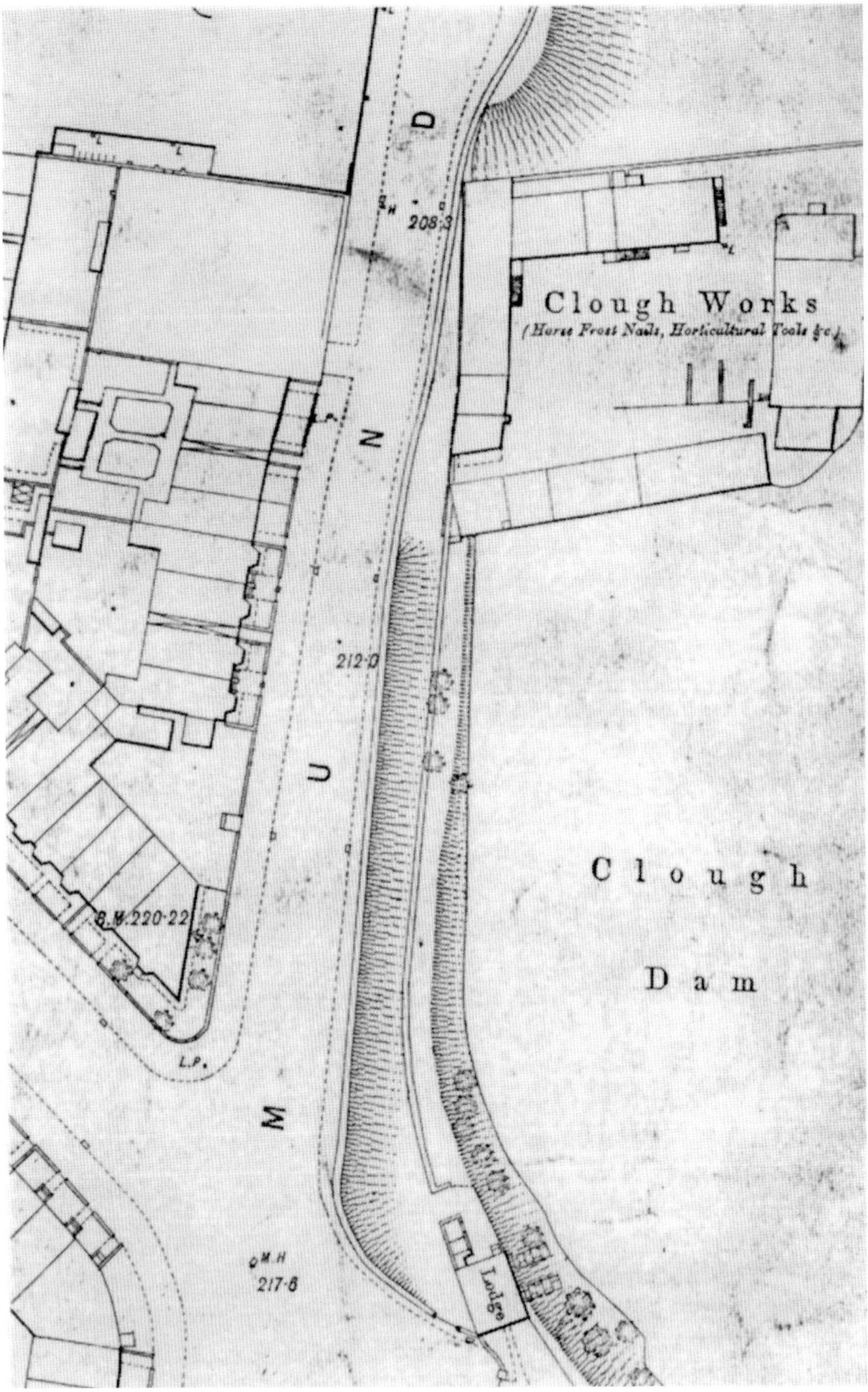
D
208·3
Clough Works
(Horse Frost Nails, Horticultural Tools &c.)
N
212·0
U
Clough
Dam
B.M. 220·22
L.P.
M
M.H
217·6
Lodge

the firm would have remained a mystery were it not for two customer order forms that had been fortuitously left inside, addressed to J. Littlewood.

An initial search for information was made in Kelly's *Sheffield Directory* which contained the following entries.

1883:	no entry,
1889:	J. Littlewood, Clough Works, Leadmill Road
1904:	J. Littlewood, Clough Works, Leadmill Road
1909:	J. Littlewood, Club Garden Walk
1912:	no entry.

Pondering on the directory entries and not being familiar with the locations mentioned (that part of Sheffield has much altered since then!), my first assumption was that Littlewood's premises would have been built in the mid 19th century and powered by a steam or gas engine.

Clough Works

Careful study of an 1889 Ordnance Survey map (scale 1:500) for that area of Sheffield revealed Clough Works clearly marked against Clough Dam. (Fig. 2.) No chimneys, boilers or engines houses are shown on the plan, thus the evidence indicates that the works were at that date still driven by water power. A further strand of evidence corroborates this; the 1845 lease for the works bore a covenant preventing the use of steam.[1]

Research shows the Clough Works site had already been in use for a number of centuries. It is first mentioned in 1581, the earliest records of rentals for the Sheffield estates of the Earls of Shrewsbury that survive.[2] Sources show that Clough Wheels enjoyed an uninterrupted occupancy by a number of leaseholders and tenants up to around 1907 when John Littlewood left. (In Sheffield the word "wheel" is used in a variety of contexts; here it reflects the building in which the grinding operation is carried out and is not associated with the grindstones themselves.)

One of the last orders to be received at Clough Wheels was from the Silent Machine and Engineering Co., makers of bacon slicing machines, for cleavers and lamb choppers. (Fig. 3.) It is dated January 1907 and addressed to J. Littlewood, Heeley, which is the part of Sheffield near to Clough Wheels, but a distinctly different district to Club Garden Walk, which was known as Little Sheffield, the address where Littlewood is next listed.

Interestingly, in the latter part of the 19th century the site was occupied by S. & R. Linley, who mainly produced scythes, sickles, axes and billhooks. (Fig. 4.) In 1897 Tyzack Son and Turner acquired Linley's "OLD O" trade mark, no doubt due to the previous owner wishing to retire. According to the 1889 *Sheffield Directory*, both Linley and Littlewood are shown occupying Clough Wheels. Thus the dates of Linley ceasing and Littlewood starting are quite close and I think it likely that Littlewood was a former employee of Linley who started on his own account, renting Linley's forge and, as the older firm ran down, probably fulfilling Linley's dwindling orders as well as soliciting for new orders elsewhere.

By the end of the century the premises would probably have been in a dilapidated condition, for soon after, in 1909, Clough Works was no longer listed. By this date the dam had been filled in and roads and houses were built on the site

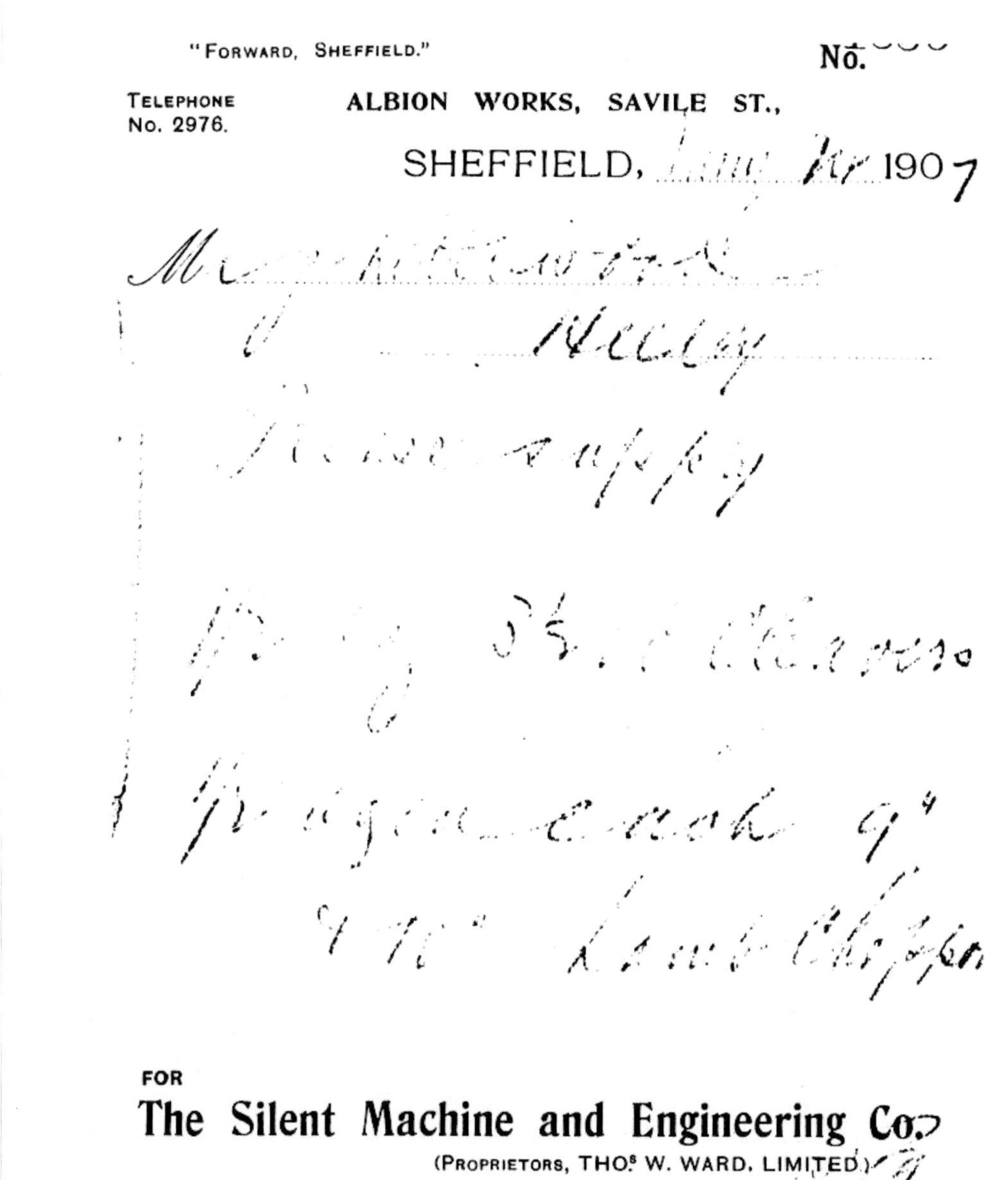

"FORWARD, SHEFFIELD."

No.

TELEPHONE
No. 2976.

ALBION WORKS, SAVILE ST.,

SHEFFIELD, 1907

FOR

The Silent Machine and Engineering Co.

(PROPRIETORS, THOS W. WARD, LIMITED.)

When Invoicing Goods please quote Order Number.

Fig. 3. The order from the Silent Machine and Engineering Co.

and Littlewood had moved to nearby Club Garden Walk, where he lasted a few more years. The *Sheffield Directory* in 1912 does not list him either at work or at home, leaving one to speculate whether he died or retired to the country!

The machinery

Not only would the premises probably have been in poor condition but the machinery also. It is most likely that the forge and tilt hammers at Clough Works had received a hard working life for over 90 years. An advertisement in the *Sheffield Iris* newspaper, dated December 1810 confirms, "NOTICE OF A SALE BY AUCTION OF A NEWLY ERECTED SCYTHE MANUFACTURY AT CLOUGH WHEELS".

A survey of Clough Wheels undertaken in 1836 for rate revaluation purposes lists the equipment in some detail, notably a 14 ft. by 7 ft. 10 in. breast wheel of 11.35 horse power having a 2 ft. 6 in. head and a 10 ft. fall, which drove eight edge tool grinding troughs (pronounced trows) and a 10 ft. by 8 ft. overshot forge wheel which produced 11.02 horsepower (enough to drive only one of the three hammers) .[3]

A forging or "tilt" hammer of this date would be of relatively simple construction of iron and wood. Most adjustments

Fig. 4. S. & R. Linley who occupied Clough Works on the latter part of the 19th century.

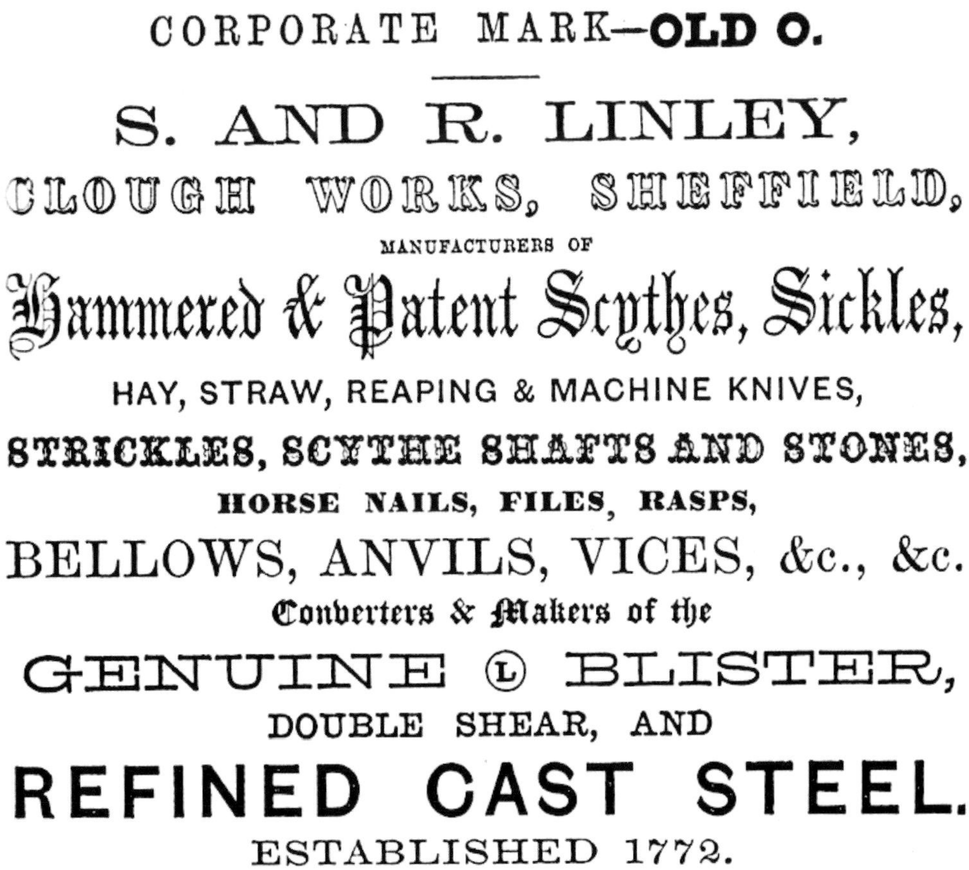

to the mechanism would have been made by the use of iron wedges being driven in or out (screws being virtually non-existent at that time). This sort of adjustment required great nicety of judgment, only gained by long experience. For example, each time the anvil tools were changed to forge different jobs, the tools had to be re-adjusted so that they would "kiss" accurately. Unlike steam or other mechanical hammers, tilts had a fixed force of blow and stroke, working on the radius of the helve, and consequently demanded highly skilled forgers to adjust and work them. This is further evidence to suggest that Mr. Littlewood, the new proprietor, had worked at Clough Wheels for many years.

The ledgers

The records cover a period from January 1900 to January 1909. The year for which there is most detail is 1900, which is here analysed as a representative example.

The purchase ledger

The entries follow a very simple pattern: every week the amounts paid out were recorded in the book. (Fig. 5.) An example from the week commencing Monday 22 January 1900 follows:

		£	*s*	*d*
Jan. 26	Cokes - Gas Co.		19	8
Jan. 27	Higginbottom (Wages)	3	13	0
Jan. 27	Wages	6	10	9
Jan. 22	Wheel rent		13	6
Jan. 27	Glue		2	3
	Emery		3	2
	Suet			8
	Stamps		2	0

It is interesting to discuss further the details that this entry shows.

Coke

This was purchased from the Sheffield Gas Company and was used in the hearths to provide heat for forging and hardening. It is probable that 19*s* 8*d* would purchase a cart load. No weight is specified but it is likely to be about 1 ton and it appears that a load was delivered nearly every week.

Higginbottom wages

Higginbottom was probably an outworker, as he was only on the books for three months during 1900. It is likely that he was a journeyman grinder working at nearby Smiths Wheel, for which Littlewood paid rent. A grinder such as Higginbottom would be paid on a piece-work basis and he would be responsible for paying anyone helping him. He would have likely employed a lad to perform the more menial tasks such as fetching and carrying black forgings and running errands. We tend to forget the former importance of the errand boy or girl in this telephone and fax age; you certainly cannot fetch ale to "sleek" the grinder's thirst by fax! The lads learned the trade by doing the simpler grinding jobs under the guidance of the grinder. The wages paid to Higginbottom are more than twice the average wage for a grinder (see below), thus it is probable that Higginbottom had another grinder working with him as well as the lad.

Wages

In other weeks, this entry is expanded to "Wages as per Wages Book". The wages book has not survived so there is no breakdown of the actual wages of employees.

There were probably workers to perform the following jobs: (i) coke lad, to keep the hearths fed (a ton a week!), (ii) unloading and cutting up iron and

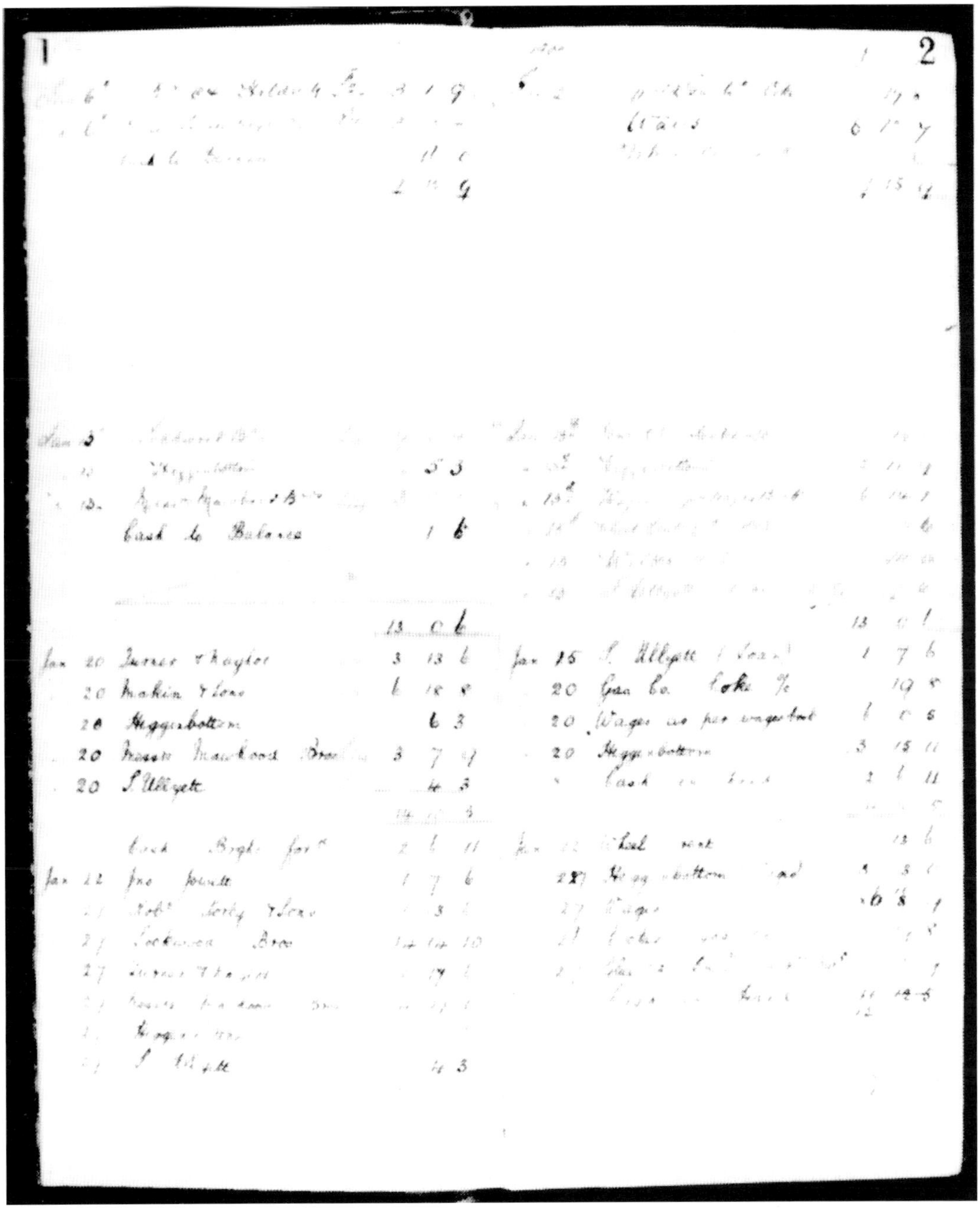

Fig. 5. One of the pages from the purchase ledger.

steel bars (ready for the forger), (iii) painting and putting handles on finished tools, (iv) warehousing and loading for delivery, performed by a warehouse man or woman who would supervise and keep the records. (Women were often employed for this task in Sheffield; I have personally known several women warehouse supervisors and hold them in the highest esteem for their knowledge of the trade!). Some idea of what the wages might have been can be deduced from the Labour Department Inquiry of 1906.[4] The average weekly wages in the edge tool trade were

Hand forgers (piece work)	£1	12*s*	1*d*
Grinders (piece work)	£1	14*s*	6*d*
Adult man	£1	11*s*	2*d*
Lads and boys		9*s*	7*d*
Women		11*s*	7*d*
Girls		6*s*	10*d*

Using these figures as a basis, Littlewood's firm probably employed something like three men workers, one women and two lads.

Wheel rent

This entry appears elsewhere as "Wheel Rent (Smiths)." There was a Smiths grinding wheel on Shoreham Street, some 400 yards distant from Clough Works. It was really a timber yard. The machinery was driven by a steam engine, the boiler being fired with coal slack and wood waste. There is a record of one of the boilers blowing up in 1875, with disastrous results. Several work-shops adjacent to the wheel took power from the engine and it was probably one of these that was rented by Littlewood as a grinding wheel. No doubt by this time Clough Dam was so silted it could only supply enough water to drive the forge at Clough Works.

Glue, emery, suet

These items were used in the process of glazing which gives the tools a final finish to the grinding. A leather head, or rim, was attached to the wooden disc some 18 in. diameter and 6 in. wide, which was fixed onto a metal spindle and belt driven via a pulley. The head was dressed with hot fish glue and rolled in emery grit. This process was usually performed last thing at night so that it would have set hard and be ready for use the following morning. After setting the glazer in its frame and attaching the driving band (belt), the suet was applied to the rotating wheel causing it to "load" the grit. When the tool was pressed against the glazer the suet acted as a lubricant, preventing the frictional heat created by the glazer from drawing the temper of the tool. Also, some of the suet was impregnated into the surface of the work, thus providing a protective "coating" and helping to prevent the bright tool surface from going rusty. This process was especially useful for goods that were being exported. The glue and emery would have been bought at any one of any number of small shops supplying grinders' needs. The suet would have come from the local butchers and rendered down over a fire (a very smelly job, most likely given to the lad!).

A further list of items purchased is shown in Table 1 which covers the period 1900–1908 and shows the wide range of supplies needed to keep the firm in production.

The sales ledgers

The sales ledgers list several tool manufacturers with worldwide reputations such as Aaron Hildick, Lockwood Brothers, Turner Naylor, Robert Sorby and Ward & Payne. Also supplied were well known names in the cutlery industry such as Saynor, Cooke and Ridal (a company who specialised in horticultural cutlery such as pruning and budding knives)

Fig.6. Clough Wheels. Painting by W. Topham, 1878

who regularly ordered bill hooks; and Michael Hunter who ordered a variety of items including axes, slashers and bill and brushing hooks. A list of customers, products ordered and the number of transactions for the year 1900 is given in Table 2.

Sheffield steel and tool firms were inter-dependent. This can partly be explained by fluctuations in orders. When, for example, Ward & Payne (an internationally renowned firm) accepted "shipping orders" that it was unable to fulfil in its own works within the specified time, the "extra" work was put out to firms such as John Littlewood's. It was this sort of trade which Littlewood specialised in. The quality of the work demanded by the contracting firms would be high, at least equal to the standard of the mark which is struck on the tool.[5] Shoddy work would not be tolerated and when tools where transferred from Littlewood's to Ward & Payne's warehouse they would be examined (or "looked over" in trade terminology) by the department manager. Any not up to the mark (literally) would be returned as "cuckoos" to be reworked. They did not get paid for until made good!

Littlewood's seem to have produced tools of the required standard, for there were many repeat orders from the major firms. In the year 1900, over 16,500 edge tools were produced, 11,700 of these being axes. Ward & Payne had twenty orders fulfilled and Turner Naylor, thirty-two. An analysis of the total production for 1900 is shown in Table 3.

It is perhaps interesting to draw some conclusions from the scale of production at Littlewood's and relate these to the

Fig. 7. Tilt hammer at Little London, on the River Sheaf near Clough Wheels.

tool manufacturing trade of Sheffield as a whole. The *Sheffield Directory* of 1900 gives ninety entries for edge tool makers, although a small proportion of these would represent "factors" rather than manufacturers. Littlewood's firm was small by comparison with many of these makers. For example, in the 1920s William Marples' edge tool department consisted of sixty-six employees: some ten times the size of Littlewood and his firm. Using simple arithmetic we might assume that Marples produced a minimum of 160,000 edge tools annually. This figure was actually much greater as a result of economies of scale and the more modern forging hammers in use, with an annual production of some 300,000 pieces.[6] Therefore, at a conservative estimate of an annual average production of 100,000 edge tools per manufacturer, with a likelihood of about 80 manufacturers, there was something like 8 million (or more) edge tools being turned out in Sheffield at the turn of the century! Such a figure throws a light on the prominence of the Sheffield tool industry, especially when it is realised that the edge tool trade was only one of the many specialist tool producing trades such as those making saws, files, engineers' tools, joiners' tools, augers, sickles, scythes, trowels, hammers, spades, forks, shovels (*ad infinitum*).

Endpiece

Table 4 is a putative profit and loss account for the firm prepared from the entries in the ledgers for the year 1900. This shows a net profit of £57 1s. 1d., only some 8% of turnover. As the stocks at the beginning and end of year are not known, this account is, of course, conjectural as far as the profit is concerned but the figures are accurate. The profit margin at 8% at best (there may have been further write-offs in the prepared accounts) certainly looks slim. The proprietor was apparently earning less than his men! This figure reminds me of a recent conversation I had with a retired man, who said of his working life, "I've been too busy earning a living to make a fortune." Mr Littlewood no doubt fell into this category.

How fortunate it is that these simple documents have survived eighty years, for they give an insight into a facet of the Sheffield tool trade that might otherwise go unconsidered and are an intimate reminder of the blood, sweat and water that drove the forge and wheel at Clough Works for over three hundred years.

Notes:

1. Sheffield City Archives. Norfolk Collection. Arundel Castle Manuscripts, ref. 158. Rentals 1701-1889 (1851-60 missing).
2. *Ibid.* ref.114. Rentals.
3. Notebook No. 29 of the Sheffield firm of surveyors, Fairbanks, in Sheffield Library (Local Collection).
4. Pollard, S. *A History of Labour in Sheffield*, Liverpool University Press, 1959, App. B.
5. The reader should however remember that large firms had a range of different marks that denoted different qualities.
6. Personal conversation with Mr. Stanley Barton, former works manager of Wm. Marples & Sons Ltd.

Acknowledgements:
I would like to thank my friend Mr "Ted" Spencer who is that rare person, a retired company accountant with an interest in local history and things historical, amongst many other attributes, who diligently worked through the books to provide what available figures there were as a balance sheet.

Thanks also to my son, Duncan Hawley, who read through the manuscript and provided many suggestions for improvements, Dennis Smith for finding the photograph of Clough Wheels in Sheffield City Libraries and the late Mr. Stanley Barton, former works manager of Wm. Marples & Sons Ltd. for production information.

Table 1: Goods and services purchased 1900 - 1908.

In the forge:

coke	used to heat the iron and steel.
iron	this formed the "mould" of the tool.[1]
steel	this formed the cutting edge of the tool.[2]
tueiron	the air blast from the bellows into the fire passes through this; although it is water cooled, the heat of the fire gradually burns it away.
bellows repair	
borax	used to create a good weld between iron and steel
hardening pan	used to hold oil or water for hardening
coke baskets	an oval shaped willow or woven wire receptacle to carry coke to the hearth.

In the grinding wheel:

wheel rent, glue,	
emery, suet	see text
grindstone	a costly item which would have been of sandstone, 6 ft. dia by 1 ft. thick.
horsing robin	a metal strap fastened to the front of a grinder's seat or horsing, it enables great pressure to be put on the articles being ground.
axle turning	a repair to the grinding wheel's spindle.

In the warehouse:

axe shafts	to handle axes when requested.
brand	to burn owners' mark onto tool handles.
varnish	to finish and protect tools.
string	to tie bundles of smaller tools together for transport.

Miscellaneous:

coal	for heating premises.
gas	for lighting.
pony shoeing, hay, chop, corn, cart repair	

Notes

1. The "mould" is the body of the tool. Even at this period (early twentieth century) it should be remembered that most edge tools were still being made from iron with appropriate steel edges fire-welded to the iron, in spite of solid steel tools made from the Bessemer and Siemens processes of steel-making taking over from the earlier processes.
2. In view of the small quantities of iron and steel bought, it seems likely that larger customers, such as Ward & Payne, Turner Naylor, etc. would supply the raw material from their own stocks. No doubt they could buy more cheaply owing to the larger quantities involved.

Table 2: Customers, products ordered and number of transactions during 1900.

Firm	Items	No. of orders received
Atkinson Bros. Ltd.	hoes	1
Milton Works, (cutlers) Bendall (not Sheffield)	hatchets	1
Britt, Chesterfield, (ironmonger)	axes	1
Brookes (?Crookes) St. Phillips Rd., Sheffield (cutlers)	axes, brushing hooks	3
Camm & Bagshaw, Leadmill Steel Works, Matilda Lane, Sheffield	axes, adzes	2
T. Firth, Norfolk Steel Works Saville St., Sheffield	drawknives	1
Aaron Hildick, 57½ Bridge St. Sheffield (edge & joiners' tool makers)	drawknives, socket chisels, lock mortice chisels, bruzzes	7
M. Hunter, Talbot Works, Saville St., Sheffield (merchants & manufacturers)	axes, bills, brushing hooks, slashers, cleavers	8
Wm. Jackson, Sheaf Island Works, Pond Hill, Sheffield (merchants & manufacturers)	axes	3
John Jowitt, Albion Works, Countess Rd., Sheffield (manufacturers of engineering tools and edge and joiners' tools)	adzes	2
Lewis & Co., 92 Bridge St., Sheffield (engineering tools etc.)	hatchets, axes	6
Machin (no address)	hatchets, axes	3
Makin & Sons, Sheffield	axes	1
Needham, Veall, Tyzack, Sheffield, (cutlers)	hoes, hatchets	1
Saynor, Cooke & Ridal, Sheffield (cutlers)	hatchets, bills, hooks, hoes	6
Robert Sorby, Sheffield (tool manufacturers)	hatchets	11
Turner Naylor, Sheffield (tool manufacturers)	hatchets, hoes	32
Ward & Payne, Sheffield (tool manufacturers)	axes, hatchets, bills	20

Table 3: Analysis of sales ledger 1900 showing the number of items produced.

	adzes, axes, hatchets	billhooks, hoes, etc.	socket chisels	draw-knives	total pieces
Jan.	300	-	771	90	1161
Feb.	1103	-	528	84	1715
Mar.	3137	-	918	264	4319
Apr.	816	132	198	-	1146
May	540	81	636	-	1257
June	620	66	-	-	686
July	918	60	-	-	978
Aug.	929	144	-	-	1073
Sept.	626	12	-	-	638
Oct.	942	165	-	-	1107
Nov.	848	220	216	144	1428
Dec.	956	62	-	-	1018
Totals	11735	942	3267	582	16526

The maximum production per month was in March with 4319 tools being produced. If a six day week was worked (five and a half was normal) there would be twenty-seven working days each of, say, ten hours, which averages a finished tool being produced every three and three-quarter minutes.

Table 4: Profit and loss account for the year 1900.

Materials purchased[1]	steel	£37	15*s*	0*d*	
	iron	£129	9*s*	3*d*	
	handles & shafts	£29	1*s*	7*d*	
	sundries	£14	7*s*	9*d*	
Total		**£210**	**13*s***	**7*d***	
Value added wages		£287	14*s*	9*d*	
Higginbottom		£43	9*s*	11*d*	
		£541	18*s*	3*d*	cost of sales
Sold for		£715	2*s*	1*d*	100% sales
		£173	**3*s***	**10*d***	24% gain
Manufacturing costs[2]		£101	10*s*	8*d*	
		£71	**13*s***	**2*d***	10% gross profit
Other costs[3]		£14	12*s*	1*d*	
		£57	**1*s***	**1*d***	8% net profit

Notes:

1. Opening and closing stocks not known.

2. Manufacturing cost	wheel rent	£26	6*s*	6*d*
	cokes	£52	4*s*	8*d*
	grindstones	£22	7*s*	0*d*
	horsing robin		7*s*	0*d*
		£101	**10*s***	**8*d***
3. Other costs	shop rent	£5	0*s*	0*d*
	printing		6*s*	6*d*
	cart repairs	£1	14*s*	0*d*
	Hollingworth	£3	8*s*	0*d*
	brand		4*s*	10*d*
	wedges		17*s*	10*d*
	wood	£2	13*s*	6*d*
	loss on loan		8*s*	3*d*
		£14	**12*s***	**1*d***

The Jones family of turners

A. W. Jones

Tools and Trades Volume 8: 1995

The trade of hardwood-and-ivory turning was followed in this family for at least three generations back and possibly more. Lewis Jones (1850-1914) lived by his skill as a turner and carver. In pre-plastic days everything was made of natural materials: ivory, bone, horn, woods, etc. It was usual for journeymen turners to stick to turning and carvers to stick to carving. Lewis did both with equal facility, one of his best lines being bone and ivory carved parasol handles with mice and squirrels running up trees. The remuneration for craftsmen in those days meant that in order to live they had to work incredibly fast. Firms which made chessmen employed a team of craftsmen, both turners and carvers, each following his own craft. As an example of payment, the turner making "Old English" pawns before the First World War probably got one old penny (1/240 of a pound) each, yes, and lived very well on it. With such a team of experts specifically engaged on the one job, firms like Jacques could produce beautiful ivory chessmen in handsome boxes at very reasonable prices which allowed for good profits. By contrast, the lone turner/carver who attempted chessmen as part of his repertoire could not compete with the mass-production firms like Jacques.

On the other hand, the work of one craftsman who made the whole set himself, should have commanded far more appreciation and value than, in fact, it actually received. Imagine making a modern car alone and unaided and then trying to sell it. "You're miles out old man", they'd say, "Fords can supply a car at half that!" Ludicrous isn't it? So the lone turner usually did hackwork and often had to repair and replace old and broken chess pieces that required more skill than was entailed for the original maker. As a matter of fact I know no-one outside this family who did make chess pieces single handed professionally, although many have been produced by amateurs – not for sale.

The competition was tremendous in those days when so many good craftsmen were staying in work simply because they could get down a half-penny cheaper than the others. Lewis Jones was a first-class artist on the lathe and made chessmen among myriads of other things. He worked in and around London sometimes as an attic master - as the self-employed craftsmen were called - and sometimes working for others for he was one of the old school who could knock up money quickly and then blow it in the pub. Like Rhett Butler he "didn't give a damn"! You could not help liking him, although he occasionally had to do a moonlight flit!

His son, Bertram Jones (1885-1969) has many chess sets of all types to his credit – all individually made, selecting, cutting, turning, carving, polishing and staining – the lot. Not many in this world could say that. His brothers Cyril and Arthur were also turners but only in a limited capacity whereas Bertram, after touring round Walsall and Sheffield as a

Fig. 1. Lewis Jones, 1850 - 1914

journeyman turner working for others at a wide variety of jobs, including such items as sickle handles at 1*s* 2*d* a gross, found himself in the King's Royal Rifle Brigade as a Lewis gunner when the war came along. Fortunately, he had an argument with a shell at Passchendaele in 1917 and received a "blighty one" which enabled him to set up as an attic master in 1919. His first workshop was a coal cellar in Barretts Grove, Stoke Newington, where he rigged up a treadle lathe. After a year or so he moved into a decent-sized workshop in Dalston, London, set up six lathes, and employed his brother and a couple of other turners. He had a three H. P. motor driving a long shafting which powered all the lathes. His son, Alfred William Lewis Jones – known as "Bill" (except by Walther Bach who always calls me "Sir William"!) was born in 1920 and I remember that big workshop very well. I spent all the time I could there, usually getting into mischief: setting fire to the men's working coats or narrowly escaping getting wound round the shafting. I was expendable you see! I remember a factory inspector coming and asking Bertram to show his first aid kit. He proudly produced a large tin box with a red cross on it from Boots the Chemists which contained a fair assortment of all the necessary items: bandages, dressings, iodine, etc. He was informed that he had to have some specified conglomeration of medical accoutrements in order to comply with the regulations, otherwise he could not continue! "That's quite alright, old man," replied Bertram, "I'll sack all the men and that's that!" He never had another complaint! He didn't give a damn either! Ninety per cent of the work was making bone and horn shaving brush handles. Round shank beef bones were delivered by the ton and all the waste was taken away for various uses. A bone shop can be an overpowering place with dust from the saw and the smell of boiling bones.

They were sawn and then trimmed with the chipping knife to fit an iron or a boxwood cup chuck into which the pieces were driven with a short-handled 1½ lb. hammer. When boiled and then kept moist, bone turns very well, but if attempted dry it is too brittle and hard on the tools. Horn is not soaked, but as the grain tends to lift, a chisel with a flat piece of spring steel (the type taken from women's stays – widely worn in those days) tied on top and used much like a cabinet scraper, was used and turned horn cleanly. As most of the handles were screwed in two pieces, all the turners could cut threads with the hand chasers. Bertram used to do all this ivory work in a wide variety when not engaged in rescuing defective work which often came back – for being the "guv'nor" in a turning shop can be a thankless job with much worry and little profit.

After a few years Bertram was given a week or so notice to quit the premises - just like that! The shop was disbanded and we moved into a three-storey house in De Beauvoir Town with a large garden and space at the side for a workshop about 20 feet by 8 feet. Bertram set up his shop temporarily in Busby's Mill at the top of Pentonville Hill. The mill had a great many separate workshops, each one having a driving pulley powered by a large gas engine which started up at 8 a.m. and stopped at 6 p.m. He worked very comfortably there, employing one polishing girl for a year whilst he used parts of each weekend and odd times to excavate the sloping floor of the home workshop and lay down a level concrete foundation, and erect a 12 ft. wooden bench for three lathes. When all was ready he moved his works home. He usually had one young person working for him for the repetition work, but few of them were any great shakes at the job. When I left school a month or so before my 14th birthday I began my education in the turning shop, and there I worked for five years. As I was on repetition bone and crinoid turned and screwed work all the time and although I became reasonably proficient at this, I considered myself more or less untrained when compared to my father of whom I was very proud. You see, before World War One, 'bone-grubbers' as they were sometimes derisively called, were plentiful, and although they lived reasonably well it was a hard-working age and those returning from the war either found that the trade was dying out through the onset of plastic materials necessitated by the lack of craftsmen, or they had no desire to take up that work again themselves, or to encourage their sons to do so.

Bertram, in setting up in business as an ivory turner was a rarity, and his ability at turning and carving on the lathe was so attractive to me that I never had another

ambition but to follow in the same line. In the 1920s there were dozens of old ivory turners, but over the next 20 years they all faded out one by one, leaving no-one to follow. I found myself in the R.A.F. for five years in World War Two, and on my return to civvy street I did start my own turning shop in 1947. I was separated from Bertram by more than 100 miles.

Having done no ivory turning, cutting or carving, my self-confidence was poor, but Bertram encouraged me by sending me work he knew I could do and giving me full instructions for work I had not done before. In a very short time I found that my five-year or so 'apprenticeship' had given me all I needed in ability to handle everything that came my way.

Of course, turning is not generally regarded as a romantic pursuit and the lathe is thought of widely as an instrument of drudgery. But that image comes from the "dark Satanic mills" days. It is almost unknown that some very great people indeed, including royalty and many titled gentlemen and ladies of the last century, have pursued the art of turning in ivory and African blackwood on ornamental turning lathes many of which were so superbly and handsomely made that they could be, and sometimes were, used in the drawing room! The lathe to me has always been the 'grand-daddy' of all machine tools because I have seen it used for so many different processes and there is practically no limit to what can be done on it, especially when equipped with many and various appendages.

The old professionals whom I knew mainly used second-hand head and tail-stocks which they fixed to home-made timber benches. With the passing of the treadle era the lathes were driven by flat leather belts from a shafting. To control the speed of the lathe it was usual to have fast and loose pulleys on the mandrel.

To stop, you simply pushed the belt over from the fast to the loose pulley with a tool handle or perhaps a thumb-screw-actuated fork which could be secured with the belt mid-way between the pulleys so that the turner could, by practice, get a slow speed in order to cut threads with the hand chasers. Of course, there were better variable speed devices operated by foot pedal with home-made slipping belt devices which could give you any controlled speed from zero to maximum. I said that mainly old lathes were used, and often the bearings were badly worn and the lathe had a prop between the headstock and the wall to take up the vibration. The one-inch flat belts with the clumsy fasteners used to clack and jolt round, and although very fine work was done, it could not always be described as comfortable. The couple of ancient relics I was using enabled me to work pretty well but I kept my eyes open for improvements. I soon got myself a new capstan headstock with Timken taper roller bearings driven by a "V" belt.

Fig. 2, opposite. Ivory turning. The left thumb lies alongside the tool. Note the slipping belt which gives variable speed. When the pedal is depressed the top raises the movable back carriage and tightens the flat belt for full speed. By controlling the position of the back carriage with the left foot any speed from 0 to maximum (about 2,500 RPM) can be obtained. This enables you to stop the lathe at once without switches or inconvenience and vary the speed at will to facilitate simple screw cutting and obviate tool chatter. Why, in heavens name, permit turning to be tiresome and difficult when a simple and easily made idea like this has been used for years – and no one knows it now! (Photo W.T. Jones)

Fig. 3. Turning a dome with arm rest and a square tool. The LEFT thumb can be seen pressed against the side of the tool. (Photo W. T. Jones)

Fig. 4. Hollowing with an inside tool using the armrest. Left thumb on top of the tool and supported below by the index finger. Does it look as if the armrest is useless or obsolete? Believe me it isn't, hasn't been and never will be. (Photo W. T. Jones)

This was such a vast improvement that I encouraged Bertram to use "V" belts: he was delighted.

Within two or three years I found that the variety of work I was tackling included most of the things I thought I might not be able to do, and included carving. Ivory turners carve, not with hand chisels in the vice as wood carvers, but with carving cutters, rotary files and burrs in the lathe. Many of these can be bought. But many shapes needed have to be turned and filed up by hand and one simply has to accumulate a stock of cutters gradually.

The large roughing cutter is one which all ivory turners use. Often, the ivory to be turned has to be driven with a short hammer into an iron or boxwood cup chuck, and this cutter is used free-hand to make the ivory round and slightly tapered so that it will drive firmly and evenly into the chuck. When you have been used to doing this on all sizes of material from, say, one eighth to three or four inches diameter for years, you get so used to cutter work that carving should come naturally - it did with me. Although I had never attempted chess knights before, I found very little difficulty in making my first four Staunton knights. I grant that they were not exactly Jacques(!) but they were good saleable ones and my first set of club-size Stauntons, made in the 1950s, was a real delight to me. I wish I had it today, but Alex Hammond knocked £2 off my asking price of only £14 and I needed the money. The ivory cost me £5, so you see why you have to be good to earn a living!

At this time I was relieving Bertram of much of the run-of-the-millwork, leaving him free to make ornate chess sets in wide variety. He would knock out at three sets of Stauntons a week (he would carve the 12 full-size knights in a day!). But the ornate sets took him a fortnight to a month and he worked principally for Mackett Beeson. I must tell you that Bertram, when a young man, could turn and carve beautifully – for his own satisfaction or for the Turner's Company competitions where he got the odd prize. But years of slogging to get down to a price showed him the folly of spending too long on work which paid him not a penny more for the extra time spent on it. Always he had to get work out cheaply, so often it was cheap work they got! But some of Bertram's sets were splendid, and he got what he wanted for them. They were still cheap because he did not need a lot of money and he enjoyed the work. Bertram suggested that I made the Stauntons that Mackett Beeson wanted along with the rare sets. But as my prices were a couple of pounds per set dearer (no more!) Mackett Beeson would not pay! So Bertram had to grind out many Stauntons when he could have made lots more fascinating sets than he did! He would have them photographed if there was time, but often, if the photographer was busy, the urgency prevented them from being recorded; so I know not what sets Bertram made or when they might turn up, which they do from time to time.

Meanwhile, I came across a Holtzapffel ornamental turning lathe of mid-nineteenth-century vintage, and this extended my range of work and the perfection thereof. I gained much experience by chess piece repairs and replacements over a number of years and consequently was able to design and make my own ornate sets. Over the years I have had to repair lots of crudely-made sets which have value merely because they are old. I still do some repairs, simply because some old sets are worth it and there are few indeed left who can now take on such work. But I love to make my own fine sets which, I can say, within their limitations, can stand with any made in the past.

Richard Clyburn and his screw spanner

Dennis Chapman

Tools and Trades Volume 8: 1995

This is an account of the origin of a simple tool, a screw spanner, first made in 1842 and still in production.

The spanner is the simplest of all the many tools, machines and implements designed by Richard Clyburn but it embodies the essential principles of his engineering skills.

Clyburn's work was the product of a particular engineering culture associated with textile manufacture and high farming in Gloucestershire and Somerset in the second quarter of the 19th century.

At that time engineering in these counties was on a relatively small scale compared with that of the Midlands, the North of England, the Clyde Valley and the South East of Scotland.

Fig. 1. Clyburn spanners, 1875 and 1975.

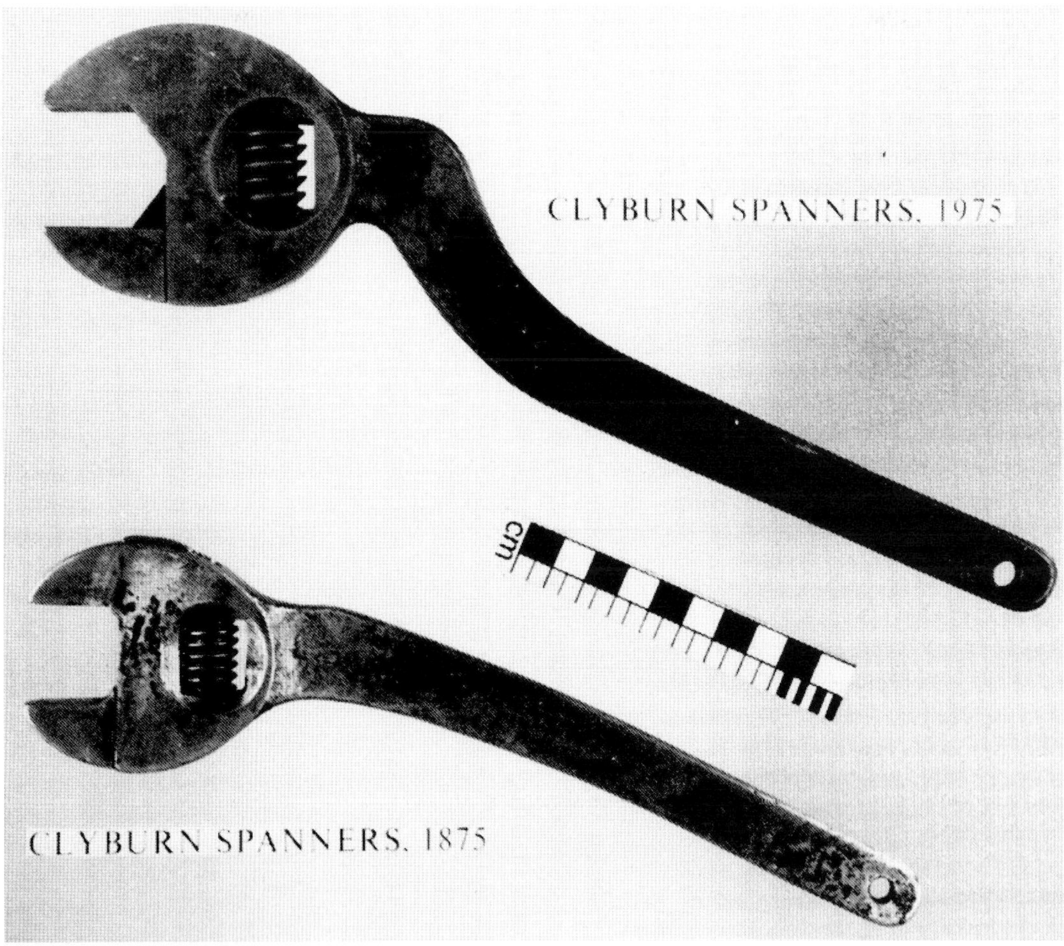

Fig. 2. The Uley Cultivator

In both counties the engineering activities were supported by the landed gentry with a curious result: when the agricultural engineering manufacturers in the United States of America and the rest of the United Kingdom were designing mowing and reaping machines, the industry of the Stroud Valley produced the spiral cutter lawn mower!

Richard Clyburn is first recorded in Gloucestershire in 1828 when he was a consulting engineer. By 1836 he was a partner in the Uley Iron Works with George Lister. In 1841 the Earl of Ducie took over the works and Clyburn became engineering manager until the Duke closed the works in 1847. Until his death he continued to work as a consultant and a designer and traded on his own account.

Almost all of Clyburn's designs were created at the Uley works but many of them were transferred to Somerset. A few implements were taken up by Ferrabee and the best known of all, the Uley Cultivator, was made by others until the last quarter of the century. (Fig. 2.)

In both counties the land owner was important: in Gloucestershire the Earl of Ducie, in Somerset Lord Portman; in both counties their stewards played a critical role – in Gloucestershire John Morton, a distinguished Scottish agriculturalist, in Somerset George Parsons, a leading English farmer. In both counties there were textile industries which supported local engineering industry: woollen manufacture in the Stroud Valley, relatively technically advanced; in Somerset sailcloth-making, technically backward.

During the first three quarters of the 19th century there were a number of engineers who were associated in partnership, or in design and patents. They were William Lewis, Edwin Beard Budding, George Lister, John and James Ferrabee and Richard Clyburn. In the first half of the century much of this activity was concerned with the woollen industry and agriculture but at the date of the 1862 International Exhibition, Ferrabees were general engineers making a range of steam engines and hydraulic machines. Edwin B. Budding and John Ferrabee made spanners which competed with those of Clyburn.

The relationship of these engineers is shown in a series of patents describing the application of the spiral rotating cutter. The first was by Lewis in 1815 describing a machine for shearing the nap on woollen cloth. The second, in 1830, was by Budding for its use in a lawn mower – this patent was financed by Ferrabee. The third, in 1840, was in the names of the Earl of Ducie, Clyburn, and Budding for "machinery for cutting vegetable and other substances"; this was applied in a chaff cutter. The fourth patent was by Ferrabee for an improved lawn mower in 1850.

Clyburn's influence was shown in a patent for a power loom taken out in 1836 with Ferrabee. In this there was "a weight suspended on an arm ... to ... render its vibrations smooth and uniform in the manner of a pendulum". This was a departure from normal power loom practice.

The relationship between Clyburn and Parsons dates from a remarkable project: the establishment of the Whitfield Example Farm by the Honourable Henry George Francis Morton, later the second Earl of Ducie.

In 1838 the Earl of Ducie invited John Morton, a leading agricultural scientist from Ayrshire, to make a complete study of his poorest and worst-managed farm. The "Report on the Present State of Whitfield Farm" was published in 1840 and proposed a six-year plan to create a farm working at the highest level of efficiency and profitability. In his Report John Morton set out his requirements for new machinery.

In 1841 "Clyburn and Lister" of Uley became "The Earl of Ducie's Iron Works" with John Morton as Director and Richard Clyburn as Engineer and Manager. The works immediately began producing the implements required at Whitfield, one of which was the famous "Uley Cultivator". In pursuit of the Earl's objectives they began at once to exhibit at the meetings of the Royal Agricultural Society of England beginning with the meeting at Liverpool in 1841.

George Parsons of West Lambrook in Somerset had already begun to develop as an engineer and with the assistance of Clyburn this produced a joint patent of 1843 No. 8660: "Certain Improvements in Machinery for Beating, Cleansing, and Crushing Various Animal and Vegetable Materials or Substances". In fact a complete range of barn machinery. A number of the Parsons - Clyburn machines were made at Uley and after the works closed Parsons continued to make some of them.

The work of Clyburn was characterised by its high quality of design, construction, workmanship and finish as attested to by the praise of the judges at the meetings of the Royal Agricultural Society of England. Each implement was made to solve a specific practical problem and, where possible, designed so that its performance could be controlled and

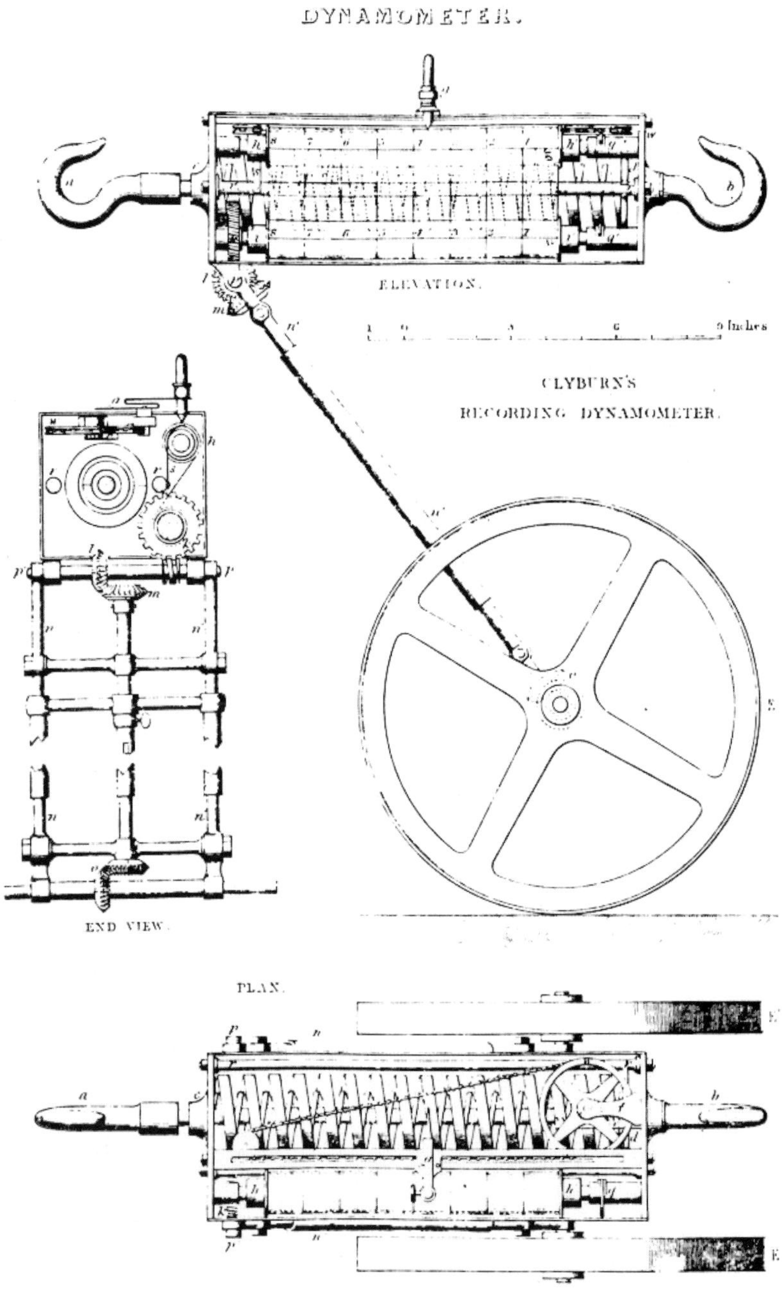

Fig. 3. Clyburn's dynamometer for measuring the laod of different ploughs.

measured. Clyburn preferred to use wrought iron rather than cast although in some cases he offered both. His implements were made with replaceable parts. The implements being made to meet the requirements of the Whitfield Example Farm together formed a system for a productive unit.

It would be out of place to describe all Clyburn's work but three examples will

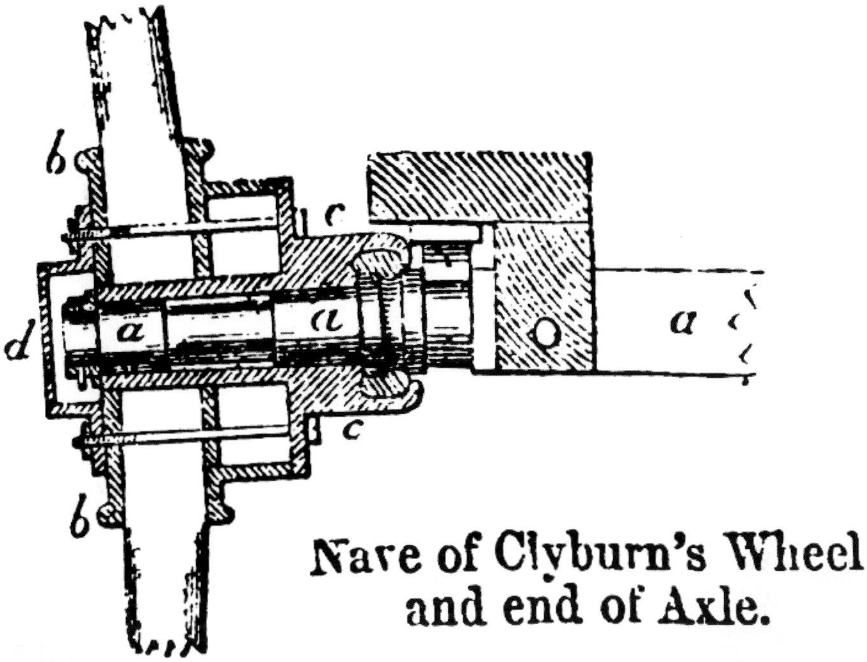

Fig. 4. Clyburn's waterproof oil bath bearing for cart and wagon wheels

suffice. The Uley Cultivator produced even rows the depth of which could be regulated by a pointer on a dial plate. His recording drawbar dynamometer measured the load, for example of different ploughs in the same soil, and provided a printout of the result on a continuous strip of paper. (Fig. 3.) A waterproof oil bath bearing for cart and wagon wheels which he designed was a piece of precision engineering, a complete break with the wheelwright tradition. (Fig. 4.)

The Whitfield Example Farm under John Morton, with the machinery and implements designed by Clyburn and made at Uley, became a highly mechanised production organisation based on steam power and served by a system of rail tracks. When the Uley works closed Clyburn joined Parsons at West Lambrook where they created an equally advanced mechanised farm. The machinery and implements were made locally. This was the origin of the subsequent career of Parsons as an engineer.

John C. Morton in his *Cyclopaedia Of Agriculture*, 1856, described and compared the two farms and their equipment; he wrote that there were only two other comparable farms in Britain although a third was being established at Windsor for His Royal Highness the Prince of Wales.

It was in keeping with Clyburn's attention to detail that even with his wide range of interests he would design a spanner.

The first record of Clyburn's spanner is in an account dated November 22nd, 1842 from the Earl of Ducie's Iron Works to a Mr. C. C. Clyford. In a list of implements and iron work is the item, "An improved screw spanner £1.5.0." The price suggests a larger size than those shown later, probably a size 6. In 1844 a set of the spanners was exhibited at the meeting of the Royal Agricultural Society of England at Southampton. In the report of the meeting they were described thus:

" Article No. 11. (New Tool) A Set of Improved Screw Spanners or Wrenches; invented and manufactured by Richard Clybum of Uley, near Dursley.

This improvement in screw-wrenches or spanners consists in the application of an adjustable jaw, opening at the end instead of the side of the handle or lever, by which it may be more readily used in confined situations. It will be found a very useful tool to the farmer in his machinery or implements, there being generally so many different-sized nuts about them. The easy manner of adjustment is a sufficient recommendation.

Price: No. 1 size	7*s* 6*d*
" 2	lls 6*d*
" 3	14*s* 6*d*
" 4	18*s* 6*d* "

The spanners were awarded a Silver Medal.

At the meeting of the R.A.S.E. at Newcastle in 1846 the spanners were shown by Parsons. They were described as "made by Richard Clyburn" who was still at Uley. In 1853 Parsons had eight exhibits at the meeting of the R.A.S.E. at Gloucester including a set of "Clyburn screw spanners made by the exhibitor, invented by the late Richard Clyburn". The spanners had travelled a full circle, from Gloucestershire to Somerset and back. There is no record of the spanners being made in Somerset after 1853.

In 1847 John Ferrabee took over the manufacture of many of the Morton, Parsons, C1yburn designs from the Earl of Ducie's Iron Works when it closed, but not the spanners.

Ferrabee showed the Budding spanners at the R.A.S.E. meeting at Northampton in 1847, where it was his 14th item. (Fig. 5.)

The spanners were again shown at the R.A.S.E. meetings at Chester in 1858 and at Canterbury in 1860.

In 1859 Ferrabee obtained a patent, No. 2904, for an improved Budding spanner and in this the jaws were tightened by the action of a wedge in addition to that of the worm and rack. This tool and a modified pattern of the original Budding were shown at the International Exhibition in London in 1862. (Fig. 6.)

The operation of the wedge spanner is best understood from Ferrabee's own account and a drawing from the patent. It is clear that Ferrabee was addressing problems that had already been solved by Clyburn years before.

The design of C1yburn's spanner shows the result of his examination of the forces involved in its use. This can be

Fig. 5. Budding's Improved Adjusting Wrench.

No. 14.—BUDDING'S IMPROVED ADJUSTING WRENCH.

This tool is adjusted by means of a worm working in a rack, and is applicable to nuts and pins of all sizes, and in almost every situation. It is very strong and light.

The following sizes are made: No. 1—7 inches long, and 1 inch range, *price* 5s. 6d. No. 2—10in. long, 1¼in. range, 8s. 6d. No. 3—12in. long, 1½in. range, 9s. 6d. No. 4—14in. long, 2in. range, 11s. 6d. No. 5—16in. long, 2¼in. range, 12s. 6d. No. 6—18in. long, 3in. range, 14s. 6d. No. 7—20in. long, 3in. range, 18s. No. 8—24in. long, 3½in. range, 20s.

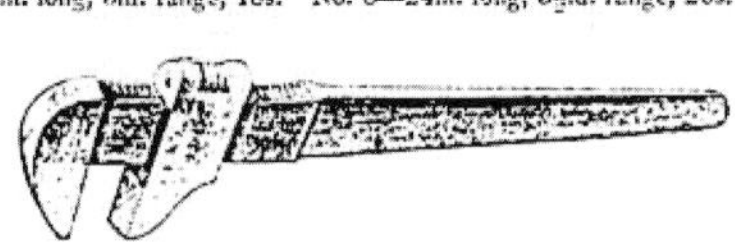

shown by comparing it with its rival, the Budding, made at the same time and in the same area.

In the C1yburn spanner there are two forces being applied when the nut is being tightened or loosened. The first is a rotary force around the nut which is its centre. The handle is a lever and its length will

Fig. 6. Patent drawings for Ferrabee's ajustable screww wrench.

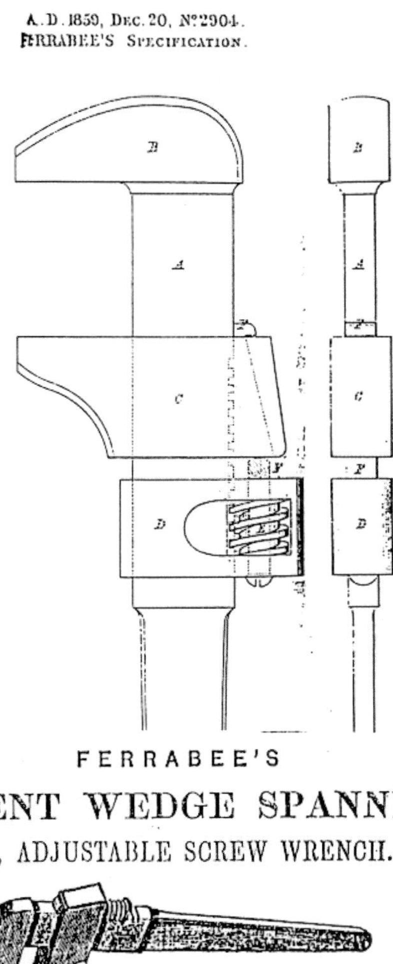

FERRABEE'S

PATENT WEDGE SPANNER,

OR, ADJUSTABLE SCREW WRENCH.

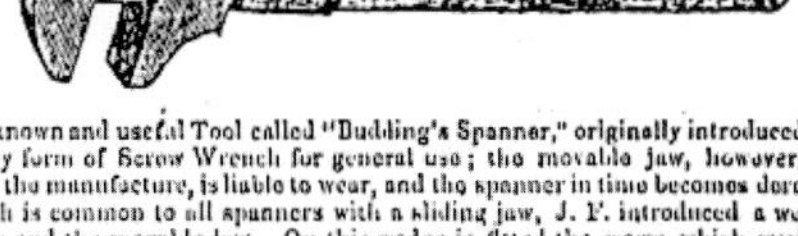

The well known and useful Tool called "Budding's Spanner," originally introduced by Mr. Ferrabee, is the most handy form of Screw Wrench for general use; the movable jaw, however, notwithstanding the care taken in the manufacture, is liable to wear, and the spanner in time becomes deranged. To obviate this defect, which is common to all spanners with a sliding jaw, J. F. introduced a wedge between the back of the stem and the movable jaw. On this wedge is fitted the worm which works into the teeth on the stem and moves the jaw up or down as may be desired. The wedge slides with the jaw, and when a strain is applied, the fit of the jaw to the stem and the wedge is so perfect, and the thrust so direct, that the spanner acquires all the strength of a solid one. The stem and upper jaw are made in one piece, and, together with the movable jaw, are of the best forged iron, all accurately fitted by machinery, and case hardened. Thus constructed it is a tool of unrivalled strength, durability, and simplicity, which may be used with confidence under all circumstances and in all situations where an adjusting spanner can be serviceable.

Length	8	10	12	14	15	16	18	20	24	Inches.
Range	1	1¼	1½	2	2¼	2½	3	3	3½	"
Price	6s.	7s. 6d.	9s	11s	12s.	13s	14s	17s.	20s	

OTHER LENGTHS MADE TO ORDER.

STROUD, GLOUCESTERSHIRE.

be proportionate to the expected force required, which will in turn depend on the size of the nut and bolt. In a Sorby catalogue of 1938 there are 13 sizes of Clyburn spanners from 6 inches in length with a span of ⅜ in. to 30 ins. long with a span of 3 in.; the ratio of span to length is 1 to 10. This ratio is found in a number of spanners of different sizes made by different firms over a period of at least 100 years. The second force is directed from the handle towards the centre of the nut and bolt. There is no conflict between these forces.

With the Budding spanner and all other spanners with the jaws at right angles to the handle, the handle is not in line with the centre of the nut but on a line parallel to this line. When the spanner is used there is a rotary force applied to tighten or loosen the nut and at the same time pressure has to be applied at the jaws in the direction of the nut to hold the spanner on the nut. These forces are not in harmony.

In practice Clyburn departed from the strict requirement that the jaws and the handle should be in line by offsetting the jaws by 20 degrees to the handle thus making fine adjustment possible by turning the handle over. This orientation of jaws to handle is now usual in

Fig. 7. Budding style spanners in the 1938 Turner, Naylor & Co. Ltd. catalogue

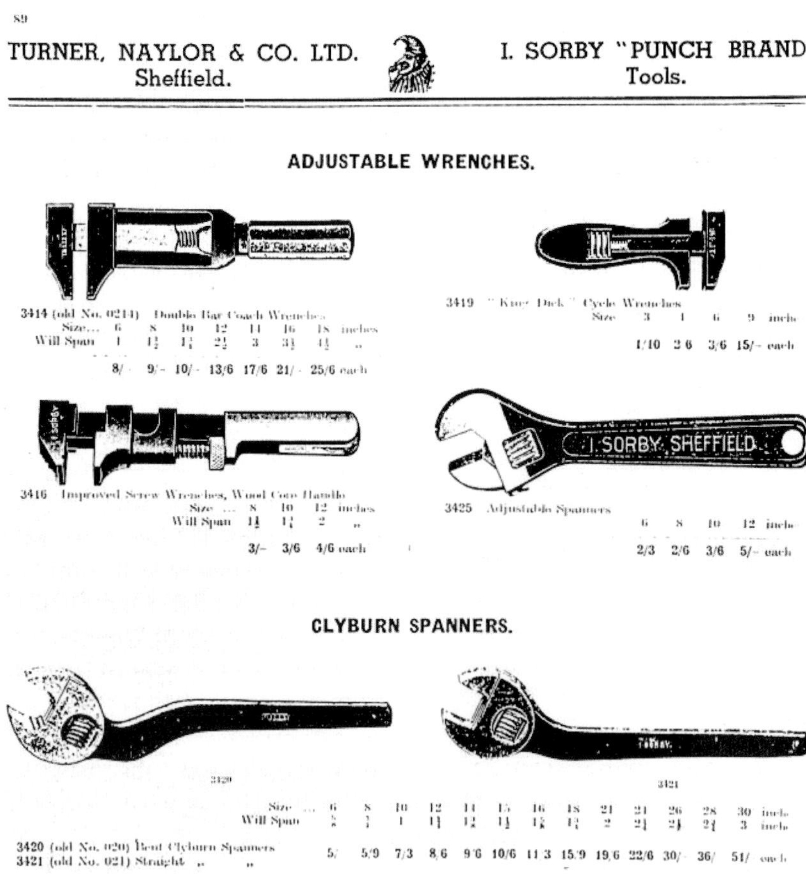

1938

simple flat spanners. Some later makers of Clyburn spanners made a model with a bent handle in which the angle of the jaws to the handle was 30 degrees. When a spanner of the Budding design is used at more or at less than a right angle to the nut the jaws can be twisted out of line. The results of this can be seen in tools that have been well used, even a high quality spanner like the "King Dick".

With the Clyburn, movement of the handle up or down affects the surface of contact of each jaw with the nut equally and in the same plane; there is no tendency to twist the jaws out of parallel.

The jaws of the Clyburn spanner are protected against strain in two ways: first each size of spanner is restricted to a prescribed maximum size of nut; secondly the design and construction of the jaws provides the greatest strength when the jaws are at their widest opening. This is achieved by the sliding part of the moving jaw being fully housed when the jaws are open to the limit. When the pressure is mainly on the fixed jaw the moving jaw is held by the cross section of the sliding bar of the jaw.

The spanners of the Budding configuration shown in the Sorby catalogue of 1938 show a number of attempts to overcome the weaknesses of the original design. (Fig. 7.)

A feature of the Clyburn spanner is the worm and rack. The Sorby catalogue shows three different patterns: there are those with a square section to the teeth in the worm and the rack, as in Sorby's No. 3414 and No. 4316. This gives positive control. There are those with symmetrical teeth with an angle of about 45 degrees as in Sorby's No. 3425, this is relatively unstable. Clyburn's asymmetrical teeth attempt to combine the advantages of both forms. With the buttress tooth when the spanner is tight two vertical surfaces mate, when the pressure is released the touching surfaces are at an angle and free to move.

The Clyburn spanner, because of its shape, can be misused as a hammer. The end of the sliding bar of the moving jaw can be riveted over the head making the tool difficult or impossible to use. This has happened to a number in the writer's collection, but the damage is easily corrected.

No spanner made by Clyburn or Parsons has been found, but the writer has a well-used example with an oval stamp on one side of the handle which reads:

"THE ORIGINAL"
"CLYBURN No 5"
"BRITISH MADE"

At the end of the handle "5" over "96" is stamped; the significance of this is not known. On the other side, again in an oval stamp is

"FORGED"
"STEEL"

Fig. 8. Drawing of the section of the sliding rack.

It cannot be certain that this is Clyburn's original pattern but it can be compared with others of known makers. The first point to be made is that the tool has been made to a very high standard of precision. The overall length of the spanner is 13 inches long, the head is 3 inches wide and 3¼ inches deep and it is set at an angle of 20 degrees to the entire line of the handle. The buttress thread on the worm and rack is deeply cut and close fitting. The total play between the ends of the worm and the body is 6 one thousandths of an inch. The spindle passes through the head and is riveted at each end. The jaws have been hardened and ground to form. This is shown by 10 segments of circles scratched on one side of the head where the spanner has been in a tight place, only one of the segments continues on to a jaw, and there the scratch is much less deep. The maximum play between moving jaw and the head is 6 one thousandths of an inch. The section of the sliding rack is symmetrical, it prevents lateral play in the moving jaw and maintains the parallelism of the jaws under pressure. (Fig. 8.)

The description "British Made" suggests manufacture after the end of World War One when competition began to be important. Variations from the "Original" pattern have been found in four examples from different makers. There is also evidence from catalogues of other makers or retailers. The obvious variation is making an alternative pattern with a bent handle. This sets the angle of the jaws to the centre line of the handle at 30 degrees. A second variation is that the spindle supporting the worm is screwed into the head. In practice the spindle works loose. There are obvious attempts to fasten the spindle by riveting at the free end in some of the examples described below. A third variation is filling the corners of the jaws to occupy the space left when the nut is hexagonal. It should be observed however that in the "Original" Clyburn the weakness of

Harcourt Quincey's Improved Shifting Screw-Key 1855. From, Crom, T.R., Horological and other Shop Tools, *published by the author, Melrose, Florida, U.S.A., 1987. Reproduced by the courtesy of the author.*

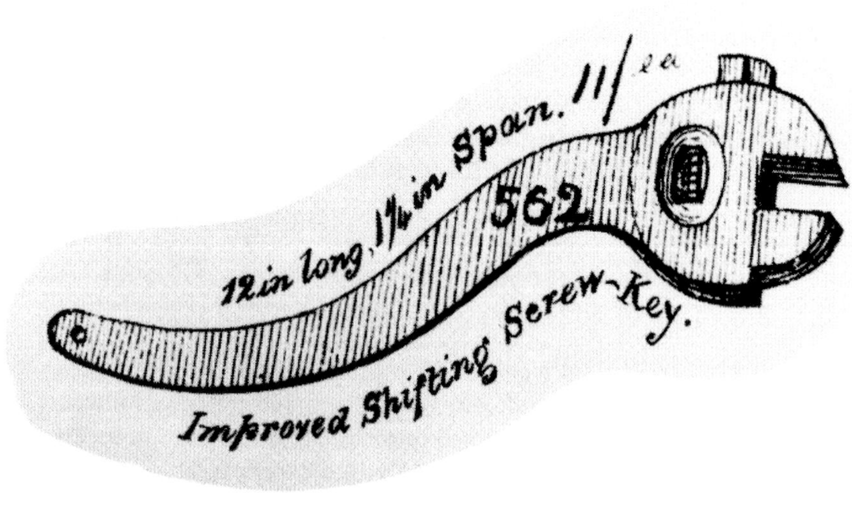

a right-angled connection between the vertical and horizontal parts of the jaws is avoided by rounding the corners.

The survival of the Clyburn spanner, originally made for farmers in 1842, unchanged in the age of high technology is a tribute to the skill of Richard Clyburn in analysing the complex forces which exist in a basic engineering task, that of making a secure fixing.

Bibliography

Morton, John, *Report on the Present State of Whitfield Farm,* London, 1840.

Morton, John C., *A Cyclopaedia of Agriculture*. Edinburgh, 1856.

Randall, H. A. "Some Mid-Gloucester Engineers and Inventors". *Transactions of the Newcomen Society,* Vol. XXVII, 1965-66.

Journal of The Royal Agricultural Society of England:

"Report of the Exhibition of Implements at Derby, 1843", Vol. IV, 1843.

"Report of the Exhibition of Implements at Southampton, 1844", Vol. V, 1845.

"Report of the Exhibition of Implements at Shrewsbury, 1845", Vol. VI, 1846.

"Report of the Exhibition of Implements at Newcastle, 1846", Vol.V11, 1847.

"Report of the Exhibition of Implements at Northampton, 1847", Vol. VIII, 1848.

"Report of the Exhibition of and Trial of Implements, at Gloucester, 1853", Vol. XIV, 1853.

Acknowledgements

The writer wishes to express his thanks to many scholars, correspondents and friends who helped with information and with gifts of Clyburn spanners, they are:

D.J.H. Smith, B.A., County Archivist of Gloucestershire, John S. Creasey, Assistant Keeper, Museum of English Rural Life, Reading, F. J. Walrond, A.M.A., Curator of The Stroud Museum, Paul H. J. Baker, J. M. Chapman, Andrew M. Hall, Paul Read, Brian Sharp, Michael Waiters, C. H. Wooliscroft.

Table 1. The following information comes from spanners that have been found.

Maker	Description	Date	Sliding Section
Josh. Evans & Sons Ltd.	Size 4 Patent Unbreakable Jaw.	1875	
Easterbrook Allcard & Co. Ltd. Sheffield	Size 4 Bent Handle Improved Strong Jaw Reg. No. 323941.	20th century	
Henry Burstall & Co. Sheffield and London	Size 4 L.N.E.R. 5/45272.	1920s	
Presto made in England	Size 5 Bent Handle Improved Strong Jaw Reg. No. 323941	1975	
Unknown	Size 8 Forged Steel As the "Original Clyburn"	19th century	

Table 2. The list below is some evidence of the many firms who made or supplied Clyburn spanners. The list is in date order.

Maker	Description	Date
Joseph Fenn, London		1840s
Harcourt Quincy	One size 1¼ in. span, 12 ins. long, double curved handle. "Improved Shifting Screw-Key" price 11/-.	1855
J. Howarth, Sheffield	"Clyburn's Improved Spanners" with straight and curved handles.	1884
Nurse and Co.		circa 1900
W. Brookes and Son, Sheffield	Genuine Clyburn patent unbreakable jaw, No. 21325.	
Aird and Anderson, Liverpool	2 Clyburn spanners, sizes 1 and 4 in "Our special Roll of Tools for Motor Cars"!	1906
Fredk. Pollard and Co. Ltd. Leicester	Clyburn spanners with bent handles and hardened jaws in 13 sizes from 5/8 of an inch, span 6 in. long to 3 in. span, 30 in. long.	1924
Turner, Naylor and Co. Ltd. Sheffield and I. Sorby	"Punch" brand. Clyburn spanners with straight and bent handles in 13 sizes and 30 in. long.	1938
Garrington		
Buck and Hickman 1961	Clyburn spanners with bent handles.	
Buck and Hickman	Spark-resistant safety tools. Spark, magnetic and corrosion tools made from Telcon Beryllium copper. These tools are suitable for industries where combustible, inflammable or explosive atmospheres create a hazard to life, or installations such as the manufacturing or processing of oil and petroleum, chemicals and explosives, paints and plastics, domestic and industrial gases. Wrenches, Clyburn pattern, adjustable, 5 sizes; ¾ in. span, 6 in. long, to 1½ in. span, 14 in. long.	1993

The humble tool bass, the tote, the frail and the toat

Kenneth E. Turner

Newsletter No. 61: Summer 1998

There have been many books published about tools from the simplest to the sophisticated but few mention the tool bass, which has been a vital part of many a tool kit. Raphael Salaman has seen fit to describe and illustrate the tool bass in his *Dictionary of Woodworking Tools*, as has Alvin Sellens in his *Dictionary of American Hand Tools*, although he lists it as a tool basket rather than a tool bass. There are many books on carpentry and joinery which include chapters describing and illustrating tools and trades but the writer has found none which include reference to the tool bass. References to tool chests and tool boxes are usually prominent in the types of book mentioned but certainly not tool basses.

It is not known just when the true tool bass (woven of bast) came into being but Richard Unger in his book, *The Art of Medieval Technology,* mentions a 14th century fresco "Building of Noah's Arc" attributed to Pieru di Puccio, in which is shown a woven tool basket with tools. A woven tool bass with tools is also shown in an engraving by Theodore DeBry entitled "Orlando Building a Ship in Panama in 1509", one of the twenty four plates which appear in the volume *History of the New World* by Jeremy Benzon in 1594.

The *Shorter Oxford Dictionary* mentions a flat plaited bag having been made of bast in 1706. Much later during the period 1900 to 1938 the tool bass was as abundant and distinctive as the Model "T" Ford.

The word "bass" (pronounced as "ass" with a "b") has several meanings

Fig. 1. Orlando building a ship in Panama in 1509. *From Benzon, 1594, pl. 19. The Beinecke Rare Book and manuscript Library, Yale University*

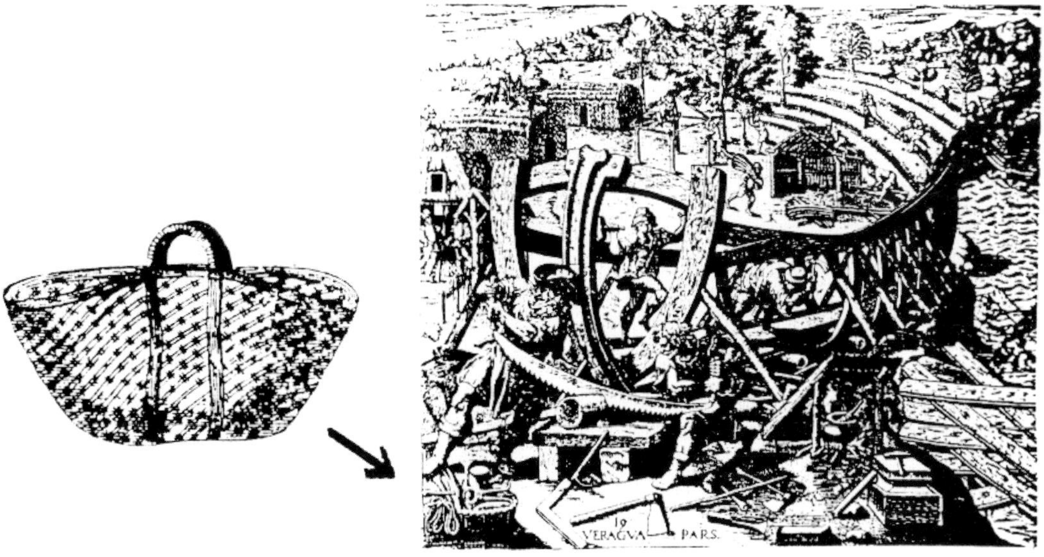

but used in the context of this article the word is a corruption of "bast." Bast is the inner bark (*phloem*) of the Lime (*tilia*) and various other trees, including certain palms, from which the strong fibrous material for making ropes, matting, hassocks, straw hats and carpenters' baskets (basses) is obtained. Loosely, bass is any similar vegetable fibre and includes flax, hemp and jute. This material in woven sheet form, was also used extensively by gardeners for covering over tender plants to protect them from frost and other injury. The raw material was stripped from the tree, beaten, soaked in water, beaten again and then in many cases, woven, as in the case of the tool bass.

Fig. 2. An empty tool bass and one caotnaing a kit of tools.

The shape of the tool bass is distinctive in that its profile always takes the form of a triangle with two sides outwardly curved and with a severely chopped off point to form the base.

The design of the tool bass is both simple and practical, its shape and open top allow easy sighting and access to its contents. It is light and convenient to carry even when filled with the usual run of carpenters' tools, saws included, in the larger size bass.

The tool bass is not meant to compete with the tool chest which is designed to house all manner of tools to suit all manner of jobs over who knows what period of time? The tool bass is designed to conveniently carry on to a site whatever tools are required to do a specific job.

A true tool bass is a tool carrier of the shape earlier described and illustrated, the exterior of which is made of woven bast, edged with webbing, lined with canvas and with handles either of rope or webbing. The more expensive basses were lined with leather, some (the very cheap) were not lined at all. While the exterior of the original basses were of woven bast, there were versions of other woven fibres, including rush. Although many carpenters' tool carriers were later made entirely of canvas (some also lined with canvas), they still retained the shape of the original woven tool bass. The all canvas (sometimes advertised as sailcloth) being stronger, were the more expensive basses. The approximate price of the lined woven bass in 1912 was ls 6*d* – 1*s* 9*d* each, rising to approximately 3*s* – 3*s* 6*d* each in 1925, about the same price as a half to three quarter pint cast iron glue pot which was about 1*s* 4*d* – 1*s* 9*d* in 1912, increasing to 2*s* 9*d* – 3*s* 6*d* in 1925.

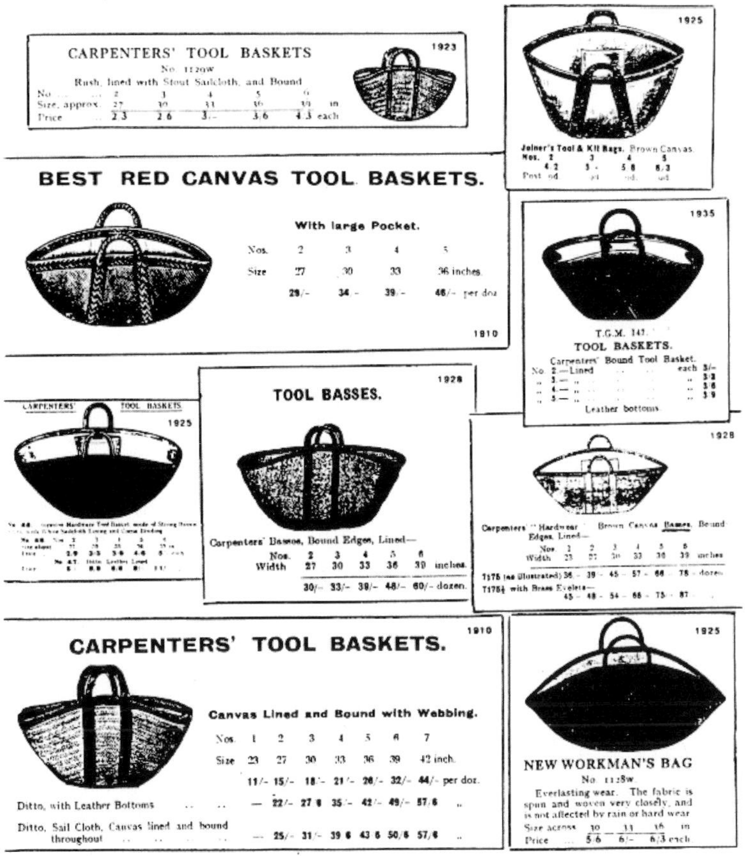

Fig. 3. A variety of tool basses from catalogues showing their prices.

For an extra 7*d* William Marples offered a tool bass with brass eyelets so that the top of the bag could be laced up.

The quality and price of tool basses varied as did their sizes. Sizes offered by merchants usually ranged from 23 ins. (No. 1) to 42 ins. (No. 7). A study of numerous suppliers' catalogues dating from 1907 to 1936, gives a fair idea of the variation in tool basses that were being offered in their heyday.

A short article on carpenters' tool chests, boxes and baskets which appeared in *The Illustrated Carpenter and Builder*, May 20th, 1898, mentions and illustrates a carpenters' frail basket.

The basket illustrated is identical in shape to the tool bass earlier described. It is interesting to note that this same illustration has been used in several suppliers' catalogues of the 1920s and 30s.

Despite extensive research, the writer

Fig. 4. Frail sticks.

Fig. 5. From The Illustrated Carpenter and Builder, *May 20th, 1898.*

has found only two references to the term "frail" in relation to a carpenters' tool basket, which perhaps suggests the term was little used in this context.

R. A. Salaman in his *Dictionary of Woodworking Tools,* as well as referring to a frail as an alternative term for bass, describes and illustrates a frail stick (carrying stick, carrying cane) – especially designed to balance on the shoulder. The stick extends backwards to support a hooked on tool bag, the front extends forwards for the hand to grip – the shoulder acts as a fulcrum.

According to the *Oxford English Dictionary* the word "frail" is in fact the name of a rush used for weaving baskets. Such baskets however, are normally of a type used for packing fruit such as figs and raisins. According to Wyld's *Universal Dictionary of the English Language,* the word "frail" derives from the French "frael, freel, fleet" meaning basket for fruit. The word in the English language however, has been used (although infrequently) to denote in the past, bags of various shapes made of materials far removed from rush and used to carry a wide variety of items – including the tools of the plasterer, plumber, mason and other tradesmen.

The advertisements shown in Figure 6 collectively illustrate the variety of tool carriers (irrespective of what they were called: bass, tote, frail, basket or bag) offered over the years to suit all manner of tradesmen.

Even though the tool bass has played an important part in the service of man, little has been recorded of these aids which were once almost as prolific as carpenters' and joiners' bit braces.

Today's equivalent of the tool bass is the usually user made wooden tote, the typical size of which is about 10 in. x 22 in. x 18 in. base to handle. A similar design tote is now available in fibre glass.

The word "tote", as well as meaning to carry, convey, or drag, is the name given to the handle of a plane. The word used in relation to planes is sometimes spelled "toat". Chamber's and Webster's dictionaries and the Goodman and Salaman works, use the spelling "toat" to denote the handle of a plane. Mercer and Dunbar, in their books use the spelling "tote" to indicate a plane's handle. Whelan brackets the alternatives (tote or toat).

Etymologically, the writer has not been able to find any connection between the words "tote" and "toat". The word "toat" seems always to be used in relation to the handle of a plane but never in relation to carrying. Whereas "tote" is used in relation to carrying as well as to the handle of a plane. It could perhaps be argued that "toat" is a corruption of the

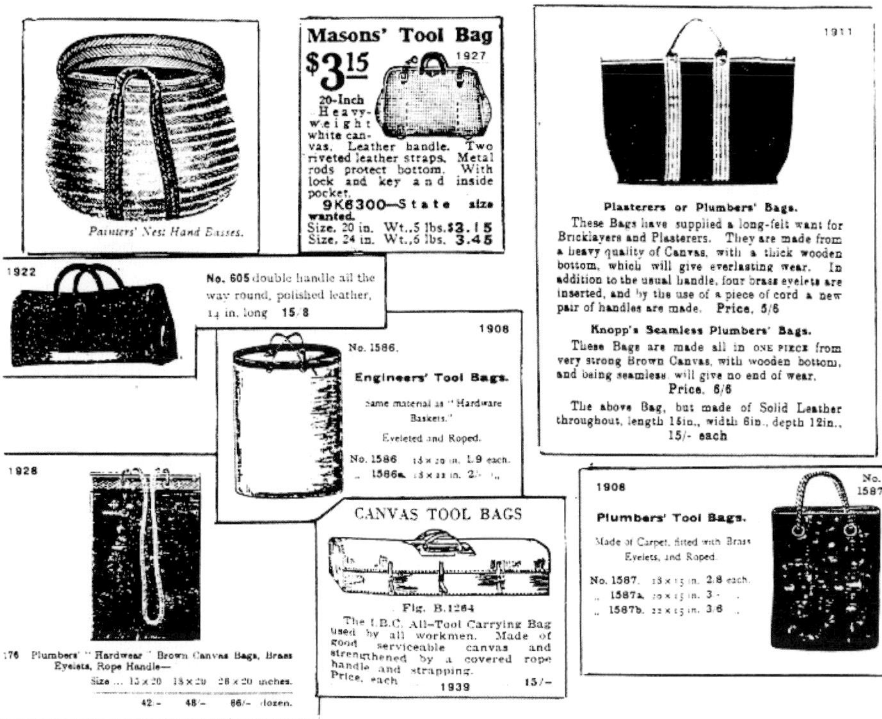

Fig. 6. A variety of advertisements for tool basses.

word "tote" or vice versa but there is no evidence of this. It could also be argued that the handle of a plane is invariably used to carry it as well as to push and pull it, hence the name given to the handle, a corruption of "tote"?

Incidentally, when the toat of a plane is referred to, one usually thinks of the back handle of a plane. It is interesting to note that Goodman in his book *The History of Woodworking Tools* also uses the word "toat" when referring to the front grip or palm knob of a plane – when there is one.

References: (others mentioned in the text)

R. W. Unger, *The Art of Mediaeval Technology*, Rutgers University Press, USA, 1991.

The Shorter Oxford Dictionary, Oxford, UK, 1950.

Chambers Encyclopaedia, Newnes, UK, 1950.

Wyld's *Universal Dictionary of the English Language*, Routledge and Keegan Paul Ltd., London, 1961.

R. A. Salaman, *Dictionary of Woodworking Tools*, Astragal Press, USA, 1997.

Trade catalogues:

S. Tyzack & Son, (UK), 1908.

Edward Preston & Sons, (UK), 1909.

John Danks & Son Prop. Ltd., (Aust.), 1912.

George Adams, (UK), 1922.

William Marples & Sons Ltd., (UK), 1928.

Army & Navy Stores, (UK), 1936.

Sailmakers' seam rubbers

Des Pawson

Newsletter No. 75: Winter 2001

These tools were used by the sailmaker to fold, rub down or flatten and smooth seams. They have been rarely illustrated in the manuals of seamanship or sailmaking yet sailmakers have used them from at least the 18th century. It is usually stated that all seams should be rubbed down smooth after sewing, but no mention is made of the tool to be used for this purpose. Seam rubbers come in two distinct forms, firstly an all wood (or ivory) tool and secondly a wood and metal tool. R. A. Salaman in his *Dictionary of Woodworking Tools c.1700-1970* shows both these types.

The all wood tool was probably individually made by the sailor or sailmaker and varied from very crude and simple to extremely ornamental. These tools appear in various museum collections but I have yet to find an early contemporary illustration. The earliest illustration of an all wood seam rubber that I can find is a photograph in *The Yankee Whale* by C. W. Ashley (1926). The wood used would be lignum vitae, greenheart, teak, mahogany or some other hard wood. The whaler would also use whale bone or whale ivory in place of wood. The simplest seam rubber may be no more than a rough shaped wedge of wood. The most ornate will have a knot carved on the top of the handle with, perhaps, the column of the tool being carved in a rope like manner and the actual rubbing part may have initials or a heart shape motif on the sides. I wonder if some of these ornate rubbers are actually more a badge of office or a token of thanks given to the sailmaker by a sailor in exchange for odd favours: "Sails" being the source of canvas used by the sailor to make his sea bag, ditty bag, to cover the top of his sea chest, even jackets and shoes and

A selection of wood and whale bone seam rubbers in the author's collection.

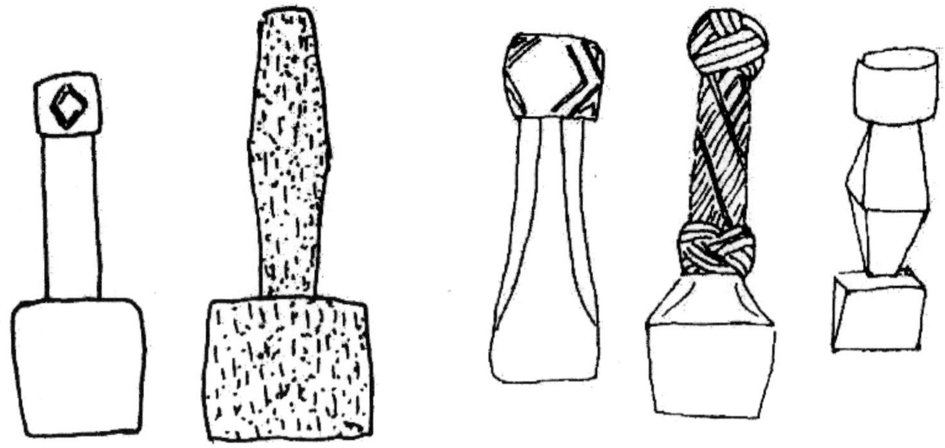

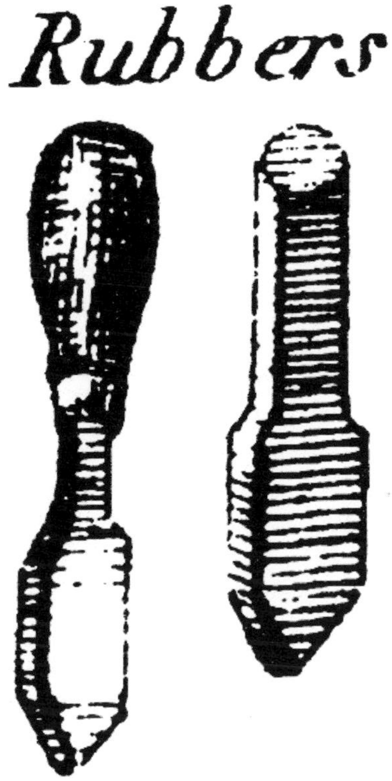

Figure 16 from David Steel, Elements of Sailmaking, *1794.*

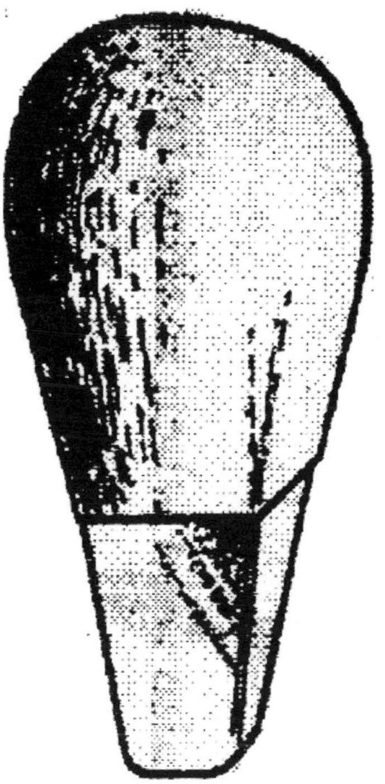

Royal Navy circa 1950s.

perhaps a hammock for the tropics. The length will vary from about 100 mm to 170 mm. Even the simplest all wood seam rubber should never be confused with a plumber's chase wedge which is larger and never has any form of swelling to the top of the handle, but may have a ferrule there instead.

The wood and metal seam rubber has a wooden handle and an iron end. The first mention, complete with illustrations, was in David Steel's *Elements of Sailmaking* (1794), where he describes it as a small iron instrument in a wooden handle to rub down or flatten the seams. It is not certain if the tool shown without a handle is all wood or all metal.

In Admiral W. H. Smyth's *The Sailors Word Book* of 1867 the rubber is described as "A small instrument used to rub or flatten down the seams of a sail, in sailmaking". No mention being made of the materials used to make the tool.

The Royal Navy Rate Book and Authorized List of Naval Stores 1909-1910 has sailmaker's rubbers as an item of stores, #1986. Unfortunately these rate books do not have any illustrations, so it is not certain if this was wood and metal or the all wood version. The rate book did state that the tool was of dockyard manufacture. It remained until 1951 for it to be shown in the *Admiralty Manual of Seamanship Volume 2* when it definitely was the wood

Davey & Co., London 1936.

and metal version.

In the 1936 copy of the *Davey and Co. of London Ltd Catalogue No.8* (and likely to be similar in earlier editions) there is an illustration of a wood and metal seam rubber with the brand name 'Willey'. 'Willey' appears to be a London maker. The trade name 'Squire' has also been found on a similar rubber. These are both similar to one shown by William Smith and Son Ltd. of Redditch in their 1980s catalogue that used old engravings.

The rubber illustrated by John James and Sons Ltd. of Redditch, circa 1925, shows a different style with a flat end, but mentions the availability of a square blade as well. 'Smiths' also supplied rubbers with this shape. J. E. Horsley in his *Tools of the Maritime Trades* suggests that this shape would enable the rubber to work close into the roped edges of a sail.

It must be noted that when the sailmaker is cutting out sails, he has occasion to turn in and rub down edges of the sail cloth for seams and tablings. The Ministry of Defence's *Sailmaker's Handbook* of 1966 suggests that a seam rubber is used for this purpose as well. In practice the sailmaker will use the back of either his shears or knife, this being the tool to hand and far more convenient than having to trouble with a second tool as he crawled about on the sail loft floor. He would use the seam rubber to flatten and smooth any hand sewn seams after they had been finished. It is doubtful if a wood and metal seam rubber would be of much use to a sailmaker at sea as the steel would easily rust and mark the sails. It is almost certain that the wooden tool (which of course he could make himself) would be preferred, the wood and metal tool with its extra weight being the tool of choice at sail lofts ashore, especially where they would have been supplied from naval stores. For those who started sailmaking in a Naval Dockyard sail loft, the habit of using a wood and metal rubber would have become ingrained and they may well have carried their preference to other sailmaking situations.